A great correspondent gives us the exciting story of Washington since 1932, spanning one of the most significant administrations of American history. The book is also an exposition of how government functions, in terms of people: what they do and how they do it. Here, for your scrutiny and appraisal, are the key men, the old dealers and the New Dealers: the Rex Tugwells and why they failed to make over the world; the heroes of the New Deal—Brandeis, Norris, the great liberals, the splendid civil officers like Elmer Irey of the Treasury, what they achieved and what their limitations are. Harold Ickes, Harry Hopkins, Wendell Willkie, and many more predominant Washington figures are here, not excluding the President himself in the various phases of his administration.

The New Deal is thoroughly aired by Mr. Childs. The absorbing story of TVA, the State Department and the diplomats, Congress and the hard workers like Jack Cochran and Tom Eliot, the campaign of '36, the inside story of Mexico's expropriation of the oil lands —these are only a few of the items of national interest covered in the book.

Coming to the war, Mr. Childs tells of Bernard Baruch's effort to start rearmament in the fall of '38; the ill-fated first defense council; the rise and fall of Knudsen; Leon Henderson and the OPA; the battle of the OCD and Mrs. Roosevelt; the Army and Navy chiefs; Donald Nelson and the War of Production . . . The whole picture is here, the product of faithful, brilliant reporting, of extraordinary powers of observation. Told with the dynamic impact of an accomplished writer, this is not only an enlightening and objective interpretation of a tremendous era, but an inspiring testimony to the fundamental soundness of American democracy.

I WRITE

FROM

WASHINGTON

Marquis W. Childs

I WRITE
FROM
WASHINGTON

Harper & Brothers Publishers

New York and London

☆

For my wife

☆

WHILE this is for the most part a personal book, I have had no little assistance in preparing it. I wish to acknowledge especially the help given me by John Coburn Turner in the preparation of Chapter VI. Many friends in government have been kind enough to check my memory and provide details which had slipped out of mind. I am especially indebted to Raymond P. Brandt, chief correspondent of the *Post-Dispatch* in Washington, for reading the manuscript. I wish to thank Mrs. Estelle Welsh and Mrs. Carrie Will Praeger for help in preparing the book for the printer. And, as with everything I have written, my deepest debt is to my wife whose intelligence and common sense have saved me from many errors I would otherwise have made.

TABLE OF CONTENTS

☆

SECTION I

THE NEW DEAL

Chapter I

Washington Is a State of Mind

THE line extended out into the street. These were girls reporting for work for the first time with their brand new Civil Service rating. Another line was the appointment line, run of the mine visitors. Around the desk marked "Congressional, Diplomatic, and Press" were men waiting to be identified before they could be given a badge, a pass, and an escort. The ceaseless milling of people back and forth goes on all day long every day, watched over by guards in uniform and enlisted men. This is the lobby of the Munitions building on Constitution Avenue where the tide of war flows strongest.

It is hard to believe it is the same place. Three years ago, two years ago, you stepped into a somnolent quiet, a deserted lobby with possibly an attendant who may have glanced up idly as you passed. You poked up the stairs past the portrait of Henry Stimson in his first tour as Secretary of War back in 1913; past other earlier secretaries in great, dusty gold frames. You strolled down the corridor and whether it was the head of G-2 or the secretary of war or the chief of staff you wanted to see, you usually found him in and willing enough to see you. That was peace, the long-disused apparatus of war that seemed as musty and as dim as the old secretaries looking down out of their faded gilt frames.

It has been the history of Washington from the beginning. The past is forever being caught up with by the violent present. Just when the capital is pleasantly arranged, as a monument, a museum, the theater of a debating society, then some cataclysmic event sweeps in with the force of a tornado and the pattern is forever upset. Each time it has happened, in each war.

The New Deal was some preparation for this upheaval. It was a kind of war. Thousands of new people, people utterly new to

3

Washington, came in its wake. They began the crowding and the pushing, the bursting at the seams. Often they seemed, to the settled inhabitants, like noisy visitors who had suddenly burst into a shrine. They were irreverent, impatient, indifferent to the past.

Yet before the crisis of the war, the city had begun to absorb them. The crest of the wave had been spent. A process of crystallization had begun. This was to be no more than another tidal mark in the history of the capital. The flood would subside or, rather, it would become a part of the vast, subterranean stream of government.

In 1937 and 1938 the New Deal was being brushed and tidied up toward such a peaceful future. Physically, too, the loose ends were being snipped off and the place readied up. Across Constitution Avenue from the new Department of Labor building were the old green houses of the Department of Agriculture, a shambling line of untidy structures. They were an affront to the view from the tall windows of Madame Perkins's office, an affront to the dull and empty classicism of the new building. And, of course, they were an affront to the handsome plans of the National Capital Park and Planning Commission. Out they went, with not a trace left, and where they had been was a greensward so that the Secretary of Labor could look across an agreeable vista to the white stone temple of the Department of Agriculture.

Then the storm broke and before you could say Franklin Roosevelt a long line of gray Tempos—barracklike two-story buildings—had sprouted where the green houses had been. Plans were out for the duration. Tempos were built almost at the base of the Washington Monument. Great mountains of earth from the excavations were pushed back onto the Mall. This was war again and it had come before the ruins of the last conflict had been quite righted up.

Washington is a vacuum in which opposing pressure groups struggle for power. That struggle is charted, definable. In normal times it is the news out of Washington; a victory for one side, a defeat for the other side. For eight years, more or less, I've written about that struggle.

There was never any fixed battleline. Nor was there any sharp demarcation, as between the forces of evil and the forces of virtue. Farmer, labor, industry, North, South, big business, little business, New Deal, Old Deal—the struggle is on a hundred shifting fronts. And in normal times it is possible to discern a kind of balance, precarious yet actual, that comes out of this conflict in the national arena. Franklin Roosevelt is a master at playing those forces one against the other.

In a time of crisis it is as though the stage lights were lowered. The struggle goes on but in an obscure and uncertain dusk. Something greater, more compelling, the unknown, the immeasurable, has dwarfed the contenders. How far it will go, where it will end, no one can say. Nor what will be the relative position of the opposed forces when the crisis is finally ended.

We who write from Washington day in and day out, the Washington correspondents, those of us who are not tied to any special beat but roam the town with considerable latitude, flatter ourselves that in a normal time we know pretty much what is going on all over the place. And within limits that is true. We have our own lines out here, there, and everywhere. We pool our information. Things rarely happen without some forewarning. We snatch at hints, we read meaning into cryptic intimations. Often we're fooled beyond belief.

But more often we sense the way the wind is shifting. It is a marvelous and fascinating game. Guessing, knowing, being right, you get a satisfaction out of all proportion to the event itself. There was once a correspondent in Washington called Joe Smith. You would tell Joe Smith something that was about to happen or that had just happened and his invariable reply would be, "Aw, I wrote that two weeks ago." Irreverently, behind his back, he was called "I-had-it-two-weeks-ago Joe Smith." He was a melancholy fellow whose only reward in life seemed to be that he did have it two weeks ago, if he did. And I could understand that. Most of us are more modest than Joe Smith, but we get the same compensation out of knowing a month, a week, a day or two, in advance which way the Washington weathervane is going to swing.

In a war there is no knowing, no guessing. The wind out of nowhere blows with overwhelming force. So much is happening that it is possible to know only fragments. Tremendous changes take place and are hardly reflected on the churned-up surface. We are all caught up in it, high and low. In a sense we are prisoners of this immeasurable force, prisoners with one degree of freedom or another.

It is the tenant of the White House who is most narrowly confined. At a little after nine-thirty each morning he is wheeled along the glass-enclosed walk from the house to the offices and from then on until five-thirty he is at the center of the vortex. Each word that he speaks is weighed and measured and its impact is reflected in circles that widen to the horizon's edge. And five-thirty is no release. This man, this President, is tied to telephones that are the nerve ends of a world-wide intelligence system. He must be there when they ring, for his is the final word.

Outwardly his manner is unchanged. To the world he still shows a blithe spirit; the smile, the cigarette holder cocked at an assured angle, the firm touch with doubters and dissenters. If the yoke that he labors under has galled, he does not allow outsiders to see it. His life is today far less public than it once was. This prisoner of war must be safeguarded as never before. The people who want to see him are filtered through a finer screen.

While the tenant is unchanged, the White House in his tenancy has undergone a transformation. It has lost the look of a leisurely country house deposited by some chance whim in the midst of a city. Under the burgeoning of the New Deal the cramped executive offices were expanded to sizable proportions with rooms for a fairly large staff. Now, on the opposite side, another and larger office building has been built.

It is the measure of a decade of extraordinary change. No longer is it a house that happens to have a small office attached to it. Rather, it has become a residence set down between two offices.

When you went there for parties in the past, you entered through the East carriage entrance, where the new offices now are. You went into a glass-enclosed area where there were rows upon rows of coat racks and then on into what is the basement. Here were vague rooms filled with odd, disused-looking furniture out of the President Hayes and the President Garfield eras. They had an attic quality, these rooms, stuffed with things that had a sentimental value and could not be thrown away, but which nevertheless were no longer good enough for the formal apartments abovestairs. They summed up a great deal of Washington, those rooms out of the conglomerate past; rooms full of crotchets of history that had somehow escaped the auctioneer.

This new war is sweeping out many relics. Yet surviving each such upheaval are strata out of the remote past. Washington is a vast geological sink in which nothing ever wholly vanishes. Layer on layer these strata are deposited—the monuments, the odd, irrelevant statesmen immortalized in bronze or stone, yes, and the people and prejudices, too, going a long way back into the past.

Even in the midst of this, the newest and greatest upheaval, you step into a garden in Georgetown that is just as it has been for a hundred years or more. The box hedges are higher but they give off in the heat of summer the same agreeable smell. The stones in the garden paths are worn a little smoother. But essentially nothing is changed and that goes, often, for the people in the gardens and the furniture of their minds; late Louis Seize or, possibly, a tidy Biedemeier.

Likewise in government the geologic layers overlap. A boring, even a superficial boring, will bring up bureaucrats and functionaries out of other epochs who are going through their appointed rounds with a firm determination to ignore the present. Fussy little men go on making familiar motions, repeating rituals of government as though in so doing they could exorcise the awful threat of change.

And in Washington you have, too, the same social strata that you have in any other prosperous city of similar size. In large, comfortable houses in Chevy Chase and Spring Valley are lawyers and lobbyists who have cherished for Roosevelt the same hatred as their counterparts in Cleveland and Detroit and Los Angeles. They have grown richer on the New Deal, unraveling new threads of government for wealthy clients; but their conversation in club locker rooms is identical with the conversation in all club locker rooms. And their wives say the same things over salad luncheons, with, if anything, an extra dash of resentment that may come out of inconveniences they have suffered in overcrowded Washington.

The surface of the city is hard, impervious. So much of the life that flows through it is obscured by the sterile, classical face that is turned to the world. Yet it is there, and close to the surface, with all the contrasts of dark and light of an ordinary city.

In the spring and in the fall an old Negro woman sits on the steps of the Riggs bank at the corner of Pennsylvania Avenue and Fifteenth Street, a short block from the White House. Beside her she has some violets if it is spring, a few sprays of holly or some small tight bunches of partridge berry in the fall. She never seems to make any effort to sell these wares. It is as though she had brought them along for her own quiet enjoyment. She sits in the sun looking with peaceful indifference at the hard gray stone façade of the Treasury across the street while the furious world streams noisily past. I have come to look for her there with the change of the seasons and to think of her as the other face of the city; the dark noisome slums that are so well hidden you never see them unless you go looking for them; the people, patient and submissive or darkly resentful, who come out of these warrens.

Across from the White House is Lafayette Square which was once a pleasant, informal little park with crushed gravel paths, a pleasant overgrowth of shrubbery, and Andrew Jackson on a horse in the middle of it. The New Deal changed all that. Walks, boulevard wide, were run through and new trees set out in checkerboard patterns. Gone was the air of bosky quiet. Yet in the two years that have intervened the green has grown up again. The big horse chestnuts survived the cataclysm and so did the flocks of pigeons and so did a rumpled, stained, old man who sits on a bench and feeds the birds.

The city is unregenerate, chock full of reminders of other times in spite of the high wind that blows periodically down the avenue. So many reveilles have sounded, and now this one has shattered the heavy air of the Potomac basin, louder and more compelling than any in the past.

I want to try to set down some of the things that have happened in the decade that has come after 1932, the Roosevelt decade. It is a period crowded with action. I have been lucky enough to see a good part of it happen. I came to Washington at the beginning of it to be a member of the staff of the St. Louis *Post-Dispatch*. To my way of thinking the *Post-Dispatch* is about the best newspaper you can work for. Few if any prejudices are superimposed from the top. And you have latitude to move around, to explore on your own initiative, and to write what you see and hear. That is rare. It is the reason I can try now to put together something out of the fierce, impetuous rush of the years that have led up to this moment of struggle and conflict.

In my account will be the people and the events that seemed to me to be important. I've tried to see it as it happened and not from any arbitrary perspective. Naturally, I have a healthy set of prejudices. As an outlander, a Middle Westerner, I have a deep suspicion of big government and big business. I have never been able to see how we could have a democracy if all the orders came from a few men in one city on the Eastern seaboard, whether that city was Washington or New York. These prejudices may get in the way, but not, I hope, too much to obscure the story.

Chapter II

The Hopefuls

THE house that stands at the southeast corner of Massachusetts Avenue and Twenty-first Street is a large, square pretentious pile with ornament out of a pastry tube. It is like others of its kind in that neighborhood, a part of the geologic era laid down in Washington in the late nineties and the early part of this century when certain of the newly rich elected to crash the political rather than the financial capital of the nation.

In its time it was the grandest, showiest, most expensive house that old Tom Walsh could build when, in his daughter's phrase, he struck it rich. Others before him had spread themselves in this pleasant elm-bordered neighborhood just beyond Dupont Circle— which was really almost country still; the green leisurely fringe of a capital that was no more than a sleepy Southern village.

But Father, having struck it rich, outdid them all. The Walsh ballroom and the Walsh conservatory were grander and larger than any other ballroom and conservatory, the White House excepted of course, in Washington. Each room was done in a different color of brocade, shiny brocade; stick candy shades, pink, yellow, green, light blue. In the vernacular of the period, it was elegant. And the Walshes, father, mother, and little Evalyn, had the time of their lives.

In July of 1935 the Rural Resettlement Administration took over the "Walsh Mansion" lock, stock, and barrel. For many years it had stood mournfully empty, as the Walsh-McLean fortune, along with most boom-time fortunes, dwindled in size. Now, under the impetus of what was really the beginning of Washington's never-ending office shortage, the great empty rooms were invaded by such a company as old man Walsh could never have dreamed of. These were the planners in the first, fresh enthusiasm of the reform era of the New Deal.

The house, which Mrs. McLean was happy to lease to the government, was ill adapted to its new function. In high-ceilinged rooms with saccharine frescoes, lighting was improvised. At the stipulation of the owner the brocaded walls were covered with cellophane. The place began to buzz with activity. Drafting boards were set up in the ballroom. Master bedrooms went to chief planners. Few complained about the inconveniences. On the contrary, everyone seemed extraordinarily good-natured, as though a party of happy picnickers had been allowed to camp for a time in the halls of the rich and mighty.

These men and women had reason to be elated. They were planning a new world. The tenants of the Walsh Mansion had been assigned to design the greenbelt communities that were the particular pride of the Rural Resettlement Administration. Architects and designers not merely competent but among the recognized leaders of their profession had been enlisted for this new undertaking which seemed to project so far into American life. Younger men in particular, eager to try in America housing experiments that had been carried out on such a large scale in Europe, were drawn to this venture.

The greenbelt communities were to be not merely "housing" as such, not merely "slum clearance." The vision was of a new way of life which took full advantage of the machine age; integral communities created in the country with workers going by bus or private car to near-by cities. With this, went large talk of decentralizing industry, building such garden towns around small factories.

Very soon handsome plans began to take form on the drafting boards in the big ballroom of the Walsh Mansion. Enthusiastic experts built dioramas so that one could see in miniature the life of these ideal new communities. Here no child crossed a dangerous public highway. Here no window looked out on a blank wall. Here were swimming pools and recreation courts and fine modern schools. As a starter, a sample, there were to be five such communities; one each near Washington, St. Louis, Cincinnati, Milwaukee, and at Bound Brook, New Jersey. When you asked detailed questions, it developed that the cost per room of the houses in these new communities would in all probability be such that rents, based on anything like an adequate return to the government, would probably be beyond the reach of low income families, even with a 45 per cent subsidy. But it was pointed out that this was because the initial cost of planning was so high and that when this cost should be prorated over other greenbelt communities, certain to be built once the magnificent advantages of the sample were apparent, the problem of excessive rents would disappear.

Presiding over all this flourishing activity was Doctor Rexford Guy Tugwell, a professor of economics from Columbia University who was then forty-four years old. So handsome as to be conspicuous—crisply curling black hair, an almost Hollywood profile —Doctor Tugwell was supremely self-confident. There were in fact many who thought him arrogant. He was completely sure that he was right. You had only to look around to see that American cities needed rebuilding. They were dark, congested, ugly. Doctor Tugwell was inclined to be impatient with skeptics. Benighted Southern congressmen who sniped at his ideas and his projects drew his sulphurous indignation. While it was silly and irrelevant to recall that youthful poem—about rolling up your sleeves and remaking the world—nevertheless in the Tugwell of this phase there was still something of that ebullient youth.

He attracted other intellectuals who wanted to help the inevitable new world to birth. Some were eccentrics, some were dreamy timewasters. For the most part, however, they were exceptionally keen and intelligent. Earnest, hard-working, giving off ideas like showers of meteors, they stood on the threshold of the new era, a little tremulous. Theirs was a cozy conspiracy of good will to remake America on a cleaner, truer, more secure pattern.

In their company you had the heady sense of a rarer, higher altitude. They were as bright and fresh as paint. Writers, economists, artists, sociologists, they were something brand new in government. I was still a little strange to Washington then and I remember being exhilarated and at the same time disturbed after a dinner or a lunch with these pioneers of a brave new world. I felt that somehow they didn't know the Middle West that I knew and the people in the Middle West. The whole process seemed far removed from the deeper currents of American life and no one was working to relate these exciting experiments to main currents. It was happening in Shangri-La, a classic Shangri-La that was growing at a startling rate.

I don't mean to make the young New Dealers in the early alphabetical agencies sound stuffy or humorless. They were not that, or at any rate not the best of them. They were gay, amusing, and they could laugh like hell at other people's mistakes and even occasionally at their own. They traveled a great deal, urgent expeditions to Seattle, to Los Angeles, to Kansas City, and always they returned full of a new enthusiasm. So much needed doing. People out there didn't seem quite to know that it needed doing. You had to make them understand what you were doing for them. You were a conspirator.

Soon, however, an unhappy omission became apparent. The conspirators had neglected to take the American people into their confidence; nor even any section of the American public that might have been expected to enter willingly into such a conspiracy. Naturally, real-estate dealers and property owners in Cincinnati, St. Louis, and Milwaukee did not like the prospect of such effective subsidized competition. Through Congress, through the orthodox political channels, they began to apply pressure. Doctor Tugwell and his planners found that they had been planning in limbo, a lonely and insecure purgatory. Finally, it was a minor miracle that three greenbelt communities were actually built.

Because Doctor Tugwell's dilemma was so painfully obvious, it has served as a useful symbol of this phase of the New Deal. In many respects it was typical of the effort to superimpose from Washington a ready-made Utopia. In a democracy such as ours it is difficult or impossible to confer any benefit unless there exists or can be created an articulate, organized demand for that benefit.

A benefit implies some change in the status quo, perhaps to the disadvantage of those already privileged. Therefore the privileged forces incline to unite in order to preserve what exists, at the sacrifice of what might be, no matter how intelligent and reasonable the latter.

You could find a scapegoat easily enough. The Southern congressmen. The newspapers which had heaped ridicule on the Tugwelltowns and their creator. But nevertheless the fact was inescapable that the planners had been planning in a political vacuum. The essential political backing, whether rooted in the trade-unions, the women's clubs, the National Association of Manufacturers, or whatever, had been neglected. And without some political nourishment, as Doctor Tugwell found out, it is impossible to lay down a blueprint for even a small section of society in this vast, powerful, well-nigh ungovernable country. Under dictatorship, perhaps, at the cost of everything else, but in a democracy as diffuse as ours, hardly.

In 1935, it was argued that we could afford such interesting mistakes. I think that was debatable. The money that may have been wasted was unimportant. What was far more precious was time. Even then, in that incredibly remote period, we had no time to spare. Optimistically it was argued that something was learned from this little lesson in political geometry; there were practical discoveries in architecture and construction cost. The Farm Security Administration, profiting by the errors of its predecessor, has followed a more sober course, bringing real benefits to rural areas throughout the country, if only, for the most part, on a sample basis.

But that argument, too, is highly debatable. So long as we had failed to find, or for that matter had neglected even to work toward, a real solution for the basic ills of our time, we could hardly afford any incidental excursions. Looking back, this period appears curiously dwarfed; like a view seen through the wrong end of a telescope, the noisy contemporary landscape strangely diminished.

The Hundred Days which began with that magnificent voice

on March 4, 1933, were long since history. Mr. Roosevelt had provided a magic that had restored our society, the transformation occurring so swiftly that people began to doubt the chaos and the despair of the months immediately before. With this went a kind of shame. Mr. Roosevelt had managed so easily and with such a sure dramatic touch that the rich and powerful could not bring themselves to believe that only a short time before they had looked to him with a mixture of fear and hope.

The President had completed his revolution. That was what his official biographer, Ernest Lindley, called it—a revolution. Seen from this perspective, in the light of the profound changes that have occurred in the world, that appears to have been a slight exaggeration. It was more nearly a restoration.

A bold, self-confident archeologist, Mr. Roosevelt stepped on March 4 into the ruins of the America of the 'twenties and swiftly and deliberately put the pieces back into place, or at any rate most of the pieces. He did not alter fundamental relationships in finance or, for that matter, anywhere else. True, he enacted some long-needed police measures such as the Securities and Exchange Act. And a little later he laid the foundation for the Social Security Act. But the controls remained where they had been before the Roosevelt revolution.

What the President and the men around him were able to do during the Hundred Days was extraordinary. The job of restoration was a tremendous one. It must have felt like a revolution to those who were in the middle of it. But a revolution alters fundamental relationships. Mr. Roosevelt was no revolutionist. He was a conservative, perhaps even a traditionalist, who wanted to preserve a society that he had found good.

That was the supreme irony of the attack which had already begun on him, an attack to which his friends unwittingly contributed almost as much as his enemies. He was denounced as a radical who wanted to destroy "the American way of life." If he wanted anything more than to set the wheels of the old order turning again, with a somewhat greater measure of justice for the great mass of the people, he gave no evidence of it. In September of 1935 he wrote a letter to the publisher of the Scripps-Howard newspapers, Roy Howard, in which he spoke of the "substantial completion" of his basic program.

That was the famous "breathing spell" letter. It may have been, of course, entirely political in motive, aimed at the 1936 election. There is good reason, however, to believe that Mr. Roosevelt did feel that the revolution was over. The Supreme Court had delivered a merciful death blow to the NRA, and while the President stubbornly maintained that that crazy contraption would actually have worked if only a few legal crotchets had been removed, the Court decision was a political windfall. Production levels were rising. Throughout the country there was a mounting tone of assurance and confidence, reflecting the temper of the new master of the White House.

But in the rosy picture of recovery there was one great flaw. The army of the unemployed remained a solid, disconcerting mass. Whether there were eight million or nine million or ten million no one was quite sure. They could not be ignored even though Mr. Roosevelt persistently refused to believe in them. Repeatedly the question would come up at his press conferences. What about the number of unemployed? Each time Mr. Roosevelt would launch on a monologue on how difficult or impossible it was to tell really who was unemployed. If two sons and a daughter lived in the household and the daughter, who had been teaching piano lessons, was to stop teaching, would she be unemployed? What measuring rod were you to use? The barometer of unemployment continued to hover uncertainly around the ten million mark, yet it was not until nearly a year and a half later that the President finally authorized a census of the unemployed.

There was one man in Washington who knew exactly how he intended to fit this barometer reading into his own scheme of things. That was a figure we have pushed out of sight, forgetting what he was in his time and what he might have been. Huey Long came out of the canebrake of Louisiana with all the equipment that it takes to upset the political applecart. He had great intellectual capacity. He had a tremendous emotional and psychological drive. His ambition know no bounds and he was completely ruthless. Most people never got over the idea that he was a comic figure, but that was because Huey didn't live long enough to disabuse them.

Huey knew exactly the weaknesses of the New Deal and he never ceased to hammer at them. He knew, too, how moribund were the Republicans who sat on the other side of the aisle in the Senate and he gave them no mercy. It was a situation made for him to exploit.

As an infighter he had the resourcefulness and cunning of a tiger. It was fascinating to watch him on the Senate floor skating dizzy circles around men with slower and far more orthodox minds. Occasionally he could be cruel. I remember him bearbaiting poor old Joe Robinson of Arkansas, the majority leader, through one long torrid afternoon. Robinson had made the mistake of getting down to a low personal plane and that was where Huey had no equals. Huey was the matador to poor old Joe's bull, moving in and out and stabbing deep. Huey had bested Robinson in one Arkansas election and what he proposed to do was to move in again and chop poor old Joe out of his Senate seat.

He would have done it, too. His declared intention was to explode the stored-up dynamite of the South. In Louisiana, Huey abolished the one-dollar poll tax as a voting prerequisite and, as he liked to boast, in the next election he got twice as many votes as he had ever got before. He told the poor whites, yes, and the Negroes, too, what he'd done for them. He built roads, he put books in their schools, he came out and talked rip-roaring political hellfire to them. What he did in Louisiana, Huey meant to do throughout the South, and given a year or two more the whole region would have fallen to him like an overripe plum. Joe Robinson and Pat Harrison knew what Huey meant. They didn't think he was funny. Incidentally, the issue of the poll tax, which keeps from one third to one half of all eligible white voters away from the polls in the South, has been talked about by the younger New Dealers but no direct attack has ever been made on it.

On April 5, 1935, Huey stood up in the Senate to make a speech. He stood up in the awkward, jerky fashion that characterized all his physical movements. What he said on that day he had said before and he would say again. Primarily it was a statement of intention.

"You aren't even trying to legislate. You've thrown up the sponge. You've turned your powers and duties over to the Wallaces, the Tugwells, and the Richbergs. The laws they've passed in the privacy of their offices would fill volumes even if we could find out what they are—which we can't.

"What a situation this is. We now have three major political parties—Republicans, Democrats, and the New Deal, and the New Deal is fully as reactionary as the Hooverites. . . ."

Then he turned to address himself to the Republicans who took a smug satisfaction in Huey's castigation of his fellow Democrats.

"The mossback Republicans are sitting back over there and chuckling to themselves—'ha-ha-ha' and 'he-he-he'—waiting for the New Deal to blow up, thinking that it will blow the country over to them. Well, we're not going to let it blow over to them. We don't want the reactionary government of either the Republicans or the New Deal.

"Why don't you be men? Why don't you legislate? That's what the people sent you here to do. Why don't you get up and pass legislation to make it impossible for one man to have a billion dollars when millions of men have nothing—not even a place to sleep? Why don't you do something to distribute the great wealth of this country?"

Huey knew that the Hundred Days was no revolution. He was going to bring about a revolution of his own and the familiar pieces of the old order were not to be left in their familiar places. In September, Huey was assassinated in his own gaudy capitol in Baton Rouge. He was forty-two years old. At the same age Adolf Hitler, in 1931, was somewhat further advanced on his career, but the comparison is difficult to make since Huey may well have been on the threshold of a very rapid climb.

In Washington you could almost hear a sigh of relief go up.

It was Roosevelt luck, the knowing and the cynical said. The sailing was clearer now that the course was unobstructed. There were still the unemployed, the millions who crowded the relief rolls, but people, prosperous people with jobs, seemed to forget them. It was as though they had been walled off in another watertight compartment of the economy.

They were the special charge of Harry Hopkins, a nervous, hard-driving social worker whom Roosevelt had brought down to Washington with him from Albany. In a job that had never existed before, Hopkins began a furious improvisation; he was playing by ear on a giant organ with all the stops pulled out. It is the record of his entire career in Washington—improvisation at the center of a tornado.

Not that he was in any doubt as to the direction in which he wanted to move. The doubter was his friend in the White House who was now hot, now cold, now right, now left, now black, now white. The relief system devised soon after Mr. Roosevelt's inauguration was grounded on the old English poor law base of pauperization. To be eligible for help you had to have fallen all the way down the scale, losing painfully one by one whatever vestiges of respectability or security had adhered to you. Hopkins fought that concept tooth and toenail.

He fought with his chief for a system of work relief that would not be based on the means test, and when victory came he was almost as surprised as the rest of the country. Early in November of 1933 he had written in his own hand a memorandum of three sentences recommending that four million men and women be put to work immediately. This chit was put on the President's desk and to Hopkins's amazement it came back a few hours later with the notation, "Approved, FDR."

To give jobs to the four million meant unending slavery night and day for Hopkins and the men around him, but this was their dream, their hope, and they set to it manfully. Not only ditch diggers and bricklayers but artists, teachers, architects, and accountants were to be put to work. Originally the plan had been to employ half relief and half nonrelief workers; but the pres-

sure from those who had long managed to stay off the relief
rolls, despite such privations as could only be guessed at, was so
great that this ratio was abandoned. Four million men and women
began to draw regular pay checks. They built roads, sewers,
reservoirs, parks, swimming pools, one hundred and fifty thousand
sanitary privies. They painted murals, repaired schools, destroyed
millions of rats, drained hundreds of thousands of acres of malarial
land. The nation's physical plant, neglected during the long depression, was patched and restored at many points by this concentrated attack.

Hopkins has said that he knew the Civil Works program was
to be merely a temporary expedient through the difficult winter
of 1933-34. But at the beginning he hoped it would be more
than that. Certainly his friends in the spending-to-save school
thought that CWA was the beginning of a long-time policy. One
of these friends, perhaps Hopkins's closest friend on Capitol Hill,
Senator Robert M. LaFollette, Jr., got a serious shock when in the
spring of 1934 the President told him that the rumors were true
and CWA was to be concluded now that the weather was warmer
and want less acute.

LaFollette's case is an interesting one. He comes closer to being
an intellectual—a theorist capable of arguing in general terms—
than anyone elected to the Senate in his generation. Two people
had profoundly influenced him. One was his father, old "fighting
Bob," and the other was the historian Frederick Jackson Turner.
Reading and rereading Turner* he was made aware of what the
inevitable closing of the frontier would mean in American life.
At the same time he saw how most people in America continued
to think in frontier terms. He remembered that his father in un-
tying a package invariably rolled up the string and put it in one
drawer of his desk and folded the paper and put it in another
drawer. That was an unshakable habit that had come down out
of an economy of scarcity. The best government was the government that governed least. That, too, had come down from the
era of the frontier.

* "Rise of the New West" by Frederick Jackson Turner. Harper's, 1906.

In 1928, Senator LaFollete had introduced a resolution in the Senate calling for Federal Reserve restrictions on the stock market boom. Like a latter day Jeremiah he had foreseen a reckoning and had been damned for his prescience. Watching the crisis develop in '31 and '32 he saw also what he thought was an opportunity that would never recur again to apply brakes to the financial system.

LaFollette had gone to Warm Springs to see the President-elect in February of 1933 just as the last of the nation's banks was closing its doors. He had gone to offer the President a plan of his own concoction, a plan that he felt was guaranteed to assure the new President, with his huge popular following, a continuing control over the country's financial power. In brief, it was to allow solvent banks to reopen only under a six-months' license, using the postal savings as a stop gap in those areas where no bank whatsoever could possibly be opened.

"In that way," LaFollette explained to Roosevelt, "you will be able to work out a careful system of checks and controls while you still have the banks existing at the sufferance of the federal government."

"Oh, but that isn't necessary at all," the President-elect replied. "I've just had every assurance of co-operation from the bankers."

The new President had no intention of putting the banks in bondage. Nor did he intend to establish a permanent policy of work relief, with the means test eliminated, on the vast scale of the CWA. Both proposals were radical and Mr. Roosevelt is no radical.

If Senator LaFollette argued forcefully and cogently on one side, the President's budget director, Lewis W. Douglas, argued with equal skill on the other side; that is, for curtailing all government expenditure and balancing the budget as quickly as possible. Douglas too had a broad intellectual grasp of the problem, and often he and the earnest little senator from Wisconsin would debate by the hour. Poles apart, they nevertheless respected each other's intellectual attainments. Each went in and out of the White House and each man thought from time to time that he had won the President over to his side, until Douglas finally resigned in disgust as the budget got more and more out of balance.

But there were other budget balancers within the administration to take his place. That had already become a definite Roosevelt technique, one which was to be practiced, with various refinements, right down to the present. Mr. Roosevelt relies upon opposites to coax him first to one side and then the other, believing apparently that this will insure a middle course approximately in line with the temper of the average American. The President is not interested in theories. First and last a pragmatist, he is concentrated, perhaps of necessity, not on what may happen five years from now but on next week and next month.

If it was a middle course, it was also, as Hopkins was to discover, a zigzag course. CWA, which had cost $833,960,000, ended in May of 1934. Once again Hopkins began to play by ear, under almost constant attack from every possible quarter. Even so early he grew to have the weary, harassed look that was to become chronic with him.

His office was on the top floor of the battered Walker-Johnson building a block and half from the White House. An untidy hall on the first floor was cluttered with girls from North Carolina or South Carolina or Georgia who were drinking the midmorning or the midafternoon coke, depending on which time it was. You creaked up in a slow-moving elevator. In his anteroom were hopeful people from all over the country; state administrators, humble suppliants, plain screwballs, earnest social workers. Some of them had waited there for days. Most of them would never see him.

When you got in to him, he had a sort of trapped look. That was his manner with the press. He barricaded himself behind his shabby desk, his feet up, inhaling deeply on a cigarette, snarling back at his persecutors. The press liked it, they liked him. He was rarely tactful or tactical. Only half trying, you could get out of him a fine, angry contempt for all that was contented and Republican. It was an act, but on the whole it was a good act. He

was sensitive, impressionable, and he looked as though he belonged on the other side of the desk with his tormentors.

Already he had begun to cultivate the close relations with the
White House which were to put him there finally as a permanent
boarder. Hopkins was among the first to turn to his own uses Mrs.
Roosevelt's considerable political talent. She was eager enough to
help and he appealed to her judgment on many issues. It might
almost be said that he gave her her start toward becoming assistant
President, the office which she was to make increasingly important.

At the same time Hopkins often stood up against his chief in
argument even after his almost feminine intuition had told him
there was no longer any use in arguing with the stubborn Dutchman. The indices would rise and pragmatically the President would
listen to the budget-balancers. Hopkins, doubting these upward
flurries, would fight for continued high relief. Several times he
talked despairingly of quitting. Once his friends believed that their
arguments had persuaded him to stay.

For an impressionable man it was a raw, rasping, nerve-racking
job. Hopkins knew that nowhere did the standard of relief permit
a decent scale of living. He knew that millions were kept off the
rolls who should have been on. And in those early years he was
constantly tortured by the inadequacy of the job that he was doing.
There were compensations of course. The sense of power. The
heady sense of being the greatest spender in the history of the
world. It was personalized, that power, in this frail man who a
short time before had had a modest social service job. He himself was broke all the time, drawing his pay check as far in advance as possible. He had the burden of two families, and Washington, even a smallish house in Georgetown, was expensive.

The thing was so big, so overwhelming. He could never know
a fraction of what was going on in the vast organization that
sprawled out across the country. Even his own shop in Washington
was far more than any man could cope with. But he had developed
then the facility for picking facts and impressions out of the air.
He was a sensitive device for recording in the briefest possible

time a thousand things that were going on around him. That is why he was to be so useful later on in London and Moscow.

In charge of buying surplus commodities for distribution to relief families, a phase of the program that had come to involve millions of dollars and constant operation in the commodity markets, was Jacob Baker, one of Hopkins's top assistants. He happened to say one day in the course of a conference, "By the way, Harry, do you know that you're the biggest buyer of butter in the world today?" This was news and Hopkins wanted to hear more about it. For fifteen minutes he listened to a concise explanation of the workings of the butter market and the part played by the relief administration in building up a big reserve. A week later at press conference, when he was asked a question about commodity buying, Hopkins talked learnedly about butter.

Always he was at the end of a tether. He knew, usually, how far he could go but his subordinates sometimes made grievous mistakes. Production for use by the unemployed was a concept that took hold of members of his staff, with some encouragement from Hopkins himself. Like the CWA, it was an ideal. Sewing rooms where women on relief made simple garments were all right. You could even make mattresses from surplus cotton although they hammered you pretty hard for that.

But when you came up against the limit, it was like hitting a stone wall, bang! Overeager underlings in Hopkins's absence initiated a plan to make shoes from some of the thousands of surplus hides on which the relief administration was paying cold storage charges. There were complaints to the White House when word of this leaked out and promptly the White House complained to Hopkins. The plan was immediately abandoned and the official responsible for it was exiled to farthest California.

The whole business of relief was so new to America. Brash youngsters brought on from Columbia University or from Wisconsin or Chicago or Harvard sat in solemn judgment on issues that three years before no one had dreamed of. Now and then they looked a little foolish, which is not to be wondered at. There was that solemn moment when three of the younger staff mem-

bers were allocating to the states the number of artists to be assigned to relief art projects. As a guide they had the state relief
rolls broken down by occupations. What, only fourteen artists in
South Dakota? That couldn't be. The number must be, oh, say
sixty or sixty-five. Put it down at that. Let's see, Tennessee is next.
Now in Tennessee . . . That office in the Walker-Johnson building was so remote from Tennessee. South Dakota was only a quaint
sort of name that meant nothing. The wonder was that these
planners did not look more foolish.

They welcomed people with ideas, almost anyone spunky
enough to speak up about what was wrong with the relief system
or, perhaps, with the world. It seemed to be a hopeful sign that
they should not be entirely satisfied with the way the job was
being done.

Someone had the idea—it may even have been Mrs. Roosevelt—of sending out a dozen keen young people to odd corners
of the country in an effort to find out just what was happening
to people on relief. At that point Martha Gellhorn happened to
come back from Paris interested in a job. (This was long before
Spain and Ernest Hemingway.) She qualified on every score and
almost before she realized what it was about she was on a train
for South Carolina with a wardrobe by Molyneux and a second-
best mink coat. The education was mutual, both for Marty and
the astonished relief population of South Carolina. She came back
to Washington with the blistering anger of which she is capable
to write a book that reported some of the little horrors she had
seen. That was an extra and unexpected dividend for which the
relief administration, never inclined to understate the plight of
the poor, was duly grateful.

I suppose that looking back from a longer perspective this
period will seem even more difficult to understand than it does
now. We knew that Marty's little horrors were just around the
corner, any corner, if you cared to look. Millions of them, really,
in one degree or another of poverty and malnutrition and despair.
The answer is, I suppose, that most people never looked. And

those who did hardly dared to let themselves think that it could go on week after week and month after month.

Enough recovery had occurred so that most of us could say firmly to ourselves that anyone on relief must be naturally shiftless or incompetent. Mr. Hoover's apple salesmen had long since disappeared. You had actually to look for people on relief if you lived in a respectable neighborhood. They were nothing more than a set of statistics and it is very easy to disbelieve a set of large figures.

There was a curious mirage in the sky; the bright shine of water in the long desert of the depression. With this went the comfortable sense that it had been arrived at without cost to anyone. Well, to hardly anyone. There were the rich who seemed to make a great deal of noise, but that could be put down to their ugly reluctance to surrender even a portion of their power and privilege.

Taxes and debt were talked about even by Mr. Roosevelt in this curiously dreamy period. When the subject came up he talked convincingly of the need for wholesale tax revision. It was a hodgepodge of taxes that we had, local and state and national all superimposed one on the other in a crazy-quilt fashion. Somewhere in this mess were iniquities. A scientific overhauling was called for, with state and local officials brought in for a thorough job from top to bottom.

That time never arrived. Members of Congress were horrified by any talk of taxes in an election year, and, of course, elections came every two years. Elections were a factor that you had to take into consideration, but far more serious was the effect that heavier taxation might have on the delicate plant called recovery. You nourished it with the CWA, poured on the life-giving millions, and it thrived. This time surely you could take away the supports and it would flourish on its own. But somehow then it always sickened again.

There were budget-balancers in Congress, men such as Byrd of Virginia and Burke of Nebraska, who talked about giving business a chance to recover, eliminating the false competition of government. Theirs was a logic to terrify any president in office responsible for the welfare of one hundred and thirty million people, and thinking inevitably of his party and re-election. LaFollette's logic was another kind but it, too, had its terrors. The senator from Wisconsin introduced a ten-billion-dollar public works bill, complete with a self-regulating device geared to turn the flood of millions on and off in relation to the rise and fall of the indices of private production. That was frightening enough, but with it went a special relief tax to pay for it.

Logic is a luxury that scarcely any man in high office has ever believed he could afford. Logic is the debased currency of the outs, the impossible extravagance of the ins. Each year there was a deficit. In 1934 it was $2,895,000,000, in 1935 it was $3,209,000,000.

These sums seem small to us today, absurdly small in relation to the colossal sums that are being spent in the war. Actually, of course, a great deal of the budget-balancing chorus appears from this perspective to have been irrelevant. In relation to the potential wealth of this country the debt of 1935 was not large. A peacetime debt of fifty billions should not have caused undue fears. What was so serious was that the money was being spent—and not only the money but, far more important, time and the measurable total of public tolerance for experiment and delay—with little or no progress in the direction of a solution.

To say this is not to belittle the important moves that were made on a number of fronts. The federal lending program brought down interest rates and stimulated home construction. Gradually slum clearance began to become more of a reality and less of a conversation piece. The public power program forced down the rates of power generally and thereby helped to raise the standard of living. The purchase and distribution of so-called surplus commodities, as the program passed out of the experimental stage, contributed materially. But although all of these moves added something, the fundamental paradox remained. Millions of hungry, shabby people had no money in their pockets with which to buy the vast surplus of goods that American machines could produce. That was what Huey Long was talking about. It is what another Huey Long will talk about, if we allow it to happen again when the war is ended and the war boom subsides. Even in the midst of war, a total war, it seems to me that never for a moment can we forget that.

It should be remembered, too, that not all the millions were spent on the unemployed. The latter had to be kept alive by the relief administration. In the same way the Reconstruction Finance Corporation shored up the financial structure of the railroads of the nation. It was part of the process of preserving the past; a process that was restorative rather than surgical.

Herbert Hoover established the Reconstruction Finance Corporation. To let the railroads and the banks drop the full way of deflation would be to risk a complete smash, it was argued, and it was an argument that had awesome force to a politician in office. President Roosevelt continued the Hoover policy. On October 31, 1941, the RFC balance sheet showed that the railroads had received in loans a total of $811,325,175, of which they had repaid $367,881,186.

The word loan is something of a euphemism here. In many instances they were loans, valid operating loans that have been repaid. In other instances they served either a direct and simple or a complex and remote political purpose. A little railroad called the Meridian and Bigbee River Railway, which meanders casually through Mississippi, applied to the RFC for a loan of $1,000,000. After careful study the RFC's railroad division found that the loan was not justified in the public interest. Learning of this decision, Pat Harrison of Mississippi called up to damn such niggardly misers and a little later the loan was granted. The balance sheet shows that $985,000 was disbursed to the Meridian and Bigbee River Railway all of which, on October 31, 1941, was still outstanding.

The Baltimore and Ohio Railroad received $95,343,399 of which it had repaid on October 31, 1941, $12,484,019. The Baltimore and Ohio has a passenger service that from Washington to New York duplicates the service of the Pennsylvania Railroad. This is said to entail an operating deficit of nearly a million dollars a month. Even to suggest the merger of those two services is to call forth cries of pain and rage from everyone with so much as a shadow of a vested interest in the status quo.

The loss of the millions that may or may not be ultimately repaid is of secondary importance. In our economy we have long put far too great a stress on money measurements. The serious failure was the failure even to begin to start to rationalize a railway system that has come down into the motor age trailing, yes, clouds of pioneer glory (think of all those movies about the Union Pacific and the Indians), but also a sprawling and outdated physical system and a debt structure that might have been put together by Rube Goldberg.

A little episode occurred that illustrates exactly how difficult even the most obvious surgery can be. The Minneapolis and St. Louis Railroad Company is a minor line with 1400 miles of road in Minnesota, Iowa, and Missouri. Faced with serious difficulties, the officers of the line applied to the railroad division of the RFC for a loan. A brief examination disclosed that poulticing and ice packs would be of no help.

The head of the RFC's railroad division at that time was John W. Barriger. While he is a conservative and a Republican, Barriger was in certain respects typical of the younger men who were drawn into government for the first time with the New Deal. He was typical in that he was a first-rate specialist in his field. Breathing, eating, and sleeping railroads, he had begun with practical experience on top of an engineer's education and had graduated to railroad finance in New York. And Barriger was typical, too, in that he saw in the new administration an opportunity to bring about basic and long-needed reforms. Not moral reforms, mind you, but functional reforms; and the difference is extremely important.

The Minneapolis and St. Louis provided an interesting test case. John Barriger and his assistants made the most detailed and thorough study of the entire line. From every possible angle they squinted at this specimen of an ailing railroad. What they were after was a working plan that would restore the line to some semblance of life and yet hurt as few people as possible. Finally they thought they had it. To put it this way is to telescope the thousands of hours of labor that went into that accomplishment; the conferences, the work sheets, the letters, the statistics, the physical inspection of the line.

Tentatively and a little timidly it was unveiled. What it did was to eliminate the more obvious waste, which meant cutting out territory that could be served by competing lines or by bus and truck. It meant that a certain number of jobs would be eliminated, but here careful provision was made for pensions and retirements in order to cushion the shock in such a way that it would be scarcely perceptible. But hardly had the Barriger brainchild been exposed to view when the storm broke. The Railway Brotherhoods marshaled all their political strength overnight and descended on Washington to stop this outrage. Not a single job was to be sacrificed; not at any rate so long as the legislative agents of the railway unions could give their orders on Capitol Hill. A Senate committee was called together to determine who had perpetrated the crime. Minnesota's Senator Henrik Shipstead, a gloomy dentist of Norwegian origin, aroused himself from the torpor in which he customarily exists to lead the crusade. Barriger was summoned to the Hill and drawn and quartered on the Capitol steps. When the nor'wester subsided not even a microscopic fragment of the reorganization plan could be found.

It was perfectly understandable. Earnest, hard-working John Barriger had run head on into a whole collection of vested interests, and the fact that he had sweet reason on his side may have even been a handicap. It made everyone that much more annoyed. For any consolation that it might have afforded, Barriger could rest on his sure knowledge that that collection of vested interests and a hundred others like it could not be sustained forever in midair. In announcing the RFC, Mr. Hoover had referred to "the steel beams" that he proposed to put under the nation's credit structure. The only difficulty was that once this shoring-up process had been carried out no one bothered to go up into the attic and clean out the vast accumulation of rubbish that had gathered there. That was a job to make enemies and already 1936 was in sight.

In the Congressional elections of 1934 the Democrats came back with a majority that was larger than that of 1932. But two years later a presidential election was on the horizon. The New Deal began to take on protective coloration. Doctor Tugwell was first pushed into the background and later eliminated. He was to do a long penance before being given another opportunity, this time, of all things, as governor of Puerto Rico, the tragic poor farm that is also an American naval base in the Caribbean. For all his blunders in the Rural Resettlement Administration, he deserved a better fate, for he had displayed both intelligence and courage. He was sacrificed to the political necessities of the moment, and his exile was a symbol of the beginning of the eclipse of the first phase of the New Deal; the phase of reform, full of fervor and fury, when the world seemed very young and anything, or almost anything, was possible.

The political strategy of the opposition was to lump the whole mass together and damn it all; omitting only those measures such as the Social Security Act that the public had long since been prepared to accept. Insofar as that strategy was successful, the confusion in the country was worse confounded. For it ignored vital distinctions between those efforts that had been undertaken with some roots in the needs and desires of the country and those other efforts that were related in the main only to an intellectual pattern to be superimposed from Washington.

It has been fascinating to watch during the past eight years— this effort to govern from a city on the Eastern seaboard a proud, fiercely independent people sprawled over a vast country. Wall Street had tried it through financial controls such as the holding company and had failed miserably. Yet the real meaning of that lesson was lost on the very New Dealers who fought, and successfully, to wipe out the holding company evil. They believed it could be done from Pennsylvania Avenue through direct political control, never realizing that in the approach itself were the same inherent defects.

Their view has never entirely prevailed. Other men, also within

the confines of the all-inclusive corral that is called for convenience
sake the New Deal, have fought against the domination of a remote bureaucracy as hard as they once fought the holding companies. They have fought for regional integration. They have
argued night and day unceasingly for a direct link with the people.

Chapter III

The Prophets

THERE is in the air of Washington a curious corruptibility. It is not the little black bag with the beautiful new bank notes or the shiny bonds. Teapot Domes are very rare even in periods of crisis when the Treasury doors are inevitably opened. There are far more subtle forms of influence that prevail on men and women who come from all over this broad land to the capital.

Nowhere else in America does ambition burn with such a fierce and consuming flame. For practically everyone there is a job higher up which has all the bright allure of a distant Himalaya. Even the President, in his first term at least, and, perhaps, as recent history has demonstrated, in the second term as well, is interested in keeping his job. Nowhere else in America do rank and hierarchy play such a role. There are not seven circles but seventy up which a never-ending procession of the hopeful are climbing.

All of this is natural and understandable and sometimes it even works for good. Part of it is mere chi-chi such as is recorded in the society columns of Washington newspapers. What it does that is damaging is to divorce so many Americans from their roots and from the objectives that first sent them to the capital. Too often the means becomes the end. The spurious prizes that Washington offers take on an importance overshadowing anything out in the country.

So many proud men have been shorn of their strength. Nothing is wrong with X, said a cynic of one of Washington's showier figures, that cannot be cured by an invitation to dinner. What is most curious is that the minute cachets come to have the greatest attraction; the miniscule decorations; the engraved invitations, the club memberships, the privileged week ends. And it is not only

33

the politicians who succumb to these little lures, but journalists, lobbyists, bureaucrats, all, or nearly all, of Washington.

The two men who held most steadfastly to what they were are also, it seems to me, the two men who most profoundly influenced this early reform era of the New Deal. One was, in fact, its progenitor; the other its spiritual father, its patron saint. Senator George W. Norris by long and patient toil prepared the way for many of the measures that were adopted in Roosevelt's first term. The late Justice Louis D. Brandeis provided the legal philosophy —the intellectual atmosphere—that was the background of these measures.

They were the flowering of a long tradition. Born in Kentucky, Brandeis was schooled in puritan New England, a time and a place that complemented his own Hebraic inheritance. Norris through his long career has represented the other face of pioneer America. Not the rugged individualist, but the co-operator, the Populist, the single taxer, the free soil man, spoke in him and with a voice clear and authentic; the voice of the lonely men and women of the high country in Nebraska, of the wide windswept plains of the Dakotas, of the men and women in the cutover country of Minnesota and Wisconsin. Norris never forgot those people, just as Brandeis never forgot what he had learned very early of the meaning of money and power.

Although they never worked in collaboration their careers were interrelated. Between them was a mutual recognition. Long intervals went by in which they scarcely saw each other, but when the need arose, the friendship and understanding between these two men of such dissimilar background became a source of mutual strength. They had character, the kind of integrity that even their enemies learned to respect. No part of the foolish Washington eddy ever drew them in. They stood apart not so much with any conscious or stubborn determination as with a never-failing awareness of the need to concentrate everything on the task at hand.

Norris came to the House from McCook, Nebraska, at a time when old granite-faced Uncle Joe Cannon was the absolute dictator of that body. Uncle Joe could claim all the advantages of dictatorship. There was no nonsense, the trains ran on time. Useless talk was not tolerated. When the green, new member from Nebraska asked for a place on the judiciary committee where he believed he would be most useful, the dictator promptly assigned him to public buildings and grounds and to the supervision of the election of President, Vice-President, and representatives. Uncle Joe must have sensed that this man was a meddler and a troublemaker.

It was a very simple time in our national life. The men who owned the nation's industry also exercised working control over the government at Washington. They had been challenged by that wild-eyed radical, Theodore Roosevelt, but Mr. Taft was more placid and more amenable. In the Senate, Boies Penrose of Pennsylvania was a kind of benevolent Nero whose huge enjoyment of life was only rarely disturbed by minor rebellions. The world was as he liked it. He frowned on change.

The telephone, he was often heard to say, was a damned nuisance. One reason was that he found it difficult to squeeze his massive bulk into the booths just off the Senate floor. On one occasion when he had crammed himself into one of these little torture chambers, some impertinence at the other end of the line caused him to explode with wrath. It was a long-distance call from Philadelphia, something special and rare. His colleagues, eavesdropping with sly enjoyment, heard him end the conversation as follows:

"Listen to me, goddamn it! You run the Pennsylvania Railroad and I'll run the Senate of the United States."

That was a fair division of labor. If you observed the rules and spoke only in turn, you were reasonably assured of a long and comfortable life in the marble halls of Congress. It was a pleasant life with as agreeable a set of men as you could find in the country. They knew good whisky. They played excellent poker. And among them were the finest story-tellers of a story-telling nation.

But this maverick Norris seemed to want something more. He raised his head once or twice in the first term or two and got smacked down for his pains. Like most beginning congressmen, he was puzzled and unhappy over his own impotence in the face

of a set of rigid rules intended to keep tight control of an unwieldy body in the hands of a few men. Earnestly he offered bill
after bill only to have them disappear by a species of parliamentary
magic in the deep recesses of committee. Norris recognized that
the House was too large, and being a consistent and reasonable
man he voted against enlarging it still further when Cannon and
his cohorts wanted to add forty-two members in line with a population increase, making the total 433 instead of 391. Hadn't they
told him that that was why regimentation was necessary? Its
unwieldy size? The House was enlarged.

Norris very early saw just what was wrong with procedure in
Congress. The folly of the lame duck session when men voted
out of office returned to legislate for the country. Secrecy in committees. The absolute dictatorship. The parliamentary dodges for
frustrating any action even when a majority favored it. He began
to see, too, as early as his first term, the legislative line that he
was to follow for the next thirty years. Business control of government was a fact that he refused to accept and in his refusal was
the germ of the Tennessee Valley Authority and the great public
power projects that have come into being during the past decade.

Even more important, perhaps, he developed the guile of the
serpent and the patience of Job. Too many beginning congressmen
are thrown by the system. They succumb to its complexity. Not
Norris. He learned all the parliamentary tricks and there came a
time when, with the backing of other mavericks from the Middle
West, he was to overthrow flinty old Uncle Joe. This was a major
rebellion, the prelude to Democratic control of both House and
Senate which came in a revulsion against the very tightness of the
dictatorship.

Not for a long time did Cannon speak to the rebel. After he
had moved on to the Senate, Norris happened to encounter the old
man by chance in the Republican cloakroom of the House. As they
faced each other across the room, in the minds of both was the
memory of their bitter quarrel. Yet as Norris tells the story, it was
Cannon who spoke first.

"You've been elected to the Senate and I've been defeated for re-election. I'm an old man and my public career is probably over, while you're still young and have many years of useful service ahead.

"Before we separate for the last time, I want to tell you that in my fight against you and your damned gang I've never had any personal feeling against you and I want you to know it. I also want to say to you that if any of that bunch had to be elected to the Senate I'd rather it should be you than any of them."

This was forgiveness from Lucifer dethroned and Norris accepted it in the spirit in which it was spoken. They greeted each other when they met after that.

Blandishments were held out from time to time to entice this Nebraskan with the melancholy face. But anyone naïve enough to expect him to yield to them had but little understanding of his origins. Poverty and early responsibility had been his lot. He knew the feel of the belt tightened against hunger and the smell of the early morning to a boy hardly strong enough to hold a plow in the furrow, and he never forgot. His father was fifty-four, his mother forty-three when he was born on a farm in northern Ohio. His father died while he was still a child, and his mother, of Pennsylvania-Dutch origin, was the chief influence in his life.

The struggle for education was not quite so severe as that of Lincoln but there are valid parallels. In Norris there is much that is like Lincoln. He has the same streak of melancholy, the same aloneness. Again and again it has overwhelmed him after some seemingly futile contest in which he has spent days and days of effort. There is in Norris, too, the same humility, the same tenderness and gentleness, and the same capacity for wrath. And like Lincoln, he has been conscious always of his origins. They shaped him in a mold that was to remain throughout his life unchanged. So much of modern America's beginnings went into that process. It was down close to the earth, close to the great mass of the plain people.

"I remember when I worked on the farm," he has told this same incident over and over, "there was one time in the year when I had a real harvest, the time in the year when I got two dollars a day, and that was during harvest, binding wheat. We had a rich farmer near where I lived who had forty acres of wheat in one field. I worked by the day for that farmer. I had plowed in that field, and often I had ribs I thought were broken when the plow struck a stone or a rock.

"Jim Mook, the owner of that forty acres of wheat, bought a self-binder but no one thought it would work. People had been talking a little about the self-binder. We'd heard there was such a thing, but nobody in the country had ever seen one and nobody believed we ever would. Among the poor people like myself, who had to work and were laboring for these farmers, binding wheat, we all knew that Jim Mook had bought a self-binder, but nobody thought it would work. The first self-binders that came out bound the wheat with wire, but we didn't believe anybody could invent a machine that could tie a knot with wire. However, the self-binder came, and it worked.

"They cut around that forty-acre lot one whole day, and that night some men, laboring men like myself, went into the field and they stacked up some sheaves of wheat, a dozen or two around that self-binder, and set it on fire. When I went home Saturday night, I knew what I would find. I knew—and I had worked until dark and had four or five miles to walk home—that I would find Mother in that one room which was our kitchen, sitting room and dining room. She would be waiting for me, and she wouldn't go to bed until I came home. That night she was reading the Bible by the tallow candle by which my sisters and I had to learn our lessons when we went to country school. We studied by that kind of a light.

"Mother got up and met me at the door, and the first thing she said was, 'Willie, have you heard about Jim Mook's self-binder?' I said, 'Yes, Mother, I've heard about it.' 'Wasn't that awful?' she asked. And I said I thought it was awful. The next remark came right from her honest heart, and without taking time to think, she said, 'But what are we poor people going to do?'

"She condemned the act; she knew it was wrong. She had no sympathy for the men who did it. But it seems to me this illustrated something in her character which I am proud to remember that my mother possessed. It seemed to me it showed that, while she would not tolerate a crime or any wrongdoing such as burning Jim Mook's binder, nevertheless, she felt that poor people in northern Ohio, like ourselves, working day and night from morning until night, deserved something better than we were getting; that something was being held away from us by those in power, either political or financial, even religious; that we were being kept down, when as human beings we should have had the same opportunities for enjoyment, the same privileges in all fundamental matters, that others had, regardless of wealth or political power."

This man never had to learn about technological unemployment from statistics in a textbook. In his heart he knew what the machine meant to the plain people, and what power meant. Year after year in the Senate he fought to keep for the government the millions of dollars that had been invested during the first World War in an effort to develop nitrogen for explosives at Muscle Shoals in Tennessee. He knew what an enormous potential lay untouched in the rivers of the Tennessee system and he fought through the long broiling heat of the Washington summer, first, to keep this prize from falling into private hands, and, later, to develop it as a government project.

Through the sticky twenties he succeeded merely in holding the fort. But slowly and surely he prepared the ground. The investigation of the Federal Power Commission showed the grave weaknesses in the superpower system operated from Wall Street, and as the mists of Coolidge prosperity vanished, private enterprise seemed somehow less sacred. In the rising tide that grew out of the depression came the impetus for the Hundred Days. The Tennessee Valley Authority was created in that period.

Norris had won. Not only the TVA but the Farm Credit Administration, the Rural Electrification Administration, and other major New Deal measures had been foreshadowed in bills he had introduced long before, when a bill by Norris was no more than a gesture.

In triumph he was remarkably as he had been in adversity. The same solitary man made his solitary way in the old familiar places. The New Dealers would have made a public hero of him if he had given them the least encouragement. But that would have been foreign to his nature. In 1935 he went down to Knoxville to see the dams and the power lines and the great lakes that are the TVA system. Norris Dam is named for him and in the big, beautiful power room at Norris the one nonfunctional object is, fittingly, Kathleen Wheeler's bust of the senator.

In a poll of correspondents in the Press Gallery in 1941, Norris was chosen as the most useful member of the Senate. It was a shrewd judgment, characteristic of the men who regularly cover the Senate. Many of the correspondents who cast their vote for him had little or no sympathy for his views. But they saw him at his desk on the Senate floor day after day, following with rare persistence the course of the legislative stream. They knew that he could be sentimental but never demagogic. His voice, rarely raised in oratory, carried the weight of knowledge and conviction. The public's business is his business and he has had no other.

Often I've gone to him for one reason or another and always I've come away with a deep sense of the American past and the character that has come out of it. His face might have been carved by a journeyman woodcarver, one of the clever untaught men who roamed New England and the frontier West. When you talk to him there is at first something between him and you; a veil of skepticism, a patient blankness that may be self-protective. If he is very tired or if his melancholy sits heavily on him this mood may not lighten. But ordinarily he comes to life and his sweet, guileful smile shines out.

Sometimes I've brought him small specimens of skullduggery with the hope of producing a flurry in the Senate or perhaps a flare-up in some government department downtown. A story, in other words, and the kind of story that my paper, the *Post-Dispatch*, has, in its pursuit of righteousness, admired. Yes, he says, he knows the world is a wicked place. But get someone else to do it this time. Isn't there someone else? Or perhaps he agrees to try, smiling the guileful smile, carefully canvassing the principals who are involved.

Few people have got really inside the shell of his reserve. One of them was the late Paul Y. Anderson of the *Post-Dispatch*. Norris loved Paul and when poor Paul was pursued by the devils of despair Norris would go and sit with him and help him wrestle with his demon. And when at last Paul killed himself, Norris grieved.

It was Paul Anderson who by a bold bit of trickery made it difficult for Norris to withdraw from the Senate race in 1936. He said he was through. He wanted to quit. He wanted to go back to Nebraska. Paul watched a telegraph boy go out of his office with a wire Norris had just signed declining to enter the primaries. He followed the boy down the hall and told him that Senator Norris wanted to recall the telegram. It was never sent, the date of withdrawal passed, and more or less against his will Norris was a candidate for re-election.

In 1942, as his term expired, again he insisted that he would not run. This time, however, one argument was persuasive. You can't step out in the middle of a war, said his friends and admirers in Nebraska, you can't quit. Eighty-one years old, entitled to a rest, he nevertheless indicated that he would be a candidate once more. He still works hard, only a little less hard than he did twenty years ago. But even if work were beyond him, I would hope that he could stay on as a symbol of something true and important out of the past. If he were to step down, people everywhere, his friends and his foes alike, would know the loss.

It was like that when Brandeis died, even though he had retired from the Supreme Court two years before. His devotion to humanity and enlightenment was unflagging to the very end. It was a life of discipline and order, the life of a teacher and a giver of light, and the world is the poorer for his going.

The pattern is as different from that of Norris as night from day. As a young lawyer in Boston he learned early the whole complex geometry of wealth and influence in business and in government. What great concentrations of wealth meant in the democratic process, he understood with a clear reasonableness that was never to be shaken.

He had good cause to know, for among his own clients at law were the rich and the mighty of New England. For the United Shoe Machinery Corporation, a citadel of New England wealth, he helped to draw up a plan of patent controls that was ingeniously contrived to levy a tax on the shoe industry of the nation, yes, of the world. There was no limit to the riches he might himself have amassed except that in his own mind he had long before imposed a limit.

Part of his life plan was a measure of financial independence that would enable him to work unhampered toward the goals he had fixed as a young man at the beginning of his career. Already he had begun the struggle to establish savings bank life insurance in Massachusetts. This was a direct, clear-cut objective in line with his deepest conviction, which was that the control of wealth should be in the hands of the many and not of the few. The insurance companies knew how important this objective was and the fight was a long and bitter one. Victory in his own state meant only that the goal had been enlarged. If savings bank life insurance at exceptionally low rates was good for Massachusetts, then it was good also for the other forty-seven states of the Union. Throughout his life Brandeis worked for that cause.

On the Supreme Court through the roaring 'twenties he set himself the task of imposing a kind of surgical reason on the convenient legalisms of the day. It was the function of one minority opinion after another. And he used language not as an ornament for the display of his own prejudices but as a device to say what he believed to be the truth beyond all comfortable shams and illusions. Often he dissented in company with his friend Oliver Wendell Holmes. Holmes was also a reasoning man but he was a skeptic too. Brandeis believed in humanity, he believed in progress. It is the bright thread that runs through everything he wrote.

His impress on the law is there for the learned to see, but even more important may have been his influence on the lives of people around him. The justice and his wife lived in a way that was almost ascetic in its simplicity. The arduous confining work of the Court tended, as it does with all the conscientious justices, to seal him off from the ordinary world. In addition he devoted hours of his time to the reforms which he had taken as his own.

Yet he did not shut himself away in saintly seclusion. By a process as disciplined, as regulated, as everything else in his life, he brought the world to him. Each Sunday afternoon through the winter a company gathered for tea in the Brandeis living room. Here were men and women representing every phase of government, each one touching some interest of the justice whose intellectual curiosity knew no arbitrary bounds.

Those teas became a wonderful and slightly awesome institution, particularly for the younger generation in whom the justice took a special interest. Mrs. Brandeis presided as umpire over a game of musical chairs, designed to give the justice ten or fifteen minutes of individual conversation with as many of the guests as could be talked to in an hour and a half. The rules were strictly observed. If you stayed too long in the privileged chair, Mrs. Brandeis would gently but firmly supplant you with the next person to be honored.

I doubt if the living room had been altered in the thirty-five years that the Brandeises lived in the spacious old apartment on California Street. The same sparse, somewhat uncomfortable furniture. The same framed photographs of classical ruins on the walls. Even, or so it usually appeared, the same young law clerk passing tea or making stiff conversation with newly arrived guests. The justice had always the same air of quick, bright interest, and ordinarily he had for you a question that went to the heart of your specialty. The specialist was often surprised at the extent of the justice's knowledge. Whether he was talking with a member of the Interstate Commerce Commission or a curator of the Smithsonian he seemed to be sharing a common background of knowledge.

There were small and simple dinners too which ended always at ten o'clock. When he was not too hard-pressed, people came for half-hour appointments in the late afternoon. The talk was never of the personalities that obsess Washington. He was interested in the ideas that interested you and he assumed that you in turn were interested in his ideas. He had made the trend of government his special province, but this was never in terms of who was to get what job. Men came to him—senators, bright young brain-trusters, bureaucrats, idealists, and causists of every stripe—to ask his advice and he gave it generously.

Especially in the last years of his life there was about him an air of prophetic beauty. The strong lines of his face were softened but not weakened. He seemed to look into another and better world, but nevertheless he met you always on a friendly, human plane. His thin, white hair was like a nimbus about his head. A gentle oracle, the weight of his wisdom was never oppressive.

It seemed to him important that people in the confusion of the present day should plan their lives with greater care. You should know, I've heard him say a half-dozen times, what you'll be doing twenty years from now. You must live as though you meant to be at least a hundred years old and yet you should be prepared to die tomorrow.

Above all he believed that young men should plan careers in public life. There should be many men in our society preparing themselves step by step to be President of the United States. At the time of the great national party conventions the choice should not lie between two or three men or a half-dozen men but among twenty or thirty or forty candidates, all fitted by training and experience for the highest office in the land. Like Norris, he believed that growth and progress came slowly, built upon careful foundations. This was one reason for his long interest in the co-operative movement. Co-operation was built slowly by the democratic method. It became a way of life in the mind and in the heart.

Only rarely did he indulge in the luxury of pessimism. With most of the reforms of the New Deal he was in sympathy. Yet there is reason to believe that at the close of his life he had begun to doubt the method and the approach of the New Dealers, quite apart from the shock that the Court-packing bill had been to him. He was no ivory tower idealist, given to carping needlessly over ways and means. Here were the young men in government whom he had hoped to see there. But all too often, it seemed to him, they had forgotten their first objectives in the Washington scramble for power. This was his lament to an old friend who sat with him on the porch of his Cape Cod house in that last September before he came home to die.

It may have been merely the weariness of eighty-five years settling down on a life crowded with ceaseless activity. Or it may have been a more searching disillusionment at the liberalism that he embodied. Perhaps it seemed to the old man sitting on the porch at Chatham that all his striving, all his hope, had come to so little.

These two men, Norris and Brandeis, are the monuments of the phase of liberal reform that culminated in the first four years of the New Deal. They tower above their fellow liberals if only because of the positive changes that they wrought. But in the light of the holocaust over the whole world there is a question as to the reality of their place in the society of which they were a part.

An incident comes back to me vividly. Walking over to the Capitol from the Senate Office building, Senator Norris and I found our way blocked by crowds that stood watching a parade which came swinging up Pennsylvania Avenue. It was Army Day. In the sharp spring sunlight troops of the regular Army marched with their outmoded Springfield rifles and their outmoded pie plate helmets. For a moment we stood watching the procession. Then the senator turned back into the building.

"Oh, we don't want the Army," he said. "We don't want to see displays like this."

It was not that Senator Norris was ever a professional pacifist or an "appeaser." But for him, as for other liberals, and, in fact, for the great majority of Americans, the Army and the implication of war were something ominous and dread, to be kept out of sight. Out of the deep current of idealism underlying so much of American life had come the brave illusion that war was actually about to be banished. Cherishing this illusion, we could ignore in the long periods of peace the little professional Army as though it

had been a quaint survival that belonged properly in the Smithsonian Institution.

For a democracy rich in resources, in comfort, and in ease, this
was a dangerous illusion. It was a deliberate sojourn in unreality
which we can never afford again. Somehow we must achieve a
citizens' army. Pride in national service for the upbuilding and
the safety of the whole country must weld a citizens' army together. This would not necessarily imply any glorification of war.
It would be a recognition of the fact that we live in an imperfect
world in which envy, hatred, greed, and lust still exist.

In the first Roosevelt administration occurred the Senate munitions investigation which helped to confirm an inherent American
suspicion of the military. Months were spent in exhuming the
skeletons of the first World War. They were grisly enough, God
knows, all grim and phosphorescent beneath the mold of fifteen
years. There were tragic errors and the bill for everything had
been two or three times as large as it should have been. Sidling
into war, crabwise, we had improvised a vast war machine, and the
result, if scrutinized closely by an unsympathetic jury, could be
made to seem no more than a costly bit of chaos.

The report the investigating committee wrote was for the most
part a sizable lexicon of what not to do when war is threatened. It
was a messy tale of millions squandered in extravagance and folly.
While there was some effort to put this knowledge to practical use
—to profit by a painful lesson—it was largely dissipated in a great
burst of moral indignation, full of fervor and fury, but overlooking
the essential problem of defense of an enormously rich continent
governed loosely under a democracy. Frank Hanighen wrote *Merchants of Death* and Archibald MacLeish expressed his indignation
in a stirring pamphlet, "Arms and The Men."

The whole thing made excellent political capital for Senator
Nye who had been chairman of the investigating committee. Audiences all over the country heard him, for a price, denounce the
merchants of death. It was original sin that smooth, glib-talking
Senator Nye went out on the platform to exorcise. For him it was
a priceless political bank account to be drawn on whenever the

need arose. Nye and others worked up a vocabulary of indignation around this theme. "Warmonger," "international banker"—these phrases came to have a rich and fruity connotation as silver-tongued Gerald Nye rolled them out.

That was the behavior pattern of many liberals of the Nye type. It may have had some connection with the puritanism of the frontier. There is a strong resemblance to the old-time revival meeting. You round up your political sinners in the committee room. Either they confess with loud moans of repentance or you bedevil them into an admission of guilt. Then you lead the congregation in an emotional jag. The net effect, in politics as in religion, is likely to be a hangover of frustration and resentment.

Senator Wheeler conducted a long investigation into the railroad scandals of the 'twenties. The corpses buried by the brothers Van Sweringen and other solemn plunderers were brought to light and painstakingly anatomized. It was a thorough, patient job that Wheeler did. The sums of money involved were enormous. The machinations of the villain, or rather, villains, were extraordinary. But the total legislation to come out of all this was, in contrast to the volume of noise and excitement, negligible.

This behavior pattern has its grave dangers. The sense of frustration and defeat grow into a psychosis of national dimensions. It was said in Germany before 1933 that every time a mayor was exposed as crooked, the Nazi party enrolled fifty thousand new members. In a time of comparative stability we could perhaps take our "merchants of death," our "international bankers," our railroad and stockmarket plunderers. But spread across the headlines in a time of trouble such calculated "exposés" might be expected to contribute to the strength of whatever equivalent of the Nazi party was flourishing at the moment.

The same pattern can be observed in the American press or at any rate in a section of it. In fact, professional liberals of the type of Nye may have learned a thing or two from the muckrakers. You get a momentary sense of satisfaction, I know very well, from bringing into the brief light of the early city edition that swell story about how much so-and-so got in the XYZ case. When the sensation has been drained out of it, it is allowed to fade swiftly out of sight. Tomorrow there may be, fortuitously, another so-and-so in another XYZ case. This would seem to be the too-general rule to which there have been many honorable exceptions.

Norris never resorted to the camp meeting technique. If there was any end to be gained in raking muck, then he was in there with a rake twelve or fourteen hours a day. He worked long and hard to promote the investigation of superpower and its political ramifications. But once the case had been made, he started to work on a positive program to correct the evils that had been exposed. Moreover, the investigation conducted by the Federal Trade Commission had been more nearly a scientific inquiry than the dart throwing so often indulged in by congressional committees. The Securities and Exchange Commission and a strengthened Federal Power Commission and, far more important, the Tennessee Valley Authority were positive measures that came out of Norris's long, persistent campaign.

With the furious impact of the events that sweep across the world stage today we may be inclined to forget the contribution of such prophets of democracy as Norris and Brandeis. We are impatient with the past which had seemed to promise so much and yet nevertheless brought us to this difficult impasse. In a time of crisis we tend to rely on arbitrary authority summarily exercised. The temptation of our day is to play God.

But the promise is there. The hope is clear and unmistakable for a society built around the controls exercised by a strong central government; the powers of that government diffused through the life of the whole country; related directly to the needs and desires of the people. Let the authoritarians never forget that the example, yes, the working model still in a stage of hopeful experimentation, is there for anyone to see who will take the time and the trouble.

Chapter IV

Power

ABOUT the time that Washington's office shortage began to grow really acute, at the onset of the defense boom, someone had the happy idea that there were many government agencies that could function just as well in New York or Chicago or St. Louis as in the capital. Word went out to all executives to determine what bureaus or commissions could be shipped off to other cities where entire floors in unfilled buildings yawned hungrily for tenants. A great hue and cry went up and bureau chiefs talked boldly of what they intended to do in response to the presidential appeal.

When the score was added up, however, the total amount of office space that had been contributed to the cause was not enough to make even a slight impression on the mounting scarcity. After much wrenching and soul-searching the Home Owners' Loan Corporation moved eight hundred employees to New York. Other agencies made smaller contributions. In this dire extremity the Department of the Interior responded with a generous offer to move a large part of the Grazing Service farther west, perhaps even as far west as Salt Lake City.

Why the Grazing Service should have been firmly fixed in Washington two thousand miles or more from anything that could be legitimately called grazing was a question that might well have been raised even in that moment of general confusion and alarm. The answer is, of course, that authority which once becomes centralized in Washington is rarely dislodged and then only with the greatest difficulty. While the process of concentration began long before Franklin Roosevelt, it increased tremendously under the impetus of the New Deal so that the population of Washington jumped in the decade after 1930 by 36 per cent. And that was before the war boom had started. Later, as the overcrowding reached an acute stage, the budget bureau had to compel government commissions to move.

There was one major New Deal agency that contributed not at all to the overcrowding of the capital. That was the Tennessee Valley Authority. Here is an all-important experiment in decentralization and more than the mere physical decentralization it is a recognition of the fact that intelligent and sympathetic administration must be directly related to the needs of the people. Here was no ready-made Utopia to be superimposed from the well-meaning remoteness of Washington. In the TVA office in the capital are a half-dozen clerks and stenographers with a capable executive acting as liaison officer. In Knoxville, in Nashville, in Chattanooga, are more than thirty thousand employees who operate the TVA. Those who fear authoritarianism from a swollen and arrogant capital should consider carefully this experiment in regional collaboration.

Without the power generated by TVA dams the victory program would have been far more handicapped at the outset than it was. In the valley there was power for producing the aluminum vital to bomber production. Nor does the long involved record of the controversy over TVA show that private enterprise would have built this added capacity if it had not been for the competition of public enterprise. In fact, the record shows at various points arguments from utility representatives that the power of the TVA system was not needed and would never be needed. Today the brilliant engineering staff that the Authority has assembled is at work on the greatest construction project ever undertaken in this country, probably the greatest undertaking in the history of the world, building twelve new dams and hydroelectric plants and what will be the largest steam-generating plant in the South to raise the installed capacity from 1,050,000 watts to more than 2,600,000. The organization was ready to proceed at top speed the moment that Congress gave the signal.

Remarkable as this record is, I think that no less so is the contribution to government that TVA has made in the nine years of its existence. Here, it may be, is a pattern for the future. The concentration of authority in a strong central government may be inevitable in our time. But if that authority can be diffused over a wide area and related directly to the human needs at the grass roots, then there is hope that authority will not become authoritarianism.

It is just possible that those who drafted the TVA Act were not aware of all the implications when they prescribed that the Authority should function not in Washington but in the region itself. In the concept of an independent authority, responsible only to the President, there was nothing essentially new. But in the scope in which it was projected for the Tennessee Valley, covering the economic and social well-being of a far-reaching area, it was new and daring. Not even Senator Norris had foreseen the extent of the project which emerged from the TVA Act. That came when President Roosevelt related power production and the extension of power lines to the necessity for conserving the basic resources of a region which was being rapidly impoverished.

One of the original members of the TVA board is Doctor Harcourt Morgan who had been president of the University of Tennessee. Before that he had been president of the University of Louisiana and he knew his South. When it came time to establish laboratories to do tests and experiments for the diverse projects to be carried out by the Authority, Doctor Morgan's good common sense came to the fore. Look here, he said, we don't need to set up new laboratories and bring a lot of new people in here. Up at the University at Knoxville there are two or three good men who are working on the very problem that we're considering. Of course, said the doctor, they haven't got very much money and their facilities are pretty limited but they're good men.

The board decided to extend TVA funds for these laboratories already at work on essential research projects at the University of Tennessee. TVA would make it possible for the university to expand its research program and take on assistants of its own choosing. That has been the precedent followed ever since. Wherever possible, local facilities and local resources are used with TVA funds to develop and enlarge the activities of the region. In the universities, in county experiment stations, yes, in private industry, TVA has made use of the brains and the resources of the valley.

Looking at his South out of shrewd, knowing eyes, Doctor Morgan had definite practical ideas about what he wanted the board to do. The South had become a raw material colony for the industry of the North Atlantic seaboard. Agricultural produce was sold at a low price and sent north to be processed and returned in the form of finished goods which brought a high price. Doctor Morgan saw that unless this cycle was somehow interrupted, the South would never regain its independence.

In a wide variety of ways TVA has been working to make the Tennessee valley more nearly self-sustaining. The cotton-tobacco one-crop system was the root of many evils, Doctor Morgan argued. Take cotton for example. Why even the cottonseed meal, after the oil had been taken out, was shipped to the north. That cottonseed meal was vital as a fertilizer if the South was ever to have a balanced agriculture with cattle on the land. There had been no cattle in the South, that is, no cattle to speak of, since the disastrous tick fever that came with the Civil War. Here was a fundamental problem which TVA proceeded to attack.

Throughout the region were small cottonseed oil refineries owned by Southern capital and operated by Southern workers. But they were finding it increasingly difficult to compete with the big refineries in the North. One by one they were going under. What this meant, of course, was further concentration of manufacture on the North Atlantic seaboard. It meant that the South was sunk that much further into colonial dependence.

TVA researchers assigned to the problem invented a new type of cottonseed oil cooker for use in small refineries. This new cooker has begun to make it possible for the small Southern plants to compete with the large Northern plants. In the logical course of events the new device might have been manufactured by the TVA itself. Or it might simply have been thrown onto the market. The way in which it was made available to manufacturers is an interesting example of how TVA collaborates with private business. Under the patent held by the TVA board, the device was licensed for manufacture to anyone who would agree to make it at a price fixed by TVA. That price had been carefully estimated to allow a fair margin of profit to the manufacturer and yet guarantee a reasonable sale price to the cottonseed oil refiners of the South.

One of the big obstacles that keeps too many Southern farmers on the mule-and-forty-acres, the meal-molasses-and-fat-back pattern, is the cost of farm machinery. This is manufactured almost entirely in the North where labor costs are high. Without some mechanical help the average farmer is stuck behind his plow. What TVA did was to work out a side-hill terracing disk that could be manufactured for twenty-five dollars. They have worked to improve and simplify other machines especially to meet the needs of the Southern farmer. And they have tried to encourage the manufacture of these machines in the South. This program has been interrupted, in part at least, by the war, but the TVAers insist that the emergency is only an interruption and that when it is over the program will go forward again with the renewed impetus of the vastly greater power facilities in the region.

Wise, kindly old Doctor Morgan found a teammate in a young man from the North. David E. Lilienthal was a graduate of the kind of public administration that the elder LaFollette established in Wisconsin. At thirty-two he gave up a lucrative Chicago law practice to become a member of the Wisconsin Public Service Commission which is responsible for public utility regulation in that state. In that laboratory of government he learned about power, public and private.

Judging from outward appearances it seemed that if President Roosevelt had looked all over the entire country he could not have found two men less likely to pull together than Morgan and Lilienthal. The latter is hard-driving, crisp, incisive, cutting to the heart of a problem with little ceremony. Besides, he was a Northerner and therefore suspect, a carpetbagger.

Yet from the first these two dissimilar men worked in harmony and understanding. When a blowup came, precipitated by the temperamental and doctrinaire Arthur E. Morgan, chairman of the board, Lilienthal and Harcourt Morgan were ready to stand together to save TVA. That blowup was incited partly by private power interests that had not yet abandoned the hope of limiting TVA's field of operations even though they had failed to stop its authorization. After a painstaking investigation of the charges brought against Lilienthal by A. E. Morgan, Senator Norris decided to back the two board members who were under fire, the majority. So did the President who removed Morgan from office for contumacy. It remained for a Senate committee of Democrats and Republicans, with Francis Biddle as counsel, to conduct an exhaustive investigation. The committee reported little or no foundation for the charges and with that hurdle out of the way the board was ready to go on with its unfinished business.

Within a short time Lilienthal had become heart and soul a part of the region. Under the TVA Act the board had almost unlimited scope and Lilienthal's imagination was stirred by the enormous possibilities that had been opened up. He was impressed by Doctor Harcourt Morgan's penetrating insight into the dilemma of the South. It started him off on a similar tack with an equally ardent conviction that inequalities had to be righted, the inequalities that divide the North and the South.

You didn't have to look long to find inequalities. First and foremost came the freight rate differential. That was the manacle forged in the 'seventies to keep the South in a state of convenient dependence. Lilienthal assigned TVA experts to study the discriminatory freight rates that give a manufacturer in New Jersey or Massachusetts or New York an overwhelming advantage over a manufacturer in Tennessee or Georgia or Mississippi. The study that these experts made was eventually to stir the Interstate Commerce Commission out of its customary lethargy so that the whole question has now been newly reopened.

Lilienthal has become an evangel bent on removing this ancient disadvantage. He has preached the gospel of equalized freight rates not only in the Tennessee Valley but in other regions—the Southwest and the Middle West—where the handicap is almost as serious. It is his own cause now, the cause of the region of which he is a part. And always he is armed with facts and figures worked up by TVA's technical staff. In the course of a speech he is likely to use charts showing in dollars and cents exactly how Southern states are disadvantaged by the rate structure. Speaking in Texas, for example, he pointed out that there in the center of the cattle country it would be natural to expect a shoe industry to develop which would make use of the raw material close at hand. Shoes made in Dallas and shoes made in Boston should, he pointed out, compete on about equal terms in Duluth, Chicago, Indianapolis, Knoxville, and Savannah. But instead, thanks to the freight rates, Boston has a tariff wall that confers special advantages on Boston-made shoes in the part of the country where the most millions live with the most billions of dollars to spend. That is the kind of argument that keen-thinking David Lilienthal likes to make.

"No one in these days," he said in the course of that same speech, "can longer doubt that the community or the region that depends predominantly on the production of raw materials is a community or a region of a lower standard of economic prosperity than is the community or region that is more extensively engaged in the processing and manufacture into finished goods of these raw materials that grow in the fields and forests or are mined from within the earth. This close relation between low income and raw material production, between high income and manufacturing, is a fact of fundamental importance that we of these disadvantaged regions must understand thoroughly, a fact upon the basis of which we must weigh our plans and fight our battles."

He might have gone on to point out the world parallel. Hitler is fighting to keep the conquered countries of Europe as dependent raw material colonies. Having looted their machines, he is determined that they shall remain forever with a low standard of living dependent upon industrialized Germany which will enjoy a far higher standard. In the same way the Nazis have plotted to make dependent raw material colonies out of the South American republics. And our own industry, if Hitler had had his way, would have existed on German sufferance; that is, on condition that we made our government conform to the Nazi pattern. Just now we are engaged in preventing this madman from reducing the rest of the world to a German kitchen garden. When we have won the war, we must win the peace and that means facing the facts which show one part of our nation with a tremendous advantage over the other regions. The North Atlantic seaboard cannot hope to remain forever secure in its higher standard behind the Chinese Wall, the Maginot Line, of a basic economic advantage.

Working through the TVA the people of the Tennessee Valley have moved in many directions to try to overcome their handicap. TVA is producing the most highly concentrated fertilizer in the world, a hyperphosphate that came out of experiments initiated by the Authority. In test demonstrations on 35,000 farms in twenty-six states the use of this new super plant food has been related to soil conservation. TVA has developed and patented a quick-freezing machine that has opened up new cash markets for fruits and vegetables. Improvements in the curing of sorghum and flax, development of new electric methods for curing sweet potatoes and for drying hay have come out of this experiment in regional collaboration. TVA surveys and research, together with an extensive educational program, have done much for forestry in the Valley. As a result of research in TVA laboratories American ceramic plants are now using North Carolina clay in the manufacture of fine china. Most exciting of all, the TVAers have developed a process for producing aluminum from the common clay of the South which mitigates the grave threat implied in the not too distant exhaustion of Arkansas' bauxite deposits.

Morgan, Lilienthal, and James Pope, the new member of the board who took the place of Arthur Morgan, are all convinced that the achievements of TVA are inseparably bound up with the nature of its organization. They are convinced that nothing like the same accomplishment would have been brought about in, let us say, a labyrinthine TVA building in Washington. Not what TVA is doing but the way in which it is doing it is inherently, even radically, new. Heretofore, the federal government has divided its activities up into watertight compartments. Soil conservation was one. Water control and the development of public power were walled off in another government agency. Mineral resources were the special preserve of still another bureau. TVA takes in every department of life throughout a unified area. Seeing the region whole—that is TVA's revolutionary approach. It is this, in the view of Lilienthal and the other members of the board, that has made possible TVA's striking achievements.

"When statutes are enacted," Lilienthal has said, "that change the daily life and uproot the settled habits of men, those laws must as far as possible be administered at the grass roots, where the men who make and apply each regulation can see the effect of their decisions and learn the lesson of that observation. This country is too varied, the traditions and the customs of its people are too different, for general regulations to be successful from coast to coast. No man in Washington can fully foresee the impact of his several acts when he must decide for Arkansas and North Dakota, when his rules and regulations must apply alike to Florida and Maine.

"This country is not only too varied, it is too vast for centralized administration to be effective. When every recommendation, every adaptation of a general policy, and every requisition must go to Washington for consideration and approval, delays pile upon delays and thereby the confidence of its citizens, upon which a democracy must ultimately rest, is threatened by uncertainty and by delay. Day-by-day decisions should be made in the field. That is what Congress has authorized us to do and that is what we have done in TVA."

Not without a struggle has the TVA been kept in the form intended by the TVA Act. Administrators feed on authority and the TVA was too ripe and lovely a plum not to attract attention. Secretary of the Interior Harold L. Ickes, the Dickensian fat boy of the Roosevelt Administration, long looked with a covetous eye on the independence of TVA, and there is reason to believe that he has never abandoned his hope of enfolding this prize within the all-inclusive embrace of his department.

Only by some very fast footwork on the part of Lilienthal, aided by Senator Norris, was hungry Harold prevented from swallowing the whole TVA. Ickes has the most extraordinary capacity for believing that virtue rests in him alone. It is one reason that he is such a formidable foe when, armored in his righteousness, he goes forth to battle for Harold Ickes. He had convinced himself, and apparently he came close to convincing the President, that TVA, responsible to the President alone, was a fearful drain on executive energy and executive time. The truth is, of course, that once the egocentric Arthur Morgan had taken himself off, the TVA board seldom if ever deposited any problem on the White House doorstep. Annual reports and annual audits are not a burden of the President himself but of the budget bureau and the executive assistants with whom President Roosevelt has been supplied in generous measure. But Honest Harold had convinced himself that only within his Department of the Interior could TVA become a virtuous and responsible agency.

The scramble for power is one of the less edifying spectacles in Washington. For Ickes it has had an irresistible attraction. His battle to take over the Forest Service must rank as one of the great bureaucratic jousts of all time. Less spectacular but no less determined has been his struggle to gain authority over federal water power development. It began with the subtle siege that he laid to TVA, a piece of strategy that went on behind the scenes with only the principals aware of how much was at stake. Failing in that move, Ickes next sought to assure for the Department of the Interior permanent control over the great power dams in the west, Grand Coulee, Bonneville, Shasta, and the others.

A group in the Senate was just as determined that these projects should be administered by an independent authority modeled after TVA. Senator Homer Bone of the state of Washington had labored for many years in the Northwest for the development of public power. Bone has the outlander's fierce resentment of authority exercised from a distant seat. When he talks about the machinations of the eastern holding companies and their fiefdom in the Pacific Northwest, his language grows lurid with strange Pacific oaths. Having won his fight for public power, he did not propose to substitute Mr. Ickes's Department of the Interior for a holding company. It was not that he doubted for a moment Honest Harold's impeccable honesty. But somehow remote control from Washington had very much the same look as remote control from New York and Senator Bone wanted none of it.

Ickes had a bill drawn that would put control of power generated in the Northwest in the Interior Department. Through years of careful cultivation, with dams and irrigation projects doled out at strategic times and strategic places, Ickes has made friends in Congress. These friends rallied round. Moreover, the secretary let it be known that his own great and good friend, Mr. Roosevelt, the very sun of his being, agreed with him in this matter. He knew that in the rush and confusion of the war crisis there would be no opportunity for a full and fair debate on the issue. And he knew, too, that once the law was passed and the precedent established, it would be very difficult to reverse the trend.

There has come into being in Washington during the New Deal a school of political philosophy that might be called the papa-knows-best school. Mr. Ickes is only one of many well-meaning office holders who subscribe to the papa-knows-best philosophy. The people could hardly be expected to know what they need or want; one has only to look at the way in which they have been hoodwinked and bilked by big business. Light and leading must come from Washington. That is the basic tenet of this benevolent theory.

They are determined, these well-intentioned paternalists, that all is to be for the best in the best possible of worlds. But you must accept their interpretation of what is best. "I think it and therefore it is right." There is now and then an intimation of this dangerous doctrine in Ickes's pronouncements. Anyone who opposes him is ipso facto a scoundrel, yes, a heretic. And contrariwise all his acts have the odor of sanctity even though occasionally they are the very same acts for which in the past he had so roundly condemned his enemies. Political lame ducks have had a way of turning up in his department, getting a well-feathered nest when the voters have turned them down. And while Ickes has been a vociferous baiter of big business, it was curious to discover during his supervision of the oil industry that executives of the big oil companies were in positions of influence.

It is just possible that Mr. Ickes is another face of the liberalism of Brandeis and Norris. At the root of his being is an inherent suspicion of mankind. This makes for a kind of paralysis of action through the group or the community. Beyond the periphery of the individual's own righteousness there is only a wicked void. There are many Ickeses. He is the model, the archetype.

The lonely crusader, that was Ickes's Chicago background. He was an unofficial public scold to a long succession of bosses and corruptionists in corrupt Chicago. I remember him there in a huge office building on South LaSalle Street. You stepped into a small anteroom and his secretary said she would see if Mr. Ickes was busy. Mr. Ickes was rarely if ever busy. The white horse was tied just outside the door, ready for the crusader to ride off lippety-larrup with any virtuous knight who importuned his aid. As he quite frankly told you himself, he could not be elected dog-catcher. Indeed after four years as Secretary of Interior he was not able to squirm his way onto the Illinois delegation to the Convention that was to renominate his great patron; instead he was obliged to be a delegate, by crown appointment as it were, from his own fiefdom of Alaska. Elections were not his dish. He was His Majesty's perpetual opposition and happy enough in the role.

Perhaps one reason why people resented him so much was that he made the best of two worlds. He was the knight in shining armor and yet, thanks to the wealth of his first wife, he could fuss with his dahlias more or less at his leisure in suburban Winnetka. In many ways his function was a useful one. I think it was Jack Alexander who first compared him to Donald Duck. But the comparison is not altogether apt, for Donald is a passive fellow who only flies up in a quacking rage when things are done to him. Harold Ickes could never be called passive. He has spent his life setting traps and springes to catch other people.

With authority, with a vast bureaucracy under his rule, he could not overcome this habit of a lifetime. Power was an embarrassment to this suspicion-haunted opposer. I have treasured the story of the associate whom Ickes set out to fire and who resolved, with a grim humor, to leave his post at a time of his own choosing since he knew that he was innocent of any crimes or misdemeanors. There followed such a sleuthing, letters opened, telephone conversations overheard, shadows and countershadows, as had rarely been seen even in the higher reaches of bureaucracy. The victim, chuckling sardonically, was trailed to the farthest corners of the United States. For months it went on and how much it cost is a secret that is probably locked forever in the hidden vastness of the General Accounting Office. When he thought this game had gone on long enough, the victim resigned in a letter intended to scorch Mr. Ickes's ears.

He is of course invulnerable. He lives in a righteous stratosphere far beyond the range of any ordinary mortal blows. Perhaps that is why the slightest pinprick of criticism that reaches him invariably draws from Mr. Ickes a loud protest. For all his addiction to intrigue, it is nevertheless possible to believe in his innocence. Papa knows best but only because it is Papa. No Machiavellian sense of power motivates the trumpeter from Chicago.

The philosophy of power is the birthright of certain of the younger New Dealers. They were aware, as who with any sight could help not being aware, of the decline of the democratic faith, and with it democratic practice, in America. You could see so well what was happening. From the office on Park Avenue or in Wall Street the order went out that would mean the dismissal of two thousand men in Pittsburgh, and thirteen hundred men in East St. Louis. In the same way the big boss of the big union decided that dues and initiation fees would be doubled or tripled. Democracy will hardly survive under such a system.

Here was an opportunity that seemed to the New Dealers to be made to order. The footprints were big and they trod gingerly but with a growing sense of exaltation. And then as so often happens a prophet came along who told them exactly what they wanted to hear.

James Burnham in his persuasive book *The Managerial Revolution* held out a permanent lease on the promised land to these

clever new managers. Burnham develops a glib theory that confirmed the fondest hopes of many of the young men who came to
Washington with the New Deal. Power, in the Burnham thesis,
is inevitably shifting not only from the capitalist owners of industry but also from such outmoded instruments of democracy
as parliaments and congresses. In a process begun with the first
World War and now accelerated under the second, capitalism is
rapidly being replaced by state ownership. In this country the
New Deal is doing the job of taking over. So runs the Burnham
theory.

Burnham rules' out socialism, arguing that the "classless society" implied by all socialists of whatever political stamp, is only
a dream. Soviet Russia has produced, in Burnham's argument, not
the classless state of socialism but the new "managerial" order. A
class of bureaucrats, the upper 11 or 12 per cent of the Soviet
population, now receives 50 per cent of the national income, according to Burnham, a Trotskyist, who quotes Trotsky as his authority. These are the exploiting class of "managers." In the same
way, in this beautifully easy theory, the Nazis too are "managers"
and far more skillful than their opposite numbers in Soviet Russia.
With remarkable dogmatism even for a Trotskyist the author
predicted victory for Germany. Roosevelt, he characterized as "a
brilliant and demagogic popular politician who did not in the least
create, but merely rides when it fits his purpose the New Deal."
His accolade is reserved for the New Dealers themselves:

"These men include some of the clearest-headed of all managers
to be found in any country. They are confident and aggressive.
Though many of them have some background in Marxism, they
have no faith in the masses of such a sort as to lead them to believe
in the ideal of a free, classless society. At the same time, they are,
sometimes openly, scornful of capitalists and capitalist ideas. They
are ready to work with anyone and are not so squeamish as to insist that their words should coincide with their actions and aims.
They believe that they can run things, and they like to run things."

It was hardly an accident that it was David Lilienthal who set
out to riddle the pretensions of this amateur Machiavelli. He had

never been a victim of the vertigo which is the occupational disease
that goes with the heady authority of a high Washington office.
Burnham's theory could not persuade him because he had been
working to integrate a far-reaching federal organization with the
life of a region. He called the "managerial revolution" what it is
—Fascism under a fancy name. Writing in the *Public Administration Review*, he went further and hit out boldly at those New
Dealers who follow the managerial line and are susceptible to the
managerial argument.

"There is an evil tendency," Lilienthal said, "among some individuals within the new managerial group in America that leads
toward exploitation of society by those who should be its servants.
This tendency public administrators can scotch if they will but
speak out plainly before it has become accepted and habitual.

"I refer to the acceptance of public administrative responsibility with an eye to using it as a stepping stone for personal advancement. Every experienced administrator will recognize what
I am talking about. We all know of the young men who come into
public service with high-sounding talk about devoting their well-
trained brains to the public interest; we have seen them develop
a kind of Phi Beta Kappa Tammany Hall, 'placing' their friends
in important posts in the service; developing 'contacts'; active in
promoting vendettas; intent upon personal publicity. Having laid
this groundwork they then leave the public service in order to represent private concerns which seek government contracts or loans,
or clients having business before administrative agencies manned
by men indebted to them for their posts."

Obviously this reference was meant for Thomas G. (Tommy
the Cork) Corcoran who had bobbed up as a lobby lawyer on the
crest of the defense boom. The Cork had come a long way from
those blithe, carefree days when he shuttled about the town engaged at least eighteen hours out of every twenty-four in the
public endeavors of his friend and patron F.D.R. Using his
extraordinary charm, which he could turn on and off like a light,
he seemed a kind of projection of the personality of the gay, good-
humored man in the White House. The President found him

very useful, particularly in partnership with his friend, Ben Cohen, whose serious, scholarly temperament complemented the Cork's Irish abandon.

It was government by prestidigitation that Corcoran practiced in the days when his charm was fresh and undimmed. The warm persuasive voice on the telephone holding out just such hope of Heaven—say that little judgeship back in Iowa—as would resolve the doubts of a troubled senator. That was the Cork in those care-free days. He was enormously clever and his charm was almost irresistible if you took it at its surface value. His exploits were legendary. What he did to get the holding company act passed. How he succeeded in slipping an innocent-looking clause into a bill to change its purpose. These were the adventures of the Cork that regaled his young admirers as he recounted them with that merry chuckle in his voice.

When he went over to the private practice of law, out of his hat, it was an almost imperceptible transition. His method of operation was exactly the same. His friends were in government offices all over town. And he simply called them up or he went to see them as he had always done in the past. He was apparently convinced that the work he was doing was just as much in the public good as anything he had ever done in the past. Wasn't he merely facili-tating armament production by bringing the clever promoter to-gether with the government contractor? It happened of course that he was being paid very well for his services, but this could be regarded as no more than just compensation for the years when the Cork had existed meagerly on a government salary of nine thousand dollars a year.

There were people who were shocked by this. Apparently one of them was the Cork's original sponsor, Justice Felix Frankfurter, who saw his brightest protégé serving Mammon. Others of the New Deal bureaucracy defended the hero who had been Galahad and Houdini all rolled into one. They sputtered about "the press," that favorite whipping boy of all politicians and especially of the New Dealers.

Only an impossible purist would argue that sleight of hand is to be forever abjured as evil. In the great game of politics it is not only necessary but inevitable. There are, however, degrees of prestidigitation. The technique must be used sparingly at rare intervals. The trouble with the Corcorans was that they relied too heavily on their political magic.

It was their weakness as "managers." You could not "manage" the potentially violent forces of our society forever by any species of magic so comparatively innocent as that of the New Deal. Keeping the audience preoccupied if not entertained, they were nevertheless given to glancing nervously into the wings as if in fear of being supplanted by a more ruthless performer with no scruples whatsoever. It is possible that they felt as Stresemann, as Ebert, as Bruening, must have felt when Hitler began to shout offstage in the Weimar Republic.

All the time there was the example of an integrated, regional collaboration between government and people. No one, least of all its sponsors, claimed perfection for the TVA. But it was, they insisted, an experiment that suggested an alternative between an impossible dictation from Washington and the easy anarchy of "states' rights." President Roosevelt went so far in 1937 as to propose seven new regional agencies similar to TVA in the other great river valleys of the nation. It was a bold concept of regions integrated one with the other in a coherent and logical pattern.

In the swift rush of events after 1937 this concept was lost sight of. It may have disappeared forever. The jealous merchants of power in Washington used a word to exorcise it—Balkanization. The nation would be Balkanized into warring regions. This ignored the obvious fact that a process of Balkanization was already going on behind the arbitrary political borders of the states, with state tariff walls and bitter commercial jealousies. Not a little of the opposition came from that vast machine of government, the Department of Agriculture. The TVA idea threatened the Department's far-reaching hold on the nation's farms, a control that extends down below the grass roots.

In Washington, more than in any other capital in the world, I suppose, it is difficult to see the forest for the trees. The forest is so dense, so dark. Take the forest of the Department of Agriculture alone. Unless you are awfully careful you can lose your way there if you wander even ten yards off the path hewn out for you to follow. The strange thing is that new trees grow up so quickly and become a part of the general background.

That is the process of government, that constant accretion of bureaus and agencies and commissions. At the edges the clamor is often loud and angry, but back in the settled establishment the functions of government go on almost unnoticed. You discover that after you have been in Washington for a time and your eyes have become adjusted to the curious subdued light of the place.

Chapter V

The Servants

THE customary Washington bombshells, exploding noisily in the nation's headlines, are generally the by-products of the struggle for power. Martin Dies, in headlong pursuit of a new assortment of Communists, Fascists, and Hottentots, pauses only long enough to catch his breath and demand another quarter-million dollars. An executive order empowers Paul McNutt to clasp twenty million more American voters to his capacious bosom. Thurman Arnold unmasks another Axis-entangled corporation, to thunderous applause.

To the general public, and particularly to that considerable segment of the general public which becomes politically conscious only at four-year intervals, Washington is apt to present two broad aspects—neither of them pleasing. At one end of the scale lie the politicians and the political appointees, all of them naturally scheming and conniving for advancement and special favors. Ensconced in scenes of incredible, marble grandeur, they float in an atmosphere of perfumed and cocktailed intrigue, which if not positively corrupt will at least bear watching. Their motives are uniformly suspicious, their mental processes arbitrary and usually fallacious, and their activities demonstrably expensive.

Understandably, it is this side of Washington that is painstakingly and exhaustively reported. For out of this welter emerge the policies and plans under which the nation functions. But the citizen is caught in the cross fire of the front-page story, its important facts too often buried in bland journalese and in the signed column, sharp with acrimony and special pleading. He may have learned to discount the obvious windy hypocrisies, but how can he evaluate at long range the workings of a city where raw ambition and genuine zeal walk side by side, and where often enough of both are found embodied in one man? Confused, he takes refuge in suspicion, fearing the worst and accepting the good with the gloomy assurance that the bad must soon follow.

At the other end of the scale—the submerged end—are found the thousands of functionaries who make the whole thing work, who carry out the dictates handed down from above. To the citizen these folk are the embodiment of what he has been conditioned to regard as "the damned bureaucracy." They are the "government clerks" who live their lives in a sorry tangle of red tape, inefficiency, and official shortsightedness. His contact with the civil service has been confined to those occasions when his dealings with the government have required him to fill out forms in triplicate, and the man behind the desk has impressed him as being bored, chilly and unhelpful.

Moreover, if he has been overwhelmed with words reporting and explaining and interpreting to him the captains and kings, he has encountered only a deathly silence concerning the activities of their subordinates. He knows that his government plows along somehow, ponderously and blindly; he knows little, and generally cares less, about the people who operate it. He remembers, perhaps from school days, that there are ten principal executive departments, each headed by an officer of cabinet rank, plus an assortment of added commissions and bureaus, with a final overlay of New Deal "alphabetical agencies." The functions of most of these departments, he feels, are obvious enough from their names. The Post Office plays a part in his daily life; if he is a farmer he is on speaking terms with the Department of Agriculture; he is painfully conscious of the Treasury every March.

As for the rest, he accepts them, but their activities do not invade his headlines. If he makes an excursion to Washington, perhaps to see the cherry blossoms, he may witness the five o'clock stampede out of, let us say, the Interior building, and ponder a moment on the mountains of forms which have just been stamped and sorted by this horde of civil servants. He may shake his head sadly, and mutter something about "that Ickes," but he will drive on and see his cherry blossoms.

And he will be right, of course. For untold thousands of Washington's citizens spend their lives in a dreary round of typing and sorting and stamping and filing, in a never-ending effort to cope with the routine paper work which is the curse of any large organization. But it takes eight and a half pages of the Washington telephone directory simply to list the agencies that carry on the functions of government. Under this multitude of listings are to be found, in heartening numbers, bureaus and offices and *men* whose work has direct and beneficial effect upon the lives of all of us. Men and women of intelligence and imagination, patient and conscientious men and women whose research and study and administration and hard work result in services of incalculable value. Some of these services may strike us as dull, others fanciful, some absorbingly interesting, others downright amusing. They are so numerous and widespread that they can be considered only at random, but in the aggregate they bear upon every imaginable phase of our economic and political and social existence.

Our visiting citizen, sourly contemplating Mr. Ickes's monster Interior building (vaguely reminiscent of the temple at Karnak) may by chance know that it houses something called the Fish and Wild Life Service. He almost certainly does not know, however, that one of the functions of this office is the protection and conservation of the entire herd of Alaska seals, with absolute control of the seal fur industry.

When Secretary of State Seward bought the territory of Alaska from Russia in 1867, he got it at the bargain-counter price of $7,200,000. Included in the purchase were the Pribilof Islands, and with them the immense seal herd, estimated at three to four million at the time we acquired it. The revenue to the Treasury from furs alone has repaid manyfold the cost of the entire transaction, and since the Pribilof herd comprises 80 per cent of all the fur seals in the world, a profitable domestic and foreign trade has accrued to the United States.

Uncontrolled and indiscriminate killings followed immediately upon our acquisition of the islands, and in the short space of two years the herd had been reduced to 125,000, not far from the vanishing point. A measure of control was applied by the government, which in 1870 leased the sealing rights to private corporations, for two twenty-year periods. The herd was saved, but the rise of pelagic sealing, or the killing of the animals at sea rather than at their breeding grounds, became a new threat to the survival of the species. Since pelagic sealing was open to the nationals of all countries, it was impossible to eliminate the practice except by international agreement.

Accordingly, a convention was signed in 1911, by the United States, Russia, Great Britain, and Japan, prohibiting commercial pelagic sealing. The United States, which enforces the convention and administers all affairs pertaining to the herd, apportions 15 per cent of the skins taken each year to the Canadian government, and supplied an equal amount to Japan until 1940, when Japan abrogated the convention. This apportionment is in consideration of the relinquishing by these countries of their right to take seals in the waters frequented by the Alaska herd.

The Fish and Wild Life Service, which in conjunction with the Coast Guard does the actual patrolling necessary for enforcement, was charged with the responsibility for restoring the herd and for protecting it from dangerous depletion. The Service set up a procedure and technique for the taking of skins based upon a study of the odd and mysterious life-cycle of the Alaska seal. The herd's natural way of life is allowed to proceed undisturbed in most respects, and only animals that are playing no vital part in propagation are selected for killing.

Japan's sudden decision to end the treaty was based on the contention that the enlarged seal herd was inflicting severe damage on Japan's food fish industry. The Japanese government complained, in vague terms, that the seals traveled down their coastline during the winter migration, consuming enormous quantities of fish en route. Our State Department discounts this claim, but is frankly baffled as to what the real reason for the abrogation might have been. The natural assumption is that the Japanese had decided to resume the profitable, prodigal killing of seals in the water.

The aquatic life of the Pribilof herd remains something of a mystery, as it has never been established, except in a general way, where the seals go after they leave the Islands each autumn. That they do *not* frequent the Japanese coast is a matter of recorded fact, despite the claims of the Japanese government. It is known that they remain at sea, however, as the herd has never been seen on dry land anywhere but at the Pribilofs. Each spring the seals begin to gather off the coast of southern California, and by May, the first contingent of mature bulls arrives at the Islands. These bad-tempered and massive bulls, five and six times as large as their mates, establish themselves in advantageous positions along the rocks and wait the coming of the cows. Vastly polygamous, the bulls are the self-constituted guardians of their harems and are frequently forced to fight for their rights. Defeated bulls are driven away from their homes, and must either win new harems for themselves from among the ranks of the "debutantes," the young, two-year-old cows, or die in combat with their stronger contemporaries.

Since the males cannot breed until they are five years old, and reach full maturity only at six or seven, the large group of adolescent males herd together at some distance from the breeding rookeries. When they reach the size and strength that will fit them to battle their way into possession of a harem, they sally forth, full of fight, to seek their fortune. These youngsters, termed "bachelors," are the only seals ever picked for killing, and the Service determines each year how many animals at the three-year-old stage may be taken without hampering propagation.

One of the most important duties of the Service, then, is its annual computation of the population of the herd. So painstaking and accurate are the methods used that the results, instead of being tabulated in round numbers, look exactly like human census figures. Not only does the Service know how large the herd is—2,338,312 in the 1941 census, as opposed to 2,185,136 in 1940 —but it establishes subsidiary facts, such as the size of the average harem in any given year, to aid in setting the number of future husbands that must be left alive, and to tell how the birth rate is holding up. Indeed, the government knows everything that can be known about its entire tribe of protégés except perhaps their middle names and their preference in breakfast foods.

In the year following the signing of the Sealing Convention the government allowed only three thousand skins to be taken from a herd then depleted to two hundred thousand. During the thirty years following, the herd has steadily increased in size until it is now back to normal, and the yearly yield of fine, selected skins approaches a hundred thousand. All skins are treated and prepared for sale by one licensed company in the United States, and are sold to the wholesale trade at auction, under government supervision.

Here an entire industry, which was at one time on the point of disappearing altogether, has been saved by intelligent, foresighted government action, and by the knowledge and devotion of the civil servants working in this single agency. The product itself has been improved, the market stabilized, and a natural resource of great beauty and usefulness saved from destruction.

The Constitution empowered Congress to "fix the standard of weights and measures." Not until forty years after the drafting of this provision did Congress get around to doing anything about it, but in 1830 it set up an Office of Standard Weights and Measures, under direction of the Treasury Department. Weights and measures throughout the country were at that time far from uniform, and the comparison of manufacturers' standards of weight and mass with those housed in the government office was a valuable and necessary factor in establishing uniformity. But the increasing complexity of industrial processes and of scientific apparatus posed problems beyond the capacity of this small office. In many instances American manufacturers were forced to send their instruments abroad for certification by the International Bureau of Weights and Measures, established in 1875.

In 1901, Congress established the National Bureau of Standards, which now occupies an imposing row of buildings near the edge of the District of Columbia. The Bureau is still charged with maintaining the official units of weight and mass, but upon the foundation provided by the standard meter and the standard kilogram innumerable derived standards are based. Since measurement, in its varied forms, is the prime essential of the mechanized industrial process, the platinum and iridium objects that repose in a special vault at the Bureau are not mere curios but are in constant use. The existence of this highly publicized group of supremely accurate measures is known to every schoolboy, but how many Americans have the slightest idea of the many uses to which they are put, and the countless contributions to manufacturing, commerce, and pure science that have been made by the Bureau of Standards?

In addition to developing and establishing standards of measurement to fit the needs of the most highly technical scientific problems, the Bureau has been assigned the very practical, day-to-day duty of checking all goods bought by the federal government, which is of course the largest purchaser of consumer goods in the country. The government provides specifications for everything it buys and awards contracts to the manufacturers submitting the lowest bids based upon these requirements. Preliminary tests must be conducted of every type of purchasable object to determine whether it actually meets specifications. If it does, the contract is finally awarded. The Bureau is responsible for almost all of this testing, and for periodic checkups to insure continued satisfactory performance by the manufacturers.

This process has a direct bearing upon purchases by individuals, for of course what the government buys is essentially the same as what the citizen buys. The Bureau does not purport to be a general testing service, and (contrary to widespread belief) does not ordinarily endorse products as being satisfactory buys for the individual consumer, or make recommendations as between competing products. But the fact that a vast congeries of products is tested for performance and durability in government use inevitably affects the production process generally, and the benefits of this testing are felt by the individual consumer. The Bureau also conducts tests for industry, where the government can be seen to have an interest in the findings and a great deal of this work is being done by technicians employed in industry but working at the Bureau in collaboration with the Bureau staff.

Accomplishments of the Bureau within the past decade include research into a vast range of subjects ranging from dental materials to fabrics and motor fuels. Important improvements in radio broadcasting have stemmed from the Bureau of Standards. Industrial uses of silver, the behavior of construction metals under various sorts of loads and vibrations, explorations of the upper atmosphere, wearing qualities of paints, carpets, shoes, and a thousand other things—a bewildering array of problems has been attacked, and useful conclusions drawn, by this branch of the civil service. In recent years a plan has been worked out by which manufacturers guarantee on the labels of their products that they have met the requirements set up in government specifications. This scheme, in eliminating confusion between grades and qualities, is saving large amounts of money for American consumers. It is being more and more widely used, and the encouragement and furtherance of it by the Bureau is another evidence of that agency's usefulness to the public.

Here, then, is another federal bureau. It is expensive, it uses costly machinery, it maintains a large plant, and it employs over a thousand people. But little is heard about it, and its problems, scandals, and internal upheavals, if any, are not of high enough voltage to make the headlines. Its employees are scientists and technicians, and are not conspicuous for clock-watching, rubberstamping, or filling out forms in triplicate. It is a government agency that continues to justify its existence every day it operates.

Traditional belief has it that the great government departments, in addition to being wasteful, unimaginative, and inefficient, are also insular and self-sufficient. So many glaring examples can be found to substantiate this claim that one tends to forget the innumerable instances where departments have foregone the luxury of suspicion and jealousy to pave the way for joint achievements. One thoroughly competent and constructive job, which I have recently come across, is a good case in point.

John Z. Williams, a young officer of the diplomatic corps serving as American vice-consul in the Dominican Republic, found himself with considerable spare time on his hands. Our business relations with that republic, while entirely amicable, are hardly brisk. Williams interested himself in the economic problems of the country, and observed among other things that its neighbor Haiti was shipping nine thousand tons of sisal each year to the United States, for manufacture of binder twine, cordage, and so on. The Dominican Republic, however, which exports coffee, cacao, and other agricultural products, has need of bags, and has been importing jute and other fibers from Mexico and elsewhere for this purpose, to the tune of half a million dollars yearly.

Entirely on his own initiative Williams wrote a report, entitled "Observations on possible benefits to be derived from trade between Haiti and the Dominican Republic on the basis of the sisal industry." He submitted it to the State Department, and when he returned home in 1941, after a three-year absence, he found that he had carved out a new job for himself.

The report had been forwarded from the State Department to the Department of Agriculture, which maintains a Bureau of Foreign Agricultural Relations. The director of this bureau suggested that Williams be sent by his department on a survey trip through Central America to report on the production of fibers generally. Since our supply of these essential materials from the Far East has now been shut off, the question is hardly academic.

As a result of his investigations, this officer, who had had no background whatever in this particular field, is now well on the way to becoming an expert in it. First loaned by his own department to Agriculture, he has now been transferred to the directorship of a Fibers Procurement Unit of a war bureau resoundingly named Inter-Agency Coordinating Committee on Strategic and Critical Materials. His job is to direct the development and production, in the shortest possible time, of the many types of fiber that are suddenly needed in the war production program.

This is a small, unglamorous, and totally unpublicized instance of good will and intelligent co-operation between departments. But its effect, in concert with hundreds of other examples of the same sort of thing, upon governmental efficiency is obvious. And in time of war, when this kind of efficiency must somehow be attained if we are ever to develop a co-ordinated, total effort, it provides an altogether heartening note.

Useful or superfluous, efficient or top-heavy, governmental agencies are expensive. Once established, their tendency is always to grow, and almost never to wither. It is the instinct of the civil servant to find new and vital jobs, which of course can properly be executed by him alone, when his original function shows signs of melting away. And new jobs require new and ever-larger appropriations.

The Treasury Department is the proud possessor of an organization which must be conceded to be the all-time champion exception to this rule. Wholly unique in the annals of U. S. government is an agency that turns over to the Treasury, in hard cash, upwards of fifty dollars for every dollar it spends for administration.

This is the achievement of the Intelligence Unit of the Bureau of Internal Revenue, which has as its principal function the detection and apprehension of the wily income-tax dodger. Organized in 1919, it has remained small, and even today numbers between two hundred and three hundred agents. During its brief and inexpensive life it has yielded over five hundred million dollars in taxes which would otherwise never have been paid. In addition to this cash return, immense even in a wartime era of billions, the Unit has put securely behind bars some of the toughest and most vicious criminals the nation has ever known.

Waxey Gordon, one of the beer barons of the machine-gun era, had for a number of years been reporting an income of about six thousand dollars. It was entirely obvious that his actual yearly pickings had been of the million-dollar class. He had taken care, however, to dissociate himself almost entirely from the operation of his tremendous, illicit business of manufacturing and distributing beer. On one unhappy occasion in his youth he had signed a receipt for a consignment of drugs and had gone to jail as a result. He never forgot this lesson. His employees did the work and made the contacts. They deposited the fabulous profits in bank accounts taken out under fictitious names. They committed every crime in the book, not excluding murder, but Gordon's name never appeared.

The first chink in the armor appeared after the murder of a truckman who had been working with some of Waxey's bootleggers. Records led to certain checkbook stubs which showed that over six million dollars had been deposited, within a single year, in nine bank accounts, all in the names of nonexistent men. The fantastically tedious job of checking every debit sheet in each of these accounts was accepted as a matter of course by the agents of the Intelligence Unit. Their search was a fruitful one.

They first established the fact that checks from these accounts had paid for various types of equipment used in the brewing business. Then when a fourteen-hundred-dollar check from one account was found that had been used as part payment for a Pierce-Arrow car owned by Gordon himself, the agents knew they had succeeded. It was established that the account, in the name of "L. J. Sampson," was actually operated by Sam H. Gurock, known to be one of Gordon's lieutenants.

Other leads were followed down—leads that had nothing to do with the beer business. Gordon's part ownership of the Piccadilly Hotel in New York was proved. In anticipation of the agent's arrival, Gordon had ordered the hotel's books replaced with a new set which would obliterate all trace of his interest. The ink was hardly dry on these books when the Intelligence Unit examined them, but an accountant was found who swore he had come across Gordon's initials in several places on the old books.

The final step, and one which the Treasury agents have used many times to advantage, was the reconstruction of the suspect's income from an elaborate check of his known purchases and out-of-pocket expenses during a year. Gordon, reporting a six-thousand-dollar income, paid six thousand dollars in rent alone for a ten-room Manhattan apartment. He owned two Pierce-Arrows and two Lincolns. He wore custom-made shirts at $13.50 apiece, ten-dollar underwear, five-dollar neckties. The agents reached a total of over twenty-five thousand dollars in traceable expenditures of this sort. Such gigantic discrepancies could hardly be attributed to mere lapse of memory.

Gordon's eleven-day trial included 152 witnesses and over one thousand exhibits. He was found guilty, sentenced to ten years in the penitentiary, fined twenty thousand dollars, charged twenty thousand dollars in court costs, and was ordered to pay taxes and penalties of $1,120,276. A fine tribute was paid the agents of the Intelligence Unit by the trial judge, the late Judge Frank J. Coleman, who said in open court:

"It is my firm conviction that never in this court, or any other court, has there been such fine work done, either on behalf of the government or of any private client, as has been done by the agents and the government attorneys in this case. These agents, who unquestionably could have received fabulous sums had they been willing to deviate from the straight line of their duty, or even to relax their diligence, have gone ahead and have accomplished a collection of evidence such as is truly astounding."

The Gordon case is only one of a series of investigations which have brought to justice Al Capone, Johnny Torrio, Leon Gleckman, and other gangland figures, whom the agents invariably refer to scornfully as "hoodlums." Among the white-collar class of tax dodgers the Unit has bagged Joseph Schenck of the movies, "Nucky" Johnson, the political boss of Atlantic City, Moe Annenberg of tip-sheet fame, and a whole covey of major and minor underlings of the late Senator Huey Long. The list is almost endless.

What manner of men are these Treasury agents?

They are, most of them, quiet, modest, and entirely undramatic. Some of them are lawyers, some accountants; others have worked their way into this specialized and technical field through various other forms of investigative work. Their pay is not high, beginning at two thousand dollars a year for junior agents and ending below six thousand dollars for agents in charge of regional offices; their chances for advancement lie almost entirely within the service itself. Their utter devotion to their work is attested by the fact that in the Unit's twenty-two years of existence only one agent has "gone bad." They are fascinated by their jobs, and their pride of workmanship in submitting an airtight case to their chief drives them to lengths of patience and minute accuracy that are believable only after one has read their reports. Their methods of detection lie along the lines of research, deduction, and careful sifting of evidence; they are content to leave the smoking re-volvers and the screaming headlines to better-known and more widely publicized agencies.

The men in this service are perhaps best epitomized in their chief, Elmer L. Irey. This modest and unassuming man is a life-long civil servant, having been a post-office inspector at the time he was chosen, along with five others, to set up the Intelligence Unit. It is difficult to imagine Irey, bespectacled and mild-man-nered, as the unrelenting nemesis of criminals who customarily terrorized entire cities. But his passion for detail and his ability to spot the tiniest errors in apparently flawless lines of reasoning have been major factors in the success of his organization. His shrewdness, coupled with his utter incorruptibility—he scornfully brushed aside a million-dollar bribe offered by Al Capone for a mere compromise of the tax case against him—and his devotion to his job, have made him one of America's really distinguished pub-lic servants.

He has been without political ambition, but his work as chief of the Intelligence Unit, and recently co-ordinator of all Treasury enforcement agencies, has inevitably placed him in line for higher honors. He has now been made assistant to Secretary Morgenthau, devoting his entire time to his work as co-ordinator, supervis-ing the Secret Service, the Narcotics Bureau, and the Customs Bureau, in addition to his own Unit. His own long-time assistant, W. H. Woolf, has replaced him in the actual direction of the In-telligence Unit, but it is noteworthy that Woolf is serving as act-ing chief. It is unlikely that Irey will fail to return, sooner or later, to the work he has loved so long.

The career of an able, devoted public servant like Irey inevitably poses the question: Where does the government get such men? The enterprise and keen observation of Williams makes us ask,

Why can't we get more like him? In a limited degree the answers are to be found in the Civil Service Commission. But in a broader sense the questions must unhappily still go unanswered.

The Constitution granted to Congress wide, if slightly indefinite, powers concerning the appointment of administrative officials below the policy-making level. But for eighty years or more Congress paid comparatively little attention to the growing problems of personnel, devoting its energies largely to the struggle with the executive branch for control over patronage.

During the early years of the Republic the hiring of employees, together with the setting of their pay and the setting of standards of fitness and efficiency, all proceeded in a haphazard, hit-or-miss fashion. Such standards as were set were entirely at the discretion of individual appointing officers. Pay for comparable classes of service varied widely between departments.

Moreover, the conscientious attempts made under our first three or four Presidents to grant appointments on the score of ability degenerated all too quickly into what came to be known as the spoils system. A great deal of campaign oratory upon the evils of this system invariably resulted in no action and in further entrenchment of the system it condemned. A pious theory of "rotation," through which officeholders were to be retired to private life after serving a set term, failed to conceal the true motive. By the time of the Buchanan administration political interference had reached a point where not only officeholders of a defeated party were ousted, but officeholders of the prevailing party, who had been so unwise as to support the wrong man for *nomination*, were likewise thrown out. Buchanan announced the set policy of reappointing no officeholders after the expiration of their terms. No thought, apparently, was given to the enormous confusion and expense involved in training new and inexperienced officials every four years.

The first effort at reform, fumbling and ineffectual, was made by President Fillmore in 1851, and in 1853 an act was passed classifying clerks in salary groups. But the question of merit and fitness for appointment was not touched, and the mad scramble for political appointment continued unabated. Abraham Lincoln could not travel from his office to his dining room, within the White House itself, without elbowing his way through crowds of office seekers thrusting petitions into his hand. Once in desperation he said, "I seem like a man so busy letting rooms at one end of his house that he has no time left to put out the fire that is blazing and destroying at the other end."

Not until 1883, not until after President Garfield had been assassinated by a disgruntled office seeker, was public indignation sufficiently aroused to make an improvement in the system unavoidable. With the passage of the Civil Service Act, which included provision for a commission to administer it, positions were for the first time classified by function as well as by salary. Competitive examinations were instituted, with preferences for appointment chosen on a basis of the graded answers. Quotas were set, apportioning appointments equitably throughout the nation.

There has been an unending struggle ever since 1883 to make the Civil Service system more efficient, to bring under its classification provisions more and more federal jobs, and to circumvent political interference. By 1923 the Classification Act had been passed, which standardized titles and salaries horizontally through the departments. Until that point over a hundred different titles could be used for workers now filling the job styled "senior file and record clerk." Among these titles were included "skilled laborer," "Italian verifier," and "boss painter," carrying salaries ranging from $720 to $2,400.

The struggle continues. Recent acts of Congress, several of them introduced by that indefatigable advocate of the merit system, Representative Robert Ramspeck of Georgia, have included large new contingents of employees in the classified categories. The field services, that vast majority of all government employees—those working outside the District of Columbia—have now been taken in. Amid screams from the minority in Congress, President Roosevelt has blanketed in thousands of previously unclassified postmasters.

But a great deal remains to be done. Classification must extend much further. Efficiency ratings as prerequisites for promotion need to be extended. Retirement and the problems of equitable pensions must be considered further.

And the question of how the Ireys and the Williamses are to be brought into government remains unanswered. For although the merit system has wrought great improvements in the caliber of government personnel, the fact remains that the Civil Service Commission has in large measure confined its attention to the distinctly subordinate grades.

The Commission has set up a bewildering array of classes, like "clerk-typists," "junior biologists," "junior chemists," and so on endlessly, and provides an essentially efficient mechanism for filling them with qualified applicants. But the Commission's tendency, perhaps unavoidable, to think in terms of watertight compartments has resulted in an inability to provide broadly imaginative and creative workers, capable of handling unusual problems and situations not covered in the rulebook.

The process of promotion and advancement, while very definite and presumably equitable, is also such that the tendency of the really gifted and able is to by-pass it. There are, true enough, classified positions now which pay ten thousand dollars a year, in effect the governmental maximum. But as a practical matter the classified civil servant seldom rises to policy-making positions. Presidents and departmental heads are generally constrained to look outside government ranks for their key appointees.

Irey, though a lifelong civil servant, rose through the creation of a new agency, and his sudden appointment to it. Once appointed, he built his office into a brilliantly successful instrumentality, and the office in turn has carried its creator into high places. One hesitates to say that this man's ability and capacity for direction would ever have come fully to light if he had proceeded through the normal civil service channels.

Williams is an officer in the diplomatic service, the most highly selective branch of the government. Appointments to the periodic examinations are hard enough to come by; the examinations themselves are almost fantastically difficult. It can be assumed that the successful candidate for this service has the very highest mental, educational, and administrative equipment. Yet Williams's sudden advancement has resulted from activity entirely outside his regular line of duty, and it has taken the form of a temporary separation from his chosen work in favor of something altogether different. Whatever he may have to thank for his present post of responsibility, it is assuredly not the inscrutable processes of the civil service.

We have not yet developed a civil service mechanism that will provide us with original thinkers upon demand, or that can be counted upon to supply upper-case administrators in anything like the quantity now required by an incredibly complex governmental process. But it is a hopeful sign that such men are to be found, some of them already within civil service ranks, others in business or professional life, who can be prevailed upon to enter government. In many cases they sacrifice opportunities for advancement, or accept thumping wage cuts. Washington can now boast many specialists, technicians, administrators who could make many times their government pay in private life.

Even more significant is the incipient rise of a class that America has long needed—those men who educate themselves with government service in view. For the first time since the early days of the Republic such public service is considered a worthy and fruitful occupation for men and women of ability and education. Better still, exalted social position is playing no necessary part in the evolution of an American Civil Service. Snobbery and the Old School Tie have been the curse of the English system, but it now appears that our own future administrators and formulators of policy will be drawn from a wide variety of social backgrounds, limited only to demonstrable ability and a desire to serve.

No one better exemplifies this trend than the present director of the Bureau of the Budget, Harold D. Smith. His little-publicized and widely misunderstood bureau fills one of the most important needs of our present-day government. It is not a mere estimating or accounting office. It is not even essentially an expense-cutting office, as its name would imply, though it has in fact saved the taxpayers a good many millions. Its primary aim is that the enormous sums now being appropriated for governmental upkeep be spent as wisely, efficiently, and constructively as possible. It reshuffles, reorganizes, and revamps old agencies, it creates new ones, and it abolishes outworn ones. Its recommendations along these lines are embodied in drafts of executive orders, for the President's signature.

The Bureau has recently been given the duty of passing on legislative recommendations of departmental heads. It assists the President in many other administrative ways, including handling a good deal of his mail. And it concerns itself with broad questions such as the development of improved plans of administrative management, and the standardization of government accounting practices. All of this is in addition to its original function of watching income and outgo, and keeping the government from being cheated.

Thus the power now concentrated in the hands of Harold Smith makes him one of the half-dozen top men in the government. His direct, personal contact with the President is so vital a part of his job that at the President's suggestion he and his staff are now housed in the State Department building, just across the street from the executive offices. He sees more of Mr. Roosevelt than any other person except possibly Harry Hopkins, and his influence and power are such that one member of Congress recently remarked, only half-jokingly, "We grant the power and Harold Smith writes the laws."

Smith is a calm, hard-working, slow-moving man, with an enormous capacity for work and a wide knowledge of his job. He was born on a Kansas farm, and worked his way through high school and college. He took a bachelor's degree in electrical engineering at his graduation in 1922 from the University of Kansas. A religious leader in college, he found his interest shifting from religion to public administration, and on the strength of a fellowship at the University of Michigan he was able to work for a master's degree in public administration. He learned about government at first hand through internships in the Detroit Bureau of Governmental Research and the Kansas Municipal League.

In 1928 he accepted the directorship of the Michigan Municipal League. This organization then existed largely on paper, and his salary was microscopic. His firm belief, however, that governmental waste and inefficiency could be eliminated impelled him to make his new job serve a useful purpose. Before long, cities and towns were flocking to the Municipal League, and paying their dues; Smith had shown them how to save money on purchases, and how to raise their efficiency level. He wrote a number of city charters, modernizing and simplifying the outworn and wasteful municipal organization that he found. His reputation in his field naturally grew, and when Frank Murphy became governor of Michigan he quickly spotted Harold Smith as a man he wanted. In 1937 he made him his budget director.

When Daniel W. Bell, another distinguished public servant, left the Budget Bureau in 1939 to become under secretary of the Treasury, Smith's name was high on the list of possible successors which was supplied to the President by the Treasury Department. Roosevelt phoned him, asking him to take the job.

He has worked from the beginning at a hard and unrelenting tempo. Although his hours are unbelievable—for weeks on end he never gets home in time for dinner—he works slowly and deliberately, maintaining an equilibrium and demonstrating an ability that have won him wide respect. Though accessible to newspapermen, he shuns personal publicity, and has avoided all trace of the egotism that so commonly engulfs the great and powerful in Washington.

Smith is, of course, an appointive officer. While eventually his may be made a civil service post, it is now subject to the will of the chief executive. A Republican President coming into office might look on the job of budget director as a fat patronage plum to be passed out to some deserving member of the party, and Smith would in the due course of events resign to make way for his successor. But any President, whether Republican or Democrat, who failed to make use of Smith's far-reaching knowledge of government should have his head examined.

The Bureau of the Budget is an integral part of the basic machinery of government. Beneath the noisy surface the vast apparatus of the bureaucracy exists unseen and for the most part unheard. The quadrennial political storms that are a fixed part of the American system are registered in this subterranean region as only faint scratches on a distant seismograph.

Chapter VI

The Game of Congress

WHEN you take a visitor to view Congress, the result is almost always the same. They see a desultory collection of quite average-looking men who are either talking in an aimless and desultory fashion or engaging in oratory of a kind rarely heard outside of Congress. The visitor is inclined to be puzzled, unhappy, perhaps even angry or annoyed.

This was not what he had expected to see. Enshrined in memory was the image of Daniel Webster, Henry Clay, Calhoun, and Adams, the great figures out of the heroic past. And here are men, any men, talking, talking apparently about whatever happens to come into their respective heads.

What the newcomer fails to realize is that he is watching only one phase, and a minor and a superficial phase at that, of a very complicated game; a game as complicated say, as *jai alai*. I remember my own reactions when I first came to Washington. It seemed not only incredibly complicated but very unattractive and very dull. The gestures were repetitious and tiresome, the whole business weary-making, set against the frayed nineteenth-century elegance of Capitol corridors and committee rooms.

What I gradually became aware of was the importance of the personalities of the players to an appreciation or even an understanding of what it was about; not only the personalities but what had shaped them, the background, the ambitions, the desires, the weaknesses. Above all, what they owed allegiance to and why, their inmost prejudices. With a little progress in this direction, the pieces began to fit together.

Unfortunately no score cards, with batting averages, are furnished. But after you've been around for a time even the dullest hearing comes to have a special interest of its own. The ramifying personalities, ties, prejudices, leading strings can be seen to extend backward into a kind of dim infinity which is, I suppose, "the people," "the nation," "the republic"—whatever name you choose to give to it.

I, of course, am still a novice. Nine years is not enough to qualify one as an expert. And, moreover, I have never really concentrated on watching the game as do, for example, the press association boys who live in the Senate or the House press gallery. They have a sure, uncanny knowledge of every play and player from start to finish. What they write, in the formalized language of the press, is only a minute fraction of what they know.

But even being in and out of the Senate and the House now and then, as I have been, you learn some things. One of the first things you learn is that certain senators and representatives are permanent players in the game of Congress. The umpire never calls them out. These are the men—rarely a woman and then customarily a widow of a former member—from the deep South who come back year after year after year, elections casting them up as recurrently and as regularly as worn shells on an ancient shingle.

When the Democrats were out of power, during the long famine of the 'twenties, they were like poor relations at a family reunion, grateful to be there but a little resentful at being made to wait always for the second table. The Southerners during that time were at best a listless opposition, driven only rarely to oratorical revolt.

Their boss in the House was a congressman from Texas named Jack Garner, an obscure autocrat who brooked no opposition from his flock. Garner had begun coming to Washington in 1903. It was a comfortable habit. He lived with his wife, who was also his secretary, in boardinghouses or clean, respectable, fourth-rate hotels and managed to save a good half of his salary and all of hers. In the late afternoons he attended Speaker Nick Longworth's poker club, a pleasant institution combining the best features of statesmanship and conviviality. Here any semblance of opposition was abandoned. They were friends, they understood each other. Sometimes on spring afternoons Jack Garner would get on a street-

car and go out to the zoo. There he would feed peanuts to the
monkeys and the elephants and then he would get on the streetcar again and go back to his boardinghouse on Capitol Hill.

Something happened in 1930 to alter the simple pattern of his
life. A light had begun to glow on the dark horizon. The Democrats gained fifty-five seats. It was like that moment in a western
just before the rescue party arrives. You're pretty sure they're
coming but nevertheless the element of suspense is still strong.
Garner became, almost overnight, a radical crying for blood. Unhappy Mr. Hoover was in the White House, but an even better
target was Andrew Mellon who had become a fixed appurtenance
in the national shooting gallery. Garner introduced a wild proposal
calling for the expenditure of $300,000,000 to help the states meet
the problem of unemployment, and for this gesture he was roundly
denounced by all right-thinking people.

This was only the first symptom of the transformation that was
soon to come. The poor relatives had inherited the earth. They
began in 1933 to exert the powers and prerogatives that went with
their inheritance and they have never ceased in the ten years that
have intervened to assert themselves. They are out to make up
for the humiliations of the 'twenties when they sat below the salt.

The reaction of the larger public concerns them little or not
at all. Re-election is achieved with a minimum of effort. That, you
soon come to understand, is what gives them the fine feet-under-
the-mahogany assurance of the permanent boarder. The trick is
simple. It is the poll tax system which, in Louisiana, Huey Long
had his legislature abolish.

In Mississippi, Alabama, Florida, Georgia, Texas, North and
South Carolina, Tennessee, Virginia, and Arkansas you pay from
a dollar to two dollars a year for the privilege of voting. A dollar
is a very large sum of money to a tenant farmer in Mississippi, so
large that he could not possibly afford to pay so much for the
abstract privilege of voting. The result is that throughout most of
the South only about 20 per cent of the white population goes to
the polls, the Negroes having, of course, been debarred since the
carpetbag era.

In Mississippi in 1940 out of the total population of 2,183,796, 175,616 people voted, which represents only 16 per cent of the total white population. This is very simple arithmetic. If the sheriff of Galobusha County is a part of your little moss-hung, rose-bowered Tammany Hall, then his cousins and his uncles and their friends and their dependents can almost by themselves swing the county for you. The cost is very low and once you get your machine working it is, with good luck, as close to perpetual motion as anything is ever likely to be on this imperfect earth. There are obligations, of course, but in most instances these are direct and simple. You have in your state one major interest—cotton always, perhaps a patent medicine company, perhaps a power company. That is a chore but not too great a chore.

In Congress the system of seniority is inflexibly observed. In this respect not even the most select club in America guards the rights of its members so zealously. Once on the escalator of seniority you are bound to rise to a position of power and importance. The permanent boarders are now all at the head of the table, some of them surprised and even a little disconcerted by the honors and responsibilities that have fallen on them.

Take amiable old Henry Steagall. For twenty-eight years he has been coming to Congress. In 1933 he became chairman of the House Banking and Currency Committee, one of the most important committees in Congress. Henry Steagall was born in Clopton, Alabama. He took a law degree from the University of Alabama and became promptly a useful cog in the ring of courthouse politicians who run the state. He is a kindly man, a likable man, and it was the easiest thing in the world for him to drift along the sluggish political channel. Henry was county solicitor first, then a member of the legislature, prosecuting attorney, and finally on June 29, 1914, came the accolade—election to Congress.

The Banking and Currency Committee must pass on complicated economic legislation of the most far-reaching significance. The wartime price-control bill was one measure that came before Henry's committee. A draft was sent to Congress by the administration in July of 1941 and for nearly five months the Banking and Currency Committee held a kind of marathon hearing.

As the summer merged into fall, you could see Henry Steagall growing a little restive through those long drawn-out sessions. A dreamy look would come into his china-blue eyes. It was late October and Henry knew that in the hills around his home town of Ozark it was fox-hunting time, and if there's one thing in this world that Henry loves, it is fox hunting. Not your pink-coated nonsense imported from England but going out at night with a pack of hounds and sitting around a fire and listening to the magic of their baying. Henry is a very active member of the Wiregrass Fox Hunters Association and in early November he sneaked away for a little vacation back home while the wheels of the Banking and Currency Committee slowed to a dead stop.

For Henry Steagall from Ozark, Alabama, it was a confusing and unhappy time. So many people wanted so many different things. The voice that somehow was loudest was that of Senator John Bankhead of Alabama, Henry's political boss. Bankhead, of the family that makes Congress its highly successful business, speaks for cotton, the system of government subsidies that has sustained cotton culture during the past ten years. The cotton farmers wanted no ceiling on farm prices. Then there was organized labor and labor was out to prevent any ceiling over wages. Henry Steagall was left to wrestle with a problem knottier than any he had ever encountered before, and as his committee bickered over a tepid compromise he heard with the ear of memory the fox hounds baying in the hills around Ozark. What came out of Henry's committee was a sorry and bedraggled excuse for a price-fixing bill.

The case of Martin Dies is more complicated. It is a case history in ambition, by Shakespeare out of *True Story Magazine*. When Martin Dies first came to Washington from Orange, Texas, he had the most complete and utter scorn for the whole institution of Congress. A protective rind of cynicism was what he showed to the world. I doubt whether I have ever encountered a more cynical man than this lank Texan with the sallow gray face. He was a leading member of the Demagogues Club, made up of younger members like himself who had pledged themselves to vote for any appropriation bill that came onto the floor of the House, no matter what it was for. It was a hell of a good joke and they made the most of it, these young *sans culottes*. You would see Dies standing at the back of the House, surrounded by two or three fellow members of his club, a good-natured grin on his face. When a roll call came, he would stalk onto the floor and roar out his yea in a lusty voice, usually drawing tolerant laughter.

Seeing him in that phase, you would have said that here was another easygoing Texan who had patented for himself a political formula guaranteeing his return to Washington ad infinitum. What happened to him is anyone's guess. It may have been merely Washington, the frustration of obscurity and neglect, some gnawing force beneath the outer surface of cynicism. Whatever it was it fed on itself.

Dies' committee to investigate un-American activities has made thousands of headlines. In the early days especially the performance was made to order for a certain section of the press. The chairman provided everything but the pink lemonade. There were witnesses who shouted their defiance at the committee, threats of contempt, mysterious spies and agents provocateurs who were spirited into the committee room incognito. With the years came growth and dignity. Mr. Dies worked out a plan for a series of regional offices staffed by his own investigators who would be on a sort of permanent safari in the minor sewers of American political life. It was pointed out that the Federal Bureau of Investigation already had efficient offices in the same cities but Dies apparently had not a very high opinion of the FBI.

Serious opposition might have developed if Chairman Dies had not succeeded in identifying his committee with the House itself. If this was done with conscious deliberation it was a clever and subtle thing to do. But I am not at all sure that Dies is so Machiavellian. It may have been merely an extension of his ego—my committee, my House—which communicated itself to his fellow members. In any event he is now wrapped firmly in the mantle of Congress itself and any slightest criticism is taken as an affront to the very temple of democracy.

This is unfortunate since it makes it difficult to determine with any objectivity what Dies has really done. It may be, as so many of his critics on the left insist, that it is sound and fury, or, again, he may have succeeded in intimidating some of the minor menaces. One thing is certain and that is that he has never caught the big fish, either Nazi or Communist. It is the little people, the little people on committees with obscure offices on obscure streets who have come to judgment under Dies.

Perhaps the most remarkable change is in Dies himself. Gone is that carefree, good-natured grin. The expression he wears now is commonly a scowl. The man is hag-ridden. He alone can save whatever vision of righteousness and security it is that he cherishes. The gnawing force is there, more insistent, unrelenting. Whether he has framed in his own mind the hopes and fears that beset him, it is impossible to say.

I remember several of us were talking with him one day in the lobby just off the House floor. He was explaining the new offices he was going to open in Los Angeles, Chicago, Minneapolis, New Orleans, and points east and west. He was talking about secret police and what they could and could not do. "Well, of course it's true," he said, a curious smile relaxing the gray strained look of his face, "that the only kind of secret police that's any good is one that's got the power of life and death."

Take another gentleman from Texas, take Tom Connally, chairman of the Senate Foreign Relations Committee, as full of dignity as a turkey cock, with twenty-five years in Congress back of him, first in the House and then in the Senate. In action on the floor or in committee he is shrewd, penetrating, with no mercy for an opponent whom he once gets on the run. In the fight over President Roosevelt's proposal to remake the Supreme Court, Connally was wonderfully effective in heaping ridicule and abuse on those witnesses who came to testify for the President's scheme. An astute politician, knowing all the tricks, he seems to wear securely his political armor—the standup collar, the black string tie, the Southern statesman's broad-brimmed black hat.

Yet he, too, reveals at times symptoms of the insecurity that gnaws at Dies and so many of the others who come from the South. It is as though they were exiles among strangers they have never learned wholly to trust. They wear with an almost proud self-consciousness the badge of their difference. Their early conditioning is so alien to modern industrial America. It is not space alone that separates Ozark, Alabama, and Orange, Texas, from Detroit. Guarding a vision of what never was, they cannot bring themselves to accept the alien and the strange.

Of course, not all the permanent players in the game of Congress come from below the Mason and Dixon line. Here and there are others who return year after year. New England has its share. Crotchety old Allen Treadway has been returning to Washington for nearly thirty years. He is a thirty-third degree Mason, a Knight Templar, a Granger, an Elk, a member of the Royal Arcanum, a trustee of the Lee Savings Bank, a director of the New England Fire Insurance Company and the Berkshire Life Insurance Company; in short, a solid citizen who plays golf on his own private nine-hole golf course, living under the interesting illusion that hard striving and right living will earn private golf courses for all Americans.

Then there is that old antiquity George Holden Tinkham who, beard and all, is straight out of an Edward Lear limerick. Merry as an elf, he appears to be entirely indifferent to what goes on in the halls of Congress and in quieter days went off on long expeditions for big game in Africa. But whether it is his rarity or some humor that he stirs in his constituents, he has returned with clocklike regularity until he decided in 1942 not to run again. Similarly Senator Arthur Capper has a hold on the imagination or the loyalty of Kansas that has made it possible for him to survive as a Republican the high tide of the New Deal.

These fixtures are not like the fixtures from the South. They are exceptions for some special and peculiar reason. Even Allen Treadway, firmly entrenched in office as he is, is responsible under the two-party system and must stand for election and give some accounting to the voters. Congressmen from the cotton states have no such responsibility.

Political generalizations are, of course, always faulty. One of the most responsible members of the Senate is Lister Hill of Alabama who is unhappily afflicted with a predilection for Southern oratory of the worst vintage. You have Ross Collins from Mississippi, as shrewd a man as you would find in a day's walk, for long chairman of the military subcommittee on appropriations, helping the more enlightened officers to move the army out of the cavalry-and-mule back era. Perhaps it comes down to individual personality, the character or lack of character in the five hundred and thirty-one men and women who represent the people of the United States in Congress assembled.

The average of conscientious, hard-working individuals is remarkably high. One of the most effective members of Congress is Mrs. Edith Nourse Rogers, Republican of Massachusetts. While, in a sense, she inherited her seat from her husband, she never coasted on his reputation, nor has she traded on her sex. I should imagine that she knows the workings of the House as well as anyone, with, perhaps, the exception of a few parliamentary fanatics who have been around forever. Mrs. Rogers serves on three committees, civil service and war veterans' legislation, on which she is ranking minority member, and foreign affairs. An authority on veterans' legislation and the whole complicated business of bonuses and pensions, she would become chairman of the committee if the Republicans were to get a majority of the House, and she would do the job well. A woman of cultivation and charm, educated in Paris, she never seems to have any difficulty understanding the vernacular of the boys who come straight from the grass roots.

On the Senate side, you would go a long way before you found two more conscientious public officials than Prentiss Brown of Michigan and Carl Hatch of New Mexico. Brown is deeply aware of the vast industrial area that he represents and he labors on three important committees, banking and currency, finance, and manufactures, to represent the interests of that area. A Democrat, the cast of his mind is essentially conservative but not reactionary.

Carl Hatch is a rare kind of man. He is without any trace, so far as one can tell from superficial observation, of the crude egotism, the appetite for power, that seem inevitably to corrupt so many men in public life. Gentle, kindly, self-effacing, he nevertheless has an earnest objective that leads him into bold action. He has persistence, too. Troubled by the manifold ills that beset our time, he reads in spare moments, reads eagerly books and articles that seem to throw some light on the shape of things to come. There is in this man from the cattle country a contemplative quality that is Lincolnian. You would trust him—with your bank account or with your country.

If he has shown any weakness in his nine years in the Senate, it is in his trust in the efficaciousness of law to correct deep-seated ills. This comes out of the strain of idealism that is at the center of his nature. The Hatch "clean politics" act was a splendid gesture but it failed to keep the big money out of the presidential campaign of 1940. There were too many ways of getting around the five-thousand-dollar limitation and the big money boys on both sides took advantage of every loophole. But Carl Hatch will try again when the time is right, having learned his lesson.

On the Republican side of the Senate, you can match Brown and Hatch with Harold Burton of Ohio and peppery, ginger-haired John Danaher of Connecticut. Both men work hard at the job of senator. While they are comparative newcomers, they have nevertheless caught on quickly to the system. Danaher in particular got the hang of it almost from the start, and on the floor and in committee he was in action before the oldsters knew he had arrived.

That is what counts, of course, the know-how. For know-how I would give the prize to Congressman John J. Cochran of St. Louis, confessing at the same time to a deep prejudice in Jack's favor for all his efforts to educate me. The general public rarely hears of him. He is a congressman's congressman. As chairman of the Committee on Expenditures in the executive departments, later as chairman of the Committee on Accounts, he knows the intricacy of government, the wheels within wheels within wheels. Both shrewd and honest, he has been able to do a yeoman's job for the public and I would not trade him for ten—no, twenty—of your well-meaning talkers.

If Jack should ever be in a frame of mind to write his autobiography, he could call it, in all honesty, "The Education of a Politician." His was the perfect preparation. He began as an office boy on the St. Louis *Post-Dispatch*, learning more about newspapers in the course of that novitiate than most people who work on them ever know. Early in life he showed that he knew his way around politically. With the easy Irish humor, the utter lack of self-consciousness that is his, he made friends among the politicians in the Irish and the German wards in North St. Louis. What it got him eventually was a job as secretary to a congressman. For a smart lad this was a postgraduate course at Harvard with Oxford thrown in on the side.

Very often these are the men who make Congress run; the secretaries, the clerks, with years of experience. They do the work for amiable old fuddlers, being kind enough to see that the stuffing in the senator's shirt doesn't spill out in public. They know the dull, important details of government that almost no one else, either in Congress or out, takes time to bother with.

What was remarkable about Jack Cochran was that he had both gifts; the capacity for painstaking detail and the politician's flair. Later on, during the first World War, he was secretary to old Senator Stone of Missouri who was then chairman of the Senate Foreign Relations Committee. That meant access to a laboratory for the observation of human behavior of a very rare sort, comparable, on the scientific side, perhaps, to those privileged physicists who work at breaking up the atom. He was elected to Congress first in 1926 from a district where the voice of influential political friends went a long way. In 1934 he ran for the Senate and would have won beyond a shadow of a doubt if "Boss" Pendergast's gang had not been counting the votes in Kansas City.

But even so he was not lost to Washington, being able to run after his defeat in the senatorial primary for his old seat in the House.

Somehow I think he may be more useful where, by virtue of the Pendergast machinations, he has remained than in the chillier, loftier atmosphere of the Senate. How many millions of dollars he has saved the Treasury through his know-how it is impossible to say. He has made himself a specialist in one of the worst congressional rackets. Members are constantly pressing private claims which call for the payment of millions out of the Treasury for real or fancied damages. Some of these claims go back to the Civil War. A plague of them came out of the first World War.

One category includes solely Indian claims. After they were given the vote, the Indians found lawyers and politicians to push their demands for the value in dollars of the natural wealth of which they were deprived by the white man. The Sioux Indians, for example, have a demand in the Court of Claims for all the gold taken out of the Black Hills and all the timber forested off those pleasant small-scale mountains. Something more than thirty millions has already been paid out on Indian claims, a suspiciously large proportion of this going to lawyers. Jack Cochran succeeded in maneuvering a bill through the House allowing the Court of Claims to offset against these astronomical demands the sums paid out to the Indian tribes for food, clothing, and education, which goes a long way toward reducing the grand total.

Pending today are claims for more than three billion dollars. They arise not only from the Indians but from every conceivable source. Cochran has made himself a sort of Horatius at the bridge to stop these raids. One claim for nearly a million dollars which the House passed in spite of his best efforts was to compensate an exporter for a loss on goods he had sold in Siberia after the Russian revolution; he maintained that a War Trade Board in Vladivostok had encouraged him to go in with his wares and that therefore when the currency in which he was paid dwindled in value to zero, his government should recompense him. Powerful political lawyers were behind that move. But Cochran beat it after all when the House sustained a presidential veto by a thumping majority.

Again and again I've watched him on the floor fighting off the raiders. He has little regard for the conventions of oratory. Instead he raises a lusty voice in blunt and angry denunciation of men whom he does not hesitate to call by harsh names. The private claims racket is not the only form of brigandage that Cochran, almost singlehanded, has stepped in to stop. He discovered that promoters were availing themselves of Congress's privilege of granting the right to bridge navigable streams to promote fly-by-night bridge companies and he soon put an end to that. Similarly he stopped the big profits that a few promoters were making from the issuance of special commemorative coins which Congress was required to authorize.

It is the know-how, plus a capacity for understanding and getting along with your fellow members. Often I have seen Jack Cochran after fiercely denouncing one of his colleagues on the floor, thump that same colleague on the back in the lobby, demanding to know, "How the hell did you think you could get away with that, you big so-and-so?" And nine times out of ten the accused takes this good-naturedly.

Learning how is a slow process and there are few short cuts. I remember when Bruce Barton came to the House in 1937, he was full of ideas about what he intended to do. For one thing he started a campaign to repeal a law a day. He started the campaign but somehow it made small headway, even in the newspapers. The system, of committees, rules, procedure, convention, custom, got in his way, baffled him, afflicted him with a sense of helplessness as it does so many new members.

Once or twice I went to see him in his New York office in the great advertising firm of which he is the head. I was struck with the difference between the two worlds in which he was dividing his career. In his big private office behind his desk was a photo mural of Coney Island covering the entire wall from floor to ceiling. He had it there to remind himself that those were the people he had to reach through the medium of advertising; through all the clever, ingenious schemes that Batten, Barton, Durstine and Osborne were paid to concoct.

They were there in the photo mural, myriads of human beings as impersonal as ants, and you dealt with them, if you were Bruce Barton on this lofty pinnacle of Manhattan, three or four times removed; they were hardly ever more personal than those antlike creatures in the photo mural. In Congress it was different. There of necessity you dealt at first hand; if not with your constituents, who might be reached by remote control, then with your fellow members. In the two empty rooms assigned to him in the old House Office building, Bruce Barton always seemed a little lost. He was just beginning to get the feel of it after three years, beginning to like it, too. More men of Bruce Barton's capacities must develop the patience to learn the congressional system.

His district was New York's so-called silk-stocking district. From that district today comes Joseph Clark Baldwin, a promising freshman who seems to show the right blend of character; sufficient independence and integrity mixed with patience and a willingness to learn the geography of a special sphere. Perhaps it comes down to the elementary truth that there is no substitute for character. Party platforms no matter how grandiloquent, campaign speeches no matter how mellifluous can never conceal the deficiencies.

Nor, finally, can a thousand thousand rhinestone-studded WPA projects. The cherished example is Senator Kenneth McKellar of Tennessee. The legend is that he once held a convention of the men and women he had put on the federal payroll and the number was so large that they could not all be accommodated in the largest public hall in Memphis. What is more, it had been gently hinted by the organizers of this fete that since it was the Christmas season it would be fitting to bring gifts to the great benefactor. Room after room after room in the Peabody Hotel overflowed with thank offerings, and Senator McKellar was as surprised and as pleased as a young girl at her debut. Nothing could have been further from his imagination!

The McKellar patronage is the oil for the machine that term after term sends him back to Washington to ornament the Senate. The machine is the property of Boss Crump of Memphis who knows the whys and wherefores of the poll tax law and the status of the Negroes who form a considerable part of the population of his fiefdom. With the strong arm of Crump at his back, Senator McKellar has never had to concern himself with the petty whims of the voters of Tennessee. When the New Deal was in the money, he was a New Dealer, causing his native heath to bloom with bridges, with privies and courthouses and swimming pools. Always sensitive to change, he began early to alter his political style. In the transition period it was difficult to keep up with the nimble gentleman from Tennessee. Sometimes on the same day he hunted with the conservative hounds and ran with the New Deal hares. But as the hares found existence increasingly difficult, the lusty bay of Senator McKellar was found from thenceforth with the pack of well-fed hounds.

Beyond character is the system itself. Not all the wisdom and the virtue since the time of Hammurabi could make up for two or three of the most glaring defects in the congressional system. They are painfully obvious. They cost millions and millions of dollars. They open the way to the worst kind of chiseling. Yet no one does much of anything about them.

Most conspicuous is the custom of appointing members of the House and the Senate to committees on which they can serve the special interests of their state or community. At first glance this seems like eminent good sense. Congressman Doakes is from Nevada, therefore put him on committees dealing with irrigation projects and with mining. Senator Whosis is from the cotton South, so, put him on the committee on agriculture which determines agricultural policy.

What happens under this system is that Congress divides itself into separate legislative bodies, each concerned with promoting the sectional interests of a particular part of the country. It was summed up, all unwittingly, by the remark of a page boy outside the door of the House. I had asked him to go in and call off the floor for me a congressman from New York City. "Oh, he won't be in there," came the reply. "They're debating an agricultural bill and I doubt if he's got a single farmer in his district." This innocent answer reflected the attitude of the membership itself. The agricultural bill concerned the whole country; the prices every man, Jack, and child would pay for everything eaten and almost everything worn; but the only members on the floor were those who represented cotton or wheat or corn or tobacco.

The chairman of the Senate Committee on Agriculture and Forestry is salty old Cotton Ed Smith of South Carolina. He is the head and front of the system of agricultural subsidies that has sustained the cotton culture of the South during the past decade. Behind Cotton Ed, or, it might be more proper to say, surrounding him, is the American Farm Bureau Federation which is possibly the most powerful single lobby in the capital. Cotton is sacred to Cotton Ed Smith and any suggestion that it might be better for the South to diversify and, gradually perhaps, break away from the bondage to cotton is rank heresy. Cotton prices must be high; that is the sole political tenet which Cotton Ed will underwrite; that, and for campaign purposes at least, the sacredness of white womanhood. Serving on his committee are senators from Montana, Oklahoma, Alabama, South Dakota, Arkansas, New Mexico, Mississippi, Iowa, Louisiana, Illinois, Tennessee, Georgia, Nevada, Nebraska, Oregon, Kansas, Minnesota, Indiana, and Vermont. Only one state, Illinois, has one of the great cities in which live the consumers who must buy the produce from the farm states.

Agriculture is, of course, a striking example. The Committee on Indian Affairs is another. This last is a very specialized body, headed by Senator Thomas of Oklahoma who fights, bleeds, and dies for the Indians on every possible occasion. Only senators from states with Indian reservations are on the Indian affairs committee. Irrigation and reclamation is still another. With the exception of Chairman Bankhead, all the members come from the dry states that incessantly seek federal funds for irrigation projects. On the committee on mines and mining are only senators from states with mining interests, Senator Wiley of Wisconsin being, perhaps, an exception.

Partly, of course, this is natural and right. A senator from a mining state brings to Washington a special concern for the miners and the mine owners who are his constituents. But the work of the committees is so important, the Senate depending almost wholly on committee recommendations on the bulk of routine bills, that special interests are served by specialists and too little attention is given to the welfare of the nation as a whole. Each committee is in a sense a separate Senate concerned with plumping for its own constituency.

Almost the same thing is true in the House. The chairman of the Committee on Immigration and Naturalization is Samuel Dickstein of New York. There are congressmen on his committee from states that have no "alien problem" but they rarely attend committee meetings. Mr. Dickstein and a half-dozen members from the cities order matters to suit themselves.

When it gets down to subdivisions of the committee on appropriations, the same regionalism holds, only more so. Chairman of the subcommittee on appropriations for the Department of the Interior is one James G. Scrugham of Nevada. Mr. Scrugham and the Department of Interior have a mutual and harmonious understanding that is beautiful to see. It may be the reason why the State of Nevada is said to appear from an airplane as pitted as the surface of the moon, the pits being irrigation and reclamation projects generously bestowed by the Department of the Interior. Mr. Scrugham's committee is a tight little organization that beats down any opposition with a fine disregard for ordinary procedures. Malcolm C. Tarver, of Georgia, shows the same tender concern for that vast rabbit warren of bureaucracy, the Department of Agriculture, being chairman of the subcommittee that ministers to the wants of the department.

In the game of Congress one of the king pieces is the House Rules Committee. This committee of fourteen members is a super traffic department for the legislation that moves through the House. To understand its intricacies, you must know the game very well. Suffice it to say that without approval of the Rules Committee it is almost impossible to bring legislation up for consideration. The power of the Rules Committee has grown to such an extent that it has essayed in recent years to pass on the subject matter of legislation, which has already been considered in lengthy hearings by another committee.

It is not surprising to find the permanent players dominating this all-important committee, serving as goalies to keep out as long as possible any legislation of which they do not approve. The chairman is Adolph J. Sabath, of Chicago, now old and infirm and unable to cope with his weighty office. The three goalies who keep guard over the inner sanctum of the rules committee are Eugene Cox of Georgia, Howard Smith of Virginia, and Dies of Texas, all three beset by the dark suspicions of the South. They serve to the best of their considerable abilities the interests of that region.

This is one of the glaring weaknesses in the congressional system—men and women come to Washington and serve solely the interests of their district or their state. Shocking instances of this occur over and over. For years the Army tried to do away with certain Army posts that had become merely historic survivals of the Indian wars with no relation to any modern plan of defense. Yet each time it was seriously proposed to end the existence of Fort Frogpuddle, congressmen and senators from that state fought like tigers to keep it in existence. They were thinking, of course, of the votes of the tradesmen and the farmers who profited by the presence of Fort Frogpuddle.

This business of regional grabbing is one reason why a basic change in the rules is called for. The item veto would give the President the power to strike out of appropriation bills separate items which he wished to veto. Take, as an example of how this would work, the appropriation bill for the Department of the Interior. As a result of the happy collaboration with Mr. Scrugham, the Department of the Interior has been treated with a generosity embarrassing even to Mr. Ickes. The annual appropriation bill for the Department is as rich with plums as a Christmas pudding. If the President could veto separate items in each appropriation bill, he could, on the advice of his experts, remove at least the more obvious steals. As it is he must approve the entire bill or risk holding up important work of the Department by vetoing the measure and starting the legislative process all over again.

The power of the item veto would tend to prevent the outrageous practice of tacking onto vital bills amendments that could not possibly get by if they were sent down to the White House in the form of an independent measure. This was what the farm bloc tried to do when the Senate was debating the second war powers bill, seeking to tie on a parity plus amendment that would have increased consumer costs two or three billions of dollars. Warning against this brazen bit of skulduggery, the President found an ally in Senator Arthur Vandenberg of Michigan. Their exchange of letters on the need for this elementary reform was one of those glimpses of reason which now and then pierce the obscure landscape of partisanship.

The sharpest differences in recent years have not been so much between Republicans and Democrats as between the executive and the legislative branches of the government. This threatens at times to become a perpetual internecine warfare. It stems out of Congress's intense jealousy of the swelling, expanding, hydra-headed executive. Now, in the face of the war and the inevitable tightening of controls "downtown," Congress on its distant hill feels more and more neglected; like some relic of the past misplaced out of the Smithsonian Institution. The result is an inferiority complex of fearful proportions.

Five days after Pearl Harbor it manifested itself in a clinical form. Before the Senate was a proposal providing funds for hire of extra assistants to meet the added burden that the war crisis had put on virtually every member of House and Senate. A debate followed that was extraordinary in the light of circumstances. Congress was appropriating at a nod from the White House billions of dollars; authorizing powers undreamed of in peacetime. Yet here was the Senate debating whether members should be allowed an additional $4,500 a year to hire extra clerks or an executive assistant.

No one appeared to question the need for more help. It was pointed out that in the course of two years nine Senators had

died from the strain of overwork. Senator Mead of New York
told of the flood of mail and the constant tide of visitors pouring
through his office. On one question pending before the Senate
he had received, he said, twenty thousand letters a day for seven
days in succession and every one of those letters had to be opened
and at least cursorily examined. He told his fellow senators that
he could not long afford to remain in the Senate and pay extra
clerks who were working seven days a week. Other senators could
match this record. Yet what about the men who came from states
with sparse population? Did they need extra clerk hire? And
what would the people say about further expenditures at a time
when the cost of the war was being reckoned in astronomical
totals?

Senator LaFollette bluntly told his colleagues that they suffered
from an inferiority complex. We do not trust ourselves to use
the long-distance telephone, he said. No senator in this body can
make an official long-distance telephone call, no member of the
House of Representatives can make one, at government expense.
Yet, said the senator from Wisconsin, year after year we appropriate without question millions upon millions of dollars to
pay the official long-distance telephone bills of the executive
branch of the government. If we can trust a subordinate in one
of the numerous agencies of the United States government to
make a long-distance call from Washington to San Francisco, why
cannot members of Congress trust each other to make long-distance calls and not abuse that privilege for personal or political
reasons?

Senator O'Mahoney of Wyoming took this for his theme too.
The legislative branch of the government was constantly decreas-
ing in importance, he said, whereas the power of the bureaus
and the departments was all the time increasing. No senator
could take time to examine even the legislation which came before his committees. Senator Byrd opposed the increase. He said
the people wanted economy. For once at least, Senator Norris
agreed with him, calling the proposal a "salary grab." Undoubtedly in the back of Norris's mind was the thought of those chisel-

ing members of congress who use their clerk hire to pay their cousins and their uncles and their aunts, yes, their wives, for doing nothing or next to nothing.

For nearly four hours on the fifth day of a crisis that shook the foundations of the republic the Senate debated whether members should be allowed an additional $4,500 for clerk hire. The roll was called and in his stentorian voice the reading clerk announced that the yeas were fifty-three, the nays thirty, not voting, twelve. So, in the unadorned language of the Congressional Record, the amendment was agreed to. Later on, however, it was killed by the House.

Hardly more than a month afterward there was another piece of evidence to add to the case history of Congress's inferiority complex. This was the famous pensions-for-Congressmen law which drew such a storm from the newspapers. In the House it was slipped through without a roll-call vote. The Senate inserted a trick clause which under certain conditions would have permitted a defeated or retiring member of House or Senate to obtain a life annuity for himself by paying $1.37 on the day his term expired. The fact was that only one member of Congress, Norris, could show the requisite tenure of thirty-five years to justify the maximum annuity of $4,100 for one payment of $1.37. Other veterans could, by making one payment, get smaller annuities.

Not the fact of the annuity itself but the way in which it was adopted was evidence of Congress's deep sense of inferiority. It was done by stealth, through parliamentary sleight of hand. Again the congressional subconscious was haunted by the guilty past. There is one daughter of the War of 1812 still on the pension rolls. Just before the present war began, a move to grant new hundreds of millions in pensions to the veterans of World War I was slipped through the House. Projected into the future the pension habit is seen to be absolutely ruinous. Small wonder then that when the storm burst in the press Congress hastily backtracked and repealed its pension plan.

About this retreat was something very pathetic. A realistic case can be made out for pensioning members of Congress, especially those conscientious, hard-working congressmen who year after year give a full measure of public service. Congress for the majority of members is a costly business. Representatives and senators are paid ten thousand dollars a year. But this is by no means net income. Representatives must make a campaign every other year, a costly campaign, and a part of the cost comes out of the congressman's own pocket. There is a constant demand for contributions from every conceivable source, demands which often cannot be refused. In the old days when Congress met for two or three months in the spring and a month or two in the winter members could maintain their law practice or even their jobs back home. Now it is a full-time business with scarcely even a holiday. Living in Washington is expensive. Many members must maintain two homes, one back in the district and one in the capital. The ten thousand dollars is pared down to a very much smaller sum when essential expenses are deducted. There are wealthy men in the Senate and the House, Byrd of Virginia, Wigglesworth of Massachusetts, Taft of Ohio, but they are the exception and not the rule.

Of course, the permanent players from the South and the members returned by self-functioning Tammanies, spend very little to hold their jobs. They make a good thing out of Congress. Penurious old Muley Doughton of North Carolina, chairman of the House Ways and Means Committee, is said to have put away a tidy little fortune out of his salary. But again these are the exceptions. And it is possible that some members who remain on in Congress long past their usefulness would be encouraged to step down if they were assured of a competence. These are some of the valid arguments that can be made for congressional pensions, but Congress, fearful apparently of what people might think, was afraid to make those arguments.

In the gambling hells of the West, according to a tradition that has come down from the frontier, was a sign over the piano that said, "Don't shoot the piano player—he's doing the best he can."

There might well be a sign like that on the front of the capitol. "Don't shoot Congress—they're doing the best they can."

When I think of Congress at work I think of Sam Rayburn, the Speaker of the House; the resolute set of his mouth, the shiny dome of his head, like a well-polished ostrich egg. Quite without side, without bombast, without pretension, he works hard in session and out, making the machine go. It is a troublesome, difficult, thankless job which somehow Rayburn seems to like. For nearly thirty years he has been coming from Texas to Washington and he knows exactly what makes a congressman tick. Yet there is unmistakably the quality of Texas about him, his forthrightness, his dry humor, his skepticism. He knows about elections, what you can do in an off year and what you can't do in an election year. That is the ghostly presence which haunts the halls of Congress. There's always an election and after that another election.

Chapter VII

Campaign

ONCE every two or three decades comes an election that is for the party in power no more than a high-spirited picnic. Such was the campaign of 1936. If Mr. Roosevelt's political enemies had wanted to make it impossible for him to be defeated, they proceeded on exactly the right course. The background was the unbelievably inept Liberty League with its ermine-and-emeralds dinner at the Mayflower Hotel in Washington. Sage old Jack Garner said when it was all over that the Democratic party needn't have spent a cent, needn't have made a single speech. It was all done by an opposition that lacked any understanding of the temper of the American people.

From the beginning a buoyant sense of confidence ran through the Democratic party. At Philadelphia in June the emirs and the pashas of the city machines gathered for what would be a roistering ratification meeting. They were all there—Hague of New Jersey, Kelly and Nash of Chicago, Pendergast of Missouri, Crump of Tennessee, and the lesser figures—to make as much noise as possible. They knew which side their political bread was buttered on. The vast expenditures of the New Deal had put into their hands power they had hitherto scarcely dreamed of.

A political convention, even when there is a real contest in sight, is a curious institution. This one was purely circus, a circus with only one act and that act a set piece out of the origins of American political history. Yet it took an orthodox five days padded with traditional gestures to build up to that ancient climax.

Spreading their tents, surrounded by their retinues, the emirs and the pashas were prepared to enjoy this comfortable occasion. In the Bellevue-Stratford, in the Ritz-Carlton, in the Benjamin Franklin, they set up headquarters where whisky and good will were dispensed with equal liberality. To fill in the dull hours they gossiped with each other, moving from one royal suite to another like reigning monarchs gathered for a coronation. They were formidable men. They controlled millions of votes and votes were power. You approached them with respect and caution.

In certain respects Tom Pendergast of Kansas City was the most formidable of them all. A thick, squat man with a head set solidly on a short bull neck, he moved with commanding dignity through crowded hotel lobbies. I had been assigned to do a roundup story on the bosses. "Let's get them all in," said O. K. Bovard, then managing editor of the *Post-Dispatch*, "let's show what all this is based on." But I was to omit Pendergast who was to have special treatment from Spencer McCulloch of the St. Louis staff. There were several reasons why I was to leave out the Missouri boss, one of them being that Pendergast had sworn to knock me down on sight, and he was a man of his word.

That had come out of an encounter a year before. I had seen him off on the maiden crossing of the *Normandie*, it being one of his specialties to make the first eastward crossing on each new luxury liner. Hints of the scandal that was to dethrone him were already in the air and I followed him from his apartment in the Waldorf-Astoria Towers to the boat to ask some pointed questions. At the hotel he had been belligerent. "Yes, I told O'Malley to approve that insurance deal, and what're you going to do about it?" he growled.

At the boat it was different. For one thing I brought up to his suite Comte Bertrand de Jouvenel of *Paris-Soir* who was making the round trip on the great, gaudy new boat. Pendergast and the very blonde Mrs. Pendergast were ensconced in the living room of their suite which was almost literally filled with flowers, orchids and lilies of the valley, expensive flowers. This was Pendergast, the Maharajah of Missouri, in all his glory.

Under Bertrand's suave, flattering manner, his charm turned on full force, they both expanded. De Jouvenel had come on board with a small trunk full of books on American politics. I had advised him to forget about them and concentrate during the four-day

crossing on the massive little man who was in himself an encyclo-
pedia of American political practice.

"I am told," said de Jouvenel, "that you are the ruler of
Missouri, Mr. Pendergast. Can you tell me how it is that you
do it?"

From an American Pendergast might have taken the question
as an effrontery, as *lèse majesté*. But this was a foreigner. You
could see him turning it over in his mind.

"Well, I'll tell you how I do it," he said with a look of pride
on his face. "It's a very simple thing when you come down to it.
There's people that need things, lots of 'em, and I see to it that
they get 'em. I go to my office on South Main Street in Kansas
City at seven o'clock in the morning and I stay there when I'm in
town till about six o'clock at night and during that time I see
maybe two hundred, maybe three hundred people. One needs a
half a ton of coal. Another woman's gotta get a job for her boy.
I see to it that they get those things. That's all there is to it."

There was more in the same vein as the old man grew expansive.
Set against the background of the orchids and the lilies of the
valley, the amboina and macassar modern fittings of the B-deck
suite, it made a wonderful story and I rushed off the boat just
before sailing to write it. If he had seen it cold when he returned
a few weeks later, Pendergast might have taken it in his stride.
But one of his henchmen back in Missouri must have radioed to
him the full text of the story. When I saw de Jouvenel in Paris
some months later he told me that on the following morning
while he was being shaved in the barber shop, Pendergast had
descended on him, making wild and threatening gestures and
brandishing a sheaf of radiograms. Poor Bertrand never quite
understood the wrath of the ruler of Missouri. That was the reason
I gave Boss Tom a wide berth at the Philadelphia convention.

There was as yet no sign of his dissolution. He was riding high
and so were all the others. They had come into the promised land
and they proposed to stay there; forever, if that were possible.

President Roosevelt arrived on a special train from Washington
to be the star of that last and anticlimactic act. And so great was

his histrionic ability, his sense of timing, his sense of crowd reaction, that he converted a foregone conclusion into something like a triumph. The crowd, a hundred thousand or more, stretched away into the darkness at Franklin Field, cheering wildly at each pause, as though the roar out of the warm, sticky night came from a single throat.

That was the beginning of a big succession of triumphs, of roaring crowds, of streets full of cheering people. The President himself could scarcely have had any illusions as to the outcome of the campaign. He is too shrewd a politician, too keen a judge of trends and tempers, to have failed to realize that it was a walkaway.

At Cleveland the Republicans had nominated Governor Alf Landon of Kansas, a pleasant, cheerful man who had been waiting in the proper expectant attitude for the lightning to strike. The truth was that the really ambitious men in the party, men like Vandenberg of Michigan, had ducked the nomination. They sensed that it spelt not merely defeat but disaster. The contest in Cleveland was almost as lame as the one at Philadelphia. There were men who wanted the honor but none with any weight. Landon, looking discomfited and out of place in the glare of the floodlights and the popping of the flash bulbs, was Hobson's choice.

President Roosevelt set out in early October on a major campaign tour that was to take him as far west as Sheridan, Wyoming. The atmosphere on the ten-car campaign train that rolled out of Union Station in Washington was a gala one. The President knew that he was going to like this expedition. His campaign technique had been perfected over the years until it was almost second nature with him. Moreover, he was to visit the fiefdoms of his chief lieutenants and he knew that everywhere a royal welcome was being prepared.

Perhaps no man in American political history had ever started on a campaign under a more fortunate augury. The city bosses were preparing to put on a kind of popularity contest, each one trying to outdo the other. Earlier in Jersey City, Mayor Hague had turned out the town and half the state in an imitation of a Roman triumph. From the moment that the procession of cars rolled out of the Holland Tunnel the thunder of bombs assaulted the ear, and the whole city under a cloudless blue sky seemed one mass of flag-waving humanity. Hague, an iron-jawed master of ceremonies, rode in the presidential car with the President to Hague's great public hospital and clinic in the center of the city that Hague regarded, with the simple possessive sense of a medieval baron, as his city.

The train rolled westward. Denver was big. St. Louis, on the return, was colossal. But it remained for Mayor Kelly in Chicago to put on an act that made everything else look like a half-hearted rehearsal. In the early evening the President rode for five miles in an open car through streets so crowded that only a narrow lane was left. In spite of the protests of the Secret Service people had been allowed to swarm off the curbs and it was all that the motorcycle police could do to force a way through for the presidential cavalcade.

This was King Crowd. They were out to have a large time and they had it. Every kind of band—bagpipes, piano accordions, jazz, fife-and-drum, bugle corps—lined the narrow lane of humanity through which the presidential party passed. As the parade turned off Michigan Boulevard into West Madison Street the mass of people became denser and noisier. They shrieked from rooftops; they sang and danced; they leaned from tenement windows and loft windows to wave and shout. And all the time a rain of torn paper fluttered down, like gray snow in the half-lighted streets.

If King Crowd had its hero, it also had its hated and despised foe. Not the least remarkable thing about this extraordinary demonstration was the hostility shown toward the Chicago *Tribune*, and, in a lesser degree, toward William Randolph Hearst's Chicago *Herald-Examiner*. Because news photographers with their cameras clung to the outside of nearly every car, the crowd could spot the press. "Where's the *Tribune*?" "Down with the *Tribune*!" "To Hell with the *Tribune*!" These shouts were heard along the entire line of march but particularly in the slum areas on West Madison Street.

King Crowd in the streets was remarkable, but the real spectacle was at the stadium where the President was to deliver his address. The entire front of the great hulking building was illuminated with huge calcium flares that threw an eerie blue light for blocks around. As the presidential party arrived, earsplitting bombs burst overhead and the crowd, a hundred thousand strong, surged up in an almost irresistible tide. Sweating police struggled to keep a way clear so that the President's car could be driven into the stadium. When he appeared on the platform a blare of sound swept up and for a moment seemed to overwhelm him by its intensity. For once the composure of this master of crowds appeared shaken and it was not until he began to speak that he slipped into his customary confident manner.

In the course of this tremendous outpouring so well prepared by Mayor Kelly there was evident that iconology which was to manifest itself many times again. All along the line of march photographs and drawings of President Roosevelt were held up on sticks and poles, waved frantically as he passed. Back again on the campaign train the Secret Service men who had ridden on the running board of his car looked as though they had been through a football scrimmage, their clothes torn and bedraggled. They admitted it was the worst experience they had ever been through.

A campaign train is like nothing else under the sun. It is a transcontinental sound wagon, a glorified road company of the greatest show on earth, a traveling convention of politicians and minor prophets. Around the voice and the personality in the last car the whole machine revolves. Each climax is built up to his appearance. For the thirty or thirty-five reporters on the train, and especially for the press association men, it is a grueling, exhausting grind.

Yet it has its compensations. If there is a good crowd on board you can be sure of something diverting or something funny every minute of the day. The candidate himself is likely to supply a good many laughs. Roosevelt did this deliberately. He knew that back in the press car we were parodying the perfection of his technique. In the two dining cars were loud speakers, and for ordinary

whistle stops most correspondents did not get off the train to go
back to the rear platform but heard the speech via the loud speaker.

The little drama was almost always the same. When the microphones on the rear platform were switched on, after the train had
ground to a stop, you could hear the murmur of the crowd, a vast
buzzing noise, punctuated here and there by shrill cries and shouts.
Then, as Roosevelt emerged from the door of the car onto the
platform, on the arm of his son Jimmy or escorted, perhaps, by
a local politician, the noise of the crowd would swell to a roar,
here and there individual voices carrying over the roar, "We want
Roosevelt," "We're for you, Mr. Roosevelt . . ." Customarily a
local bigwig, the congressman from the district, or the governor,
would gallop through a conventional introduction full of loud
encomiums. Then the roar again, and Roosevelt waiting until it
died down, his infallible sense of timing . . . "My friends, I'm
happy to be here in ———. The last time I was here was ———. I see
your ——— looked excellent as I came along. . . ."

We back in the dining car knew this formula so well that someone would invariably supply a facetious name or a facetious date
well in advance of the benign voice out of the loud speaker. Another device of the old master was to remind his audience that at
some time in the past one or more of his relatives had been connected with local history, usually the settling of the place. It was
difficult to believe that so many Roosevelts and Delanos could
have been in so many different places.

The universe within a universe being drawn across the continent
in slightly shabby Pullman cars was a center for ceaseless gossip
and rumor. We had in the end car one of the most extraordinary
figures of our time who was engaged in exhibiting himself to
millions of people in the midst of that greatest of all American
institutions, a presidential election. With him was his wife, herself
no mean public figure. It was about these two that most of the
gossip centered. We watched them lead their curious public lives
and we speculated endlessly about their private lives. Every scrap
of information, every rumor, every report, became a part of the
legend of these two principals.

They were surrounded by lesser characters who took on importance and coloration from their proximity to the principals. Marvin McIntyre, wraithlike, his voice husky with fatigue, would play poker or bridge until five or six in the morning back in one of the press cars; then, cheerful as a cricket, would greet the local politicians who came on board at the first stop of the day. Judge Rosenman, the ubiquitous Sammy the Rose, was one of the speech writers on the train. Senator Wheeler of Montana, so soon to be an enemy, was part of the entourage for a time; he was afraid that Roosevelt was being too timid. Jimmy, the ebullient, the glad-faced, the smiling, the hand-shaking Jimmy, was on board and so was his wife, the gentle Betsy. This was an easy, comfortable family excursion.

One character stumped us. She was young, blonde, and pretty, and seemed to have no visible connection with the business of the campaign. She had suddenly appeared on the train out of nowhere. For two and a half days feverish curiosity burned over this mysterious figure. She rode in the parades, usually in the same car with Mrs. Roosevelt, draped with an appropriate number of orchids or gardenias or whatever it was the local committee happened to be putting out. No one in the official party seemed to know who she was, or at least they said they didn't. At last a woman reporter was delegated to ask Mrs. Roosevelt herself. The mysterious stranger's name, the report came back, was Mayris Chaney. She was a dancer, a protégée and friend of Mrs. Roosevelt. But why, why on a campaign train? Well, they had promised themselves a holiday together and when Mrs. Roosevelt discovered that she would not be on the West Coast that fall she wired for her friend, Mayris, to tour with the presidential party. It was as simple as that.

The train wound back through the Middle West, through Michigan where in each industrial city thousands of men and women stood along the railroad tracks just to catch a glimpse of the President. But of course, said the wise old heads on the train, he would never carry Michigan. What was it they said about the visitation of politicians? People would come out to look certainly;

they would come out to look at a dead whale on a flatcar. That was what the knowing correspondents said and we tended to agree with them. Look at the crowds that turned out to see Al Smith.

In Detroit, in Cadillac Square, was the same huge, yelling, roaring, almost uncontrollable crowd, or a Detroit version of it; the same struggling police lines, the same wild, frenzied cheering, the same smile from Roosevelt, the same easy, almost casual, wave of his hand. We were weary of crowds, we in the press cars. There had been no opportunity to service the Pullmans. Water flowed from the tap in trickles. The lights were a dim blur. That night a cynical correspondent included in his story a census of the train that began with one President, one President's wife, went on through thirty-two reporters, eleven Pullman porters, and ended up with one jitter-bug—Mayris Chaney. Like the old Tom shows, this road company had everything.

The contrast with Landon was painful. He had apparently never realized that campaigning in the era of the news reel and the radio calls for a technique as deliberate as that of a Hollywood star. You could be homely and homespun but if you didn't know how to put it across you looked merely inept and foolish. Landon was utterly unprepared for the fierce white light that beat on him after his nomination, just as he was unprepared to make the vital decisions that are called for each day in a national race.

Briefly, I was on the Landon train where the atmosphere was sober and uncertain. We went to Portland, Maine, for a fling at the Maine electorate just before Maine's presidential balloting (old saw: "As Maine goes, so goes the Nation"). I haven't the slightest recollection what Landon talked about. I only remember feeling pained at realizing how badly the Republicans managed these things. The rally was held in a baseball park outside of Portland and the speaker's stand had been constructed at what would be approximately center field. This left most of the audience, in the grandstand and the bleachers, removed by a considerable distance from the candidate. And about the time the speaker was to mount the rostrum a thick fog rolled in from the sea. Poor Landon might as well have been speaking from the bottom of the ocean for all the personal relationship he established with his listeners. As he began to speak, hedged in by a battery of microphones, two or three news photographers climbed a two by four not ten feet away and aimed at him. It wobbled uncertainly with their weight and Landon, glancing up from his manuscript, whispered several times audibly, "Get down from there, get down, I tell you!" He had the unhappy look of a man who has just taken his seat in the dental chair for what is certain to be a long and painful ordeal.

His managers were for the most part amateurs. It had a homemade air that might have been well enough except that it did not seem quite genuine. The men around him were frightened of the embrace of big business and moneyed professionalism. On the way back from Portland to Topeka a wire came from a wealthy publisher who announced that he intended to attach his private car to the train at the next stop. This caused consternation among Landon's earnest advisers. A private car, the ultimate symbol of money and privilege! Someone recalled, moreover, that this car was the *Wanderer* which had once belonged to Ned McLean who had had Harding as his guest on the car. Salvos of telegrams were fired off to the publisher and at the announced stop fat little Lacey Haines of Topeka, looking amazingly like Victor Moore, stood out on the railroad track to stop, if necessary by force, any wealthy boarding party from the *Wanderer*.

There were no amateurs in the Roosevelt camp. The President finished his strenuous tour in a warm glow of self-confidence, with the roars of the crowd still echoing from far out across America. It had been as successful as anyone had dared to hope and yet the strange thing was that, removed a little from the tumult and the shouting, it was difficult to realize why it had all happened. What made the enthusiasm of the tour seem all the more extraordinary was the fact that only by stretching the meaning of the phrase could Roosevelt's talks be called political speeches. They were more like the friendly sermons of a bishop come to make his quadrennial diocesan call. Bishop Roosevelt reported on the excellent state of health enjoyed throughout his vast diocese, particu-

larly as compared with the miserable state that had prevailed
before he took high office.

This was the central theme of almost every talk he made. The
issues of the campaign and the policies to be followed in the future
were touched upon only incidentally, if at all. The President
promised crop insurance and crop control of some sort. He told the
motor manufacturers that they must increase the annual wage paid
to their workers through "planning." He said that work relief
was important. But other than this he scarcely mentioned issues.
And almost invariably he referred to his Republican opposition as
one would speak of the forces of darkness, the embodiment of an
almost abstract evil, and yet tolerantly as of an inevitable counter-
poise to the good life for which he, the President, spoke. These
forces of darkness had been beaten by the New Deal Saint George,
and the President assumed in his talks that of course no one would
be so deluded as to invite the dragon back again. Sometimes he
asked the direct question of his audiences—do you want the powers
of reaction in office again? Always a roaring chorus of noes came
back.

For the last day or two Jim Farley joined the caravan. The
meaning of the crowds and the cheers and the rain of torn-up
telephone books had not escaped the big fellow. We sat with him
in a drawing room on the last afternoon and talked it over. He was
in a jovial mood. The big expanse of his bald head glistened and
the tempo of his gum chewing was if anything faster than normal.
Big Jim had worked hard for this. It was all over, he said. Nothing that the President could do or say in the two and a half weeks
that remained could lose the election for him. The only question
now was how large his majority would be, and although Farley
had not yet got down to predicting states, he was certain that it
would be large.

The Roosevelt campaign of that year was essentially Farley's
kind of campaign. There were those within the Roosevelt inner
circle who believed that issues should be discussed; the people
should be educated on the big questions that the country faced.
Henry Wallace was one of those who thought there should be

more discussion of the state of the nation. But the practical politicians scoffed at such suggestions. A campaign, they said, was how you got elected. It had nothing to do with education. Hadn't the Republicans talked about the full dinner pail for forty years or more and got away with it four times out of five? This was Roosevelt prosperity, New Deal prosperity, and the Farleys in the party proposed to ride it through.

That was what Roosevelt did in the autumn of 1936. After the Middle West we went to New England. Same company, same show, same crowd. At Providence they swarmed like ants over the capitol plaza and the approaches to it. Boston Common just at dusk appeared to be packed solid with humanity. Motoring through Cambridge in the early darkness we heard a strange and alien sound. From the sons of Harvard on the curbstone came loud boos for that other son of Harvard in the front car. He was all those things the fathers of young Harvard men called him; a renegade, a traitor to his class.

We had been motoring since eight o'clock in the morning in a long furious procession that frequently got out of control of state police; fighting the crowds through mill towns all of the way. Writing for an afternoon newspaper on such excursions is something of a trick. You use your portable typewriter in the car between stops or you scribble furiously on a pad hoping that a telegraph operator at the next stop will be able to read your illegible copy. Twelve hours of that kind of campaigning and most of the party was limp. Yet the principal appeared as blithe and confident that evening before a huge crowd in Worcester as though it had been the first speech of the day instead of the twenty-first. We conceded that he could take it.

Curiosities were always turning up. In the course of that motor tour of New England a bland, supremely self-centered, young Englishman joined the party as a reporter, of sorts, to have a look at the quaint American system of electioneering. His name was Randolph Churchill and he was the son of a Tory politician named Winston Churchill. Young Randolph had inherited a generous share of his father's poise and self-assurance which American newspapermen found rather hard to take. On the train one night, the motoring over for the day, Heywood Broun put Churchill through a mild hazing, but so bland was this young aristocrat's exterior that it had no effect whatsoever. He was a little irritating and the next day the boys saw to it that as the hours wore on he was relegated to cars successively further back in the procession, until by midafternoon he might just as well not have been with the party at all. I have often wondered how much of the kidding to which Broun and others subjected this bumptious young man found its way into the London paper he was writing for. Obviously he had not yet undergone the trial by fire that is said to have made his father the malleable man of world affairs that he is today.

This was one kind of campaigning. That same fall I was to see another kind. On orders from Bovard I sampled Norman Thomas's technique. If the Roosevelt campaign was almost straight showmanship of a very high order, the Thomas tour was a political Chautauqua. Norman and his courageous wife traveled without benefit of retinue, he in an upper berth, she in the lower. They traveled that way for weeks on end, Norman speaking from twelve to fourteen times a day, with a kind of endurance that only politicians must be endowed with. At each stop they would be met by earnest disciples who would take them in hand for the day's events. Often Thomas talked at schools and public forums, taking advantage of an audience wherever he could find one.

Almost invariably he gave them a rapid-fire harangue. The New Deal, built on the corrupt city machines, was no more suited to save the country than the reactionary G.O.P. They were both corrupt and dead, and only Socialism could save democracy, Thomas told his listeners, his voice growing hoarse, his talk sounding more like a scratchy phonograph record as he repeated it for the sixth or seventh time. His audiences were of course small. Six or seven hundred students or teachers, crowded into the auditorium of Antioch College at Yellow Springs, Ohio, was the high mark of a day of speechmaking in Ohio. Through the party organization and through the funds the party could command, through the prestige of his high office and the magnetic appeal of his personality, Roosevelt reached millions directly and on the air while the Socialist, Norman Thomas, spoke to thousands.

In the closing days the President carried his campaign to Pennsylvania. Pennsylvania was considered a doubtful state. In Pennsylvania lived the Republican party's great angel, Joseph Pew of the Sun Oil Company, who was out to elect Landon at whatever cost. But the Democrats too had an angel in Pennsylvania. On the platform with Roosevelt at Harrisburg sat John L. Lewis. I seem to recall that he had a slightly possessive air as though this had been a *fête de Versailles* that he had ordered and paid for, as indeed he had. I am frank to add, however, that this may have been merely an interpretation read into that grim and mysterious physiognomy in the light of the later knowledge that its owner had given a half-million dollars out of the United Mine Workers' Treasury to the Democratic war chest. For that matter John L. Lewis always looks possessive, and with good reason, for he has made the largest trade-union in the United States his personal property. On the platform on that blowy day, with his miner cohorts in the crowd before him, John L. may well have dreamed dreams of imperial grandeur. This was Franklin Roosevelt's inning. John L. Lewis's would come next.

One of the extraordinary things about a political campaign is the way in which the partisans are able to hypnotize themselves. Anyone with the slightest knowledge of what the American people were saying and thinking could have known that Landon hadn't a Chinaman's chance. Yet he himself was persuaded of his victory and so were many of the people around him. Weren't the newspapers for him? And didn't the *Literary Digest* poll show that he would be elected? To such frail reeds the candidate clung, resenting almost angrily any suggestion of doubt as though it had been an effort to persuade himself of victory, an effort that he did not want to have to repeat. In that last week he was a tired, harassed, unhappy man who had to cling to confidence to save his own sanity.

The Republicans in the closing week made stupid mistakes that

I believe Landon would not have made if the ultimate decisions had not long since passed out of his reach. For one thing there were the pay roll notices threatening workers with the loss of their jobs if Roosevelt should win. Similarly the Social Security pay roll deductions were made to seem part of an evil conspiracy to curtail the average man's income. Anyone with ordinary political judgment should have known that that kind of thing would produce an effect exactly opposite from the one intended.

It gave Roosevelt a chance to end his campaign in a blaze of emotion. Landon had had a huge rally earlier in Madison Square Garden. Of necessity Roosevelt's meeting had to be half again as big and twice as loud—and it was. They hate me, said Franklin Roosevelt of the rich and the mighty, and I welcome their hatred. The packed Garden exploded in a steamy torrent of sound. Only in this last speech did the President open up the New Deal stops—housing, work relief, social security—promising that these gains would be held and new goals set.

On the night of the great victory the clan Roosevelt was gathered at Hyde Park. Forty-six states in the Roosevelt column, that was something that the simplest mind could understand. Even before midnight the wise money boys were looking for a place in the Roosevelt van, repenting their sins of omission and commission. William Randolph Hearst telephoned from California to tell the ebullient Jimmy how astonished and happy he was that the man he had sought to defeat through every kind of editorial trick and incessant salvoes of type a foot high was actually the choice of the American people and by so overwhelming a majority.

There were many calls into Hyde Park that night from the repentant, eager to recant at the first opportunity. In any event most of the big corporations had had vice-presidents who were Democrats and who had made contributions to the Roosevelt campaign. They didn't give as much as the board chairmen and the directors had given to Landon, but nevertheless it amounted to having one foot in heaven.

In this moment of triumph all the oddly assorted elements within the Democratic party sang hosannahs. The President in his

campaign had covered them all in; all the faithful from tough, old
Cotton Ed Smith of South Carolina to earnest, uplooking, young
Jerry Voorhis from California. No one had been excluded. And
nothing had been altered by the great tide of votes rolled up for
the personality and the voice and the hope they implied. Nothing
had been changed, unless, perhaps, it was in the mind of the man
who was the center of the happy family party in the library of
Hyde Park House.

To many of his own class he was the figure of evil personified;
a personal devil symbolizing the forces that were stirring deeply
in American life. To millions of others he was the image of a better
life, the sign of a new day. Apart from the histrionic efforts of the
bosses, he had a personal following as large as any living American
had ever had, hero-worshipers far outnumbering those of his distant cousin, Theodore Roosevelt. What were his secret thoughts
on that night when it was known that the American people had
given him the greatest presidential majority in history? How far
ahead did he project the shadow of his destiny? We are fighting
to preserve the kind of life that we have known in the past, and if
we preserve it, as we mean to, then historians in the future are
going to have a great deal to say about this man Roosevelt. They
are going to try to appraise his thoughts on that history-making
night.

The President's more intelligent detractors, and naturally this
would not include those who regard him as personally responsible
for the depression, Hitler, the war, and the heavy snow that fell
in Washington in the early spring of 1942, insist that he is wholly
an opportunist. They say that he sails before whatever wind there
is, tacking and tacking and perhaps reaching something approaching his objective if the wind does not die. These, of course, are the
purists who for the most part stand outside the sweaty domain of
politics. They ignore the patent fact that in our political system a
straight line is never, or hardly ever, the shortest distance between
two points. Roosevelt, the strategist, the master maneuverer, has
known this very well, perhaps too well.

As for the inner being, the man behind the grin, millions of words are still to be written on that score. One thing is certain: it is not at all simple. The blind men in the fable quarreled over the shape of the elephant in much the same way that Franklin Roosevelt's friends and enemies quarrel over the shape of his character. It is false, it is true, it is deep, it is shallow, it is proud, it is humble. And, perhaps, like the blind men in the fable, they are all right.

This is a complex human being. One thing that is too often ignored is the sense of *noblesse oblige* that came out of his background, out of Hyde Park House. His detractors sneer and even some of his friends deprecate it; they say it gave him a basket-for-the-poor-family-down-the-lane approach to social problems. On the other hand, persons close to him believe that out of this has come the President's mature acceptance of obligation; yes, the endurance that has taken him through all his trials.

For whatever it is worth, it came from the woman who was probably the central figure in his life. The President's mother, Mrs. Sarah Delano Roosevelt, lived to see her son inaugurated not twice but three times. Her life covered the span of the century that ended on December 7, 1941. She went as a child to China in one of her father's clipper ships, and in Hong Kong she was respectfully presented with gifts by the rich old tea tycoons with whom her father dealt. She was a woman of strong character, unswerving will. She married a man considerably older than herself and at his death she devoted herself thenceforward to her son.

I envy the playwrights of fifty or seventy-five years from now. They will inevitably draw on this family for the raw material of drama to compare with the Lincoln story. Much of it is already at hand. Take, for example, Eleanor Roosevelt's autobiography. That is an extraordinary human document. If it does not tell all, it tells nearly all with a frankness and a sincerity such as few personal narratives ever attain. It is the story of the ugly duckling who at last came into the life of a swan and yet remembered what it was like to be an ugly duckling. For the ugly ducklings of this world Eleanor Roosevelt will fight with a fury that grows out of the secret roots of her own experience.

I think the future playwright might well use that scene in the library at Hyde Park on the night of November 4th, 1936. It is after midnight. One by one the friends of the family have departed until only those few intimates who are almost part of the family are left. It has been a strenuous day, beginning with the flare of flashlights at the polling booth in the little town in the morning and ending in the drama of an hour ago in a blaze of light, the blare of bands, the focus of the world on the moment of celebration. Now they are alone, the family, warmly united in this moment in spite of all the conflicts and jealousies that flow through every large family. A sense of the drama, of the history-making triumph, is upon them, but more important is the sense of family, full-blooded, proud, united before the world.

The elder Mrs. Roosevelt is the first to move to go. She says her good nights reluctantly, receiving from each member of each generation in turn an affectionate greeting. Then for a moment she pauses in the doorway.

"Oh Franklin, there's one thing I meant to ask you."

The President looks at her fondly, waiting.

"Now that this is all over I want you to be sure to find something for that nice Colonel X to do. I do so like to see him when I go down to Washington."

This brings a perfect uproar from them all. "Politics, Granny," they cry. "Granny's playing politics." The President joins in the laughter. The old lady smiles a little too but her dignity is unruffled. She has her sense of *noblesse* which has nothing to do with the vulgarities of politics; politics of which she does not entirely approve. Presumptuous though I know it is in the light of our limited perspective, I suggest this as the curtain for that scene for the future playwright.

The mood was to change with astonishing abruptness. Shortly after Congress convened the President read his message on the state of the union which contained little that was provocative. Then thirty days later he sent up the bill to remake the Supreme Court. It was the signal that released all the smoldering animosity that has been obscured by the tide of victory. Within the space of a few hours the lines were drawn for a battle that served in large part to nullify the thundering majority of two months before.

It has seemed to me looking back at that time that if Roosevelt had made the Court an issue in his campaign, the result might have been quite different. Certainly the Court was a legitimate campaign issue. The conservative majority had, in the definition of the minority, thwarted the will of the people as expressed by Congress. But not once had the President referred to this obstacle. True, he might have lost more than Maine and Vermont, but it is inconceivable that he could have lost the election no matter what he said about the Court. As Jim Farley put it, nothing that he could have said in that last fortnight could have lost him the election. Now, in a bill that was obviously specious in its approach, he proposed to reshape to his own liking the highest tribunal in the land. The chief opposition came from members of his own party who were uncommitted by any campaign pledges.

I suppose the issue of the Court will be argued until kingdom come. They tend, these arguments, toward the metaphysical— how many Supreme Court justices can dance on a needle point. It has so many faces, this argument. I believed at the time that if the administration had got behind the bill to grant retiring justices a pension equivalent to their full pay, the battle might have been avoided. But no one can say this with any certainty, I suppose, unless two or three old men choose to tell in their memoirs what was actually in their minds.

It was Senator Wheeler's first venture in national leadership and he made the most of it. He was resourceful, wily, incessantly working, planning, and executing the moves that one after the other undermined the position of the administration. I happened to be in Senator Wheeler's office just after he had appeared before the Senate Judiciary Committee to read the letter from Chief Justice Hughes disapproving the principal features of the Court scheme. Mrs. Wheeler came in, an exultant glow on her face. "You've done it," she said, "you've done it, I knew you would." Far from satisfying the Wheeler ambition, the victory merely fed it.

Through the summer heat the bitter fight wore on. Poor old Joe Robinson collapsed and died alone in his apartment in the Methodist Building across from the Capitol. There was a growing sense of the futility of the struggle. Long-forgotten was the election, that parade of forty-six states. The opposition did a gleeful war dance on the floor of the Senate every day.

Finally came a kind of capitulation. Then the appointment of Senator Hugo Black to the vacancy that had existed for nearly five months touched off the uproar again. Black was subjected to such an ordeal as few men have ever gone through. All the virulence toward the President that had been half concealed, half revealed, in the Court fight was now directed at this convenient victim. Much of it was irrelevant. It may have given the President a certain satisfaction to name Black to the Court, but if it was meant as reprisal it was a costly one. There are few men of Black's capacities in the Senate, and his departure for the white marble mausoleum across from the Capitol meant a loss that the administration has never made up for.

The lines of opposition that were drawn during that long and futile summer were to persist in the critical years to come. True, if it had not been that issue, it would have been another one. Yet it was an issue made to order for the opposition. And it was an issue that in the end gave the opposition the strong, hot taste of victory. All through that summer of 1937 a narrow domestic issue preoccupied the Congress and the country. It might have been 1900 or 1910. A curious haze of unreality seemed to have settled over the Washington scene. The cloud on the European horizon was scarcely discernible.

Section II
TRANSITION

Chapter VIII

Abroad at Home

THE summer and early fall of 1937 I spent in Europe. Returning on one of the big French liners I had somewhat the sense of fleeing from imminent doom, as did almost all returning travelers from that point on. It was the period when French line boats were going up like Roman candles and ours was a typical crossing. There were rumors of fire and sudden death. Apparently two or three staterooms were destroyed, the hard work of the ship's patrol preventing the flames from spreading further. At least in the cocktail lounge that was what we believed.

Back in Washington, two isolationist senators were at pains to bring me up to date on what had happened in my absence. The newest sensation was the President's speech in Chicago in which he had called for a quarantine of the aggressor nations. That had been a nine days' wonder, a broadside of big headlines, and then everyone had settled down to explain the speech away.

My isolationist senators had the easiest explanation. It was the result of a British plot. The Italians in the Mediterranean were conducting an undeclared submarine warfare against British shipping in order to deter the British from sending any aid to the beleaguered Spanish Loyalists. So from London an urgent appeal had come from the Chamberlain government: tell the President that unless he makes a strong statement we shall be forced to take a stand and war may follow. The British Ambassador was not in Washington at the time and the story even named a mysterious emissary who had been delegated to carry the urgent word to the White House.

By such convenient fables were we to delude ourselves into a belief that only through the machinations of foreign devils could pure, virtuous, isolated America become involved in the ruin of

Europe. We were more than ready to accept this legend; in fact
we helped to fabricate it. It coincided so beautifully with our desire
to live in uninterrupted peace and quietude. Looking back, it is
difficult to realize how strong a hold this illusion had on men's
minds. A stubborn legend, it still persists against the weight of
overwhelming reality in a war for our very existence.

I had been in Spain, in Valencia and Madrid, having a brief but
intensive look at the civil war, and my first job was to complete
the series of articles I had begun during the crossing on the *Ile de
France*. Spain, even the small bit that I saw, had been incredibly
strong and sharp, a struggle between life and death that could
nowhere be disguised by rhetoric. In the pleasant October haze
that lay over Washington, the shells falling in the streets of
Madrid and the trenches in University City which you could visit
by streetcar seemed very far off, as though they were part of something that was happening on another planet.

I wrote about Spain, I talked about Spain, I joined organizations
to help Spain. I was, I suppose, one of those innocents on whom
the knowing and the cynical have heaped scorn and ridicule. But
I offer no apologies. The people I saw in Spain, the people I
wanted to help, were innocents too; they were fighting desperately
to save their own country from a foreign invader.

It was not alone in Washington that the reality of Spain was lost
or obscured. I had seen it in London and Paris. In fact, once you
crossed the border, Spain, for the still comfortable democracies,
simply ceased to exist. It was only an item on an agenda at Geneva.
It was a dangerous idea to be muffled and muted in the swathings
of diplomacy, the protocol, the red tape, the sealing wax, the top
hats, the intimate little cocktail parties, all the tiresome trappings
of a moribund craft surviving out of the eighteenth century.

I was to watch with pain and loathing the Washington phase of
that diplomatic quadrille. The career diplomat who had been the
ambassador of Spain in Washington before July of 1936, when
the revolution broke out, was Juan de Cardenas who was unadulterated *ancien régime*, with a professional weariness, a professional
disdain for anything that breathed and moved and uttered sounds

of life. He quickly made his obeisance of loyalty to General Franco, in response to a peremptory telegram from El Caudillo, and went to live at the Ritz-Carlton Hotel in New York where he was Franco's unofficial ambassador. In his place the Loyalist government, which was the only government recognized by the United States, sent as ambassador Don Fernando de los Rios, a distinguished professor in the University of Madrid, a sober Republican with views about as radical as those of the late Senator Borah.

The new ambassador endured for nearly three years a species of torment which, fortunately, it is given to few men to endure. De los Rios was the legal and legitimate representative of his government in Washington. He and his family occupied the embassy on Sixteenth Street and he had the title of ambassador. Primarily a scholar, with a brilliant record in the history of Hispanic-America, De los Rios had a strong sense of his dignity and his position. Yet there were many Americans who took it on themselves to instruct him in his duty. Most of these volunteers were eager liberals who were genuinely concerned with saving democratic Spain. Others were amateur Communists exercising a lamentable passion for what they considered to be high intrigue.

And there were others whose motives were more obscure. One or two, I strongly suspected although I could never prove, were interested in their own personal gain. A fortune in gold had been brought to the United States by Spanish representatives, and one or two of the ambassador's most persistent visitors intended, if they could, to have their share of it. In this select group also were official delegates of "the party." No amateurs these, they dealt in terms of realpolitik with no sentiment allowed to interfere. These men of power were said to have their authority directly from "the party" in Spain and in Moscow, and they tended to regard poor De los Rios merely as a convenient front. Looking back I do not recall that any of these shadowy figures were ever investigated by Mr. Dies, who contented himself with running down the innocents and the amateurs whose names appeared on the lists of sponsors of the innumerable "Save Spain" organizations which had sprung up.

It was painful to watch De los Rios struggle with his dignity and his position against these interlopers. Besieged, set upon in a new environment, a new world, he bristled at each new affront, his luxuriant black beard seeming fairly to quiver with indignation. Perhaps because he realized that he had stepped outside the sphere of his own knowledge and into a strange new profession, De los Rios tried hard to live up to the canons of diplomacy even in the face of the very undiplomatic Americans whom he entertained at the Embassy.

The forms were always correctly observed at luncheon and at dinner; the requisite number of courses, the food excellent, with the correct wines. While the host was punctilious in his observance of the proprieties the same could scarcely be said for many of his guests. I remember a largish luncheon, some twenty odd, for a guest of honor who never appeared. In the midst of lunch the ambassador, who had been devoting himself to conversation with his immediate table mates, was interrupted by one of the amateur Communists. This man "suggested" in a rather firm voice that the ambassador send for some propaganda documents lately arrived from Spain so that they could be passed around while the company was still at table. The ambassador said quietly that that could wait until later. The amateur Communist repeated his "suggestion" in a louder voice. The ambassador tried hard to ignore the stentorian hint. When it was repeated even more peremptorily, he said in a voice which with difficulty he kept calm, "We will look at the pamphlets after lunch." We looked at the pamphlets after lunch.

These were the small things. In the privacy of the ambassador's study, larger and more painful controversies were fought out. They harried and hounded him. The trickle of supplies that got through to Spain in spite of the arms embargo was too small and too sluggish. The professor turned ambassador was too conscious of his own responsibilities, his own position. He would not be swept along by these rude, radical Americans who seemed so sure of themselves.

The shadow of this feud lay heavy over the Embassy. You

could almost watch the ambassador put on his public face when public necessity demanded it. At those press conferences, with cocktails, for example. We would wait in a sort of desolate patio where there were tired orange trees in pots and a tiled fountain that dripped relentlessly. The ambassador would come in bowing and smiling to the right and to the left, greeting those whom he knew with a cordial word. He would seat himself firmly, seriously, in the center of the room and then he would begin to talk. He talked well and fluently, and yet almost always the optimism he tried to radiate came out a little cracked.

It must have been like that on the visits of state which he made to Secretary Hull and Under Secretary Welles. But even if he had had the gift of persuasion of Cato and the élan of Zorina, it would apparently have made no real difference. And why? There were as many answers to that question as there were views on the Spanish issue. The arms embargo had been rushed through Congress at breakneck speed shortly after the outbreak of the rebellion. In the two and a half years that followed, it was constantly on the point of being lifted, according to the most authoritative inside reports, and yet when the terrible debacle came at the end, the embargo was still clamped tightly on.

The inside reports emanated from the liberals who called on the President to urge him to "do something." They came away encouraged, emboldened to believe that there would be action. It was they who spread the word, strictly off the record, of course, that the President intended to take steps to lift the embargo. So the report would appear in this column and that inspired story, and all through the "Save Spain" organizations would run a current of hope. It is obvious now that those hopeful rumors from the White House were a disservice.

When no action came and hope gave way to gloom, the word was that the Catholic Church was too powerful; the President did not dare to go counter to their wishes. True, a powerful group within the Church made incessant propaganda against Spain and the American friends of Spain, using the Communist tag for all that it was worth. This was the group that sponsored the notorious

Jane Anderson who was broadcasting for the Nazis from Berlin long after America was at war. On the other hand, one of the great princes of the Church, the late Cardinal Mundelein, a man of broad understanding and deep humanity, had quite another view on Spain. The diocesan papers under his jurisdiction were not afraid to discuss the Spanish rebellion in terms of the underlying realities.

If "the Church" were not explanation enough, there was the State Department. Here, it was said, were the narrow, pettifogging careerists who had access to the President and who communicated to him, in slightly different terms, their own precious predilection for the safe, the secure, and the respectable. An honest census would probably have shown that most of the permanent officers of the State Department as well as most career diplomats were on' the side of Franco, or at least uninterested in Loyalist survival. But here again was another faction, including men in high position, who looked behind the façade of noisy propaganda and emotionalism to the real meaning of the Spanish war, which was, of course, the beginning of Hitler's conquest of Europe.

The attitude of the State Department and of our career diplomats abroad may well have been determined by the British Foreign Office. The Foreign Office line was pro-Franco, inevitably. It was a hallmark of the craft of the old diplomacy. The realities in terms of the British position were obscured by what happened to your dear friends; to the dear Marqués of Y, to the charming old Duke of X, to dear Lady So-and-So's Spanish relatives. It was a repetition of the British attitude toward Russia, and it served the German purpose perfectly as the Germans themselves must have very well known.

Perhaps it is too early to say why the Germans were allowed to establish a Fascist state in that first bastion of western Europe. That must wait, perhaps, for the memoirs; those memoirs which are the luxury of the wrong-guessers who can tell why it happened and how it might have been worse. If you have been too wrong, of course, you are denied the privilege of publishing your memoirs. Then you are tortured in a Gestapo prison or tried at Riom.

The craft of diplomacy, that last refuge of a polite and ordered past, had closed its mind on Spain. Likewise it closed its doors on the representatives of Spain. For all that he was so careful to observe the canons of diplomacy, De los Rios was carefully ignored in Washington by all who wanted to be correct and proper. He was invited to official and public gatherings, but his name rarely if ever appeared on the guest lists of intimate and important parties.

The citadel of the closed world of diplomacy in Washington was the British Embassy. In the dreamy unreal period from 1937 through 1939 the massive red-brick monument on Massachusetts Avenue was a kind of fortification where the past had barricaded itself against the assault of change. The ambassador was Sir Ronald Lindsay, a mountain of a man who was as shy as a woods creature, as reserved and preoccupied as an Oxford don. His wife was an American woman who superimposed her code of snobbism on the ambassador's caution and conservatism. Their own relationship not being of the happiest, Lady Lindsay's social secretary, Miss Irenee Boyle, was intermediary between them and for them to the world. The result was a singularly cloistered existence, those admitted to the inner sanctum having for the most part only the most frivolous knowledge of American life and no knowledge whatsoever of the deeper currents of American politics.

There were pleasant dinners with bridge afterward in the cold, porphyry-columned salon that the architect, Sir Edward Lutyens, had inflicted on generations of British ambassadors. There were frequent expeditions to the movies. Rarely, there were safaris to New York for a Long Island week end or possibly for a dinner of the English Speaking Union. This was the gentle orbit in which Sir Ronald and his lady moved.

Sir Ronald had many severe critics both in London and in Washington. It was wholly unjust, however, to revile him. He was the perfect end product of a method which had, as events were to prove, outlived its usefulness. Sir Ronald was in the Curzon tradition, straight out of Harold Nicholson. Self-contained, self-assured, he went through the ritual of his career with a maximum of correctness. You received from the Foreign Office a telegram instructing you to take up a matter of importance with the Secretary of State. You made an appointment with the Secretary of State, you called on him, and you solemnly discussed with him the matter of importance to your government. You went back to your embassy and you wrote in the orotund language of your profession a dispatch to your Foreign Office. In the diplomatic pouch you duly received the handsome red moroccan dispatch boxes with their gold embossings and you duly opened them and duly read the dispatches they contained.

Those few persons who gained access to Sir Ronald discovered him to be, beneath his exterior shyness, a person of wit and charm, lacking perhaps any very strong element of curiosity in his nature. His life was completely circumscribed by his career, and the terms of his career had been laid down a very long time before and now their orthodoxy could not be questioned.

In London in the summer I had lunched with a friend who had been in the Embassy at Washington, and he had brought with him the Foreign Office official in charge of the North American desk. It had been startling to discover the gaps in this officer's knowledge of current American affairs. He had never heard, for example, of Professor Felix Frankfurter and the part that Frankfurter was, or was not, taking in the Supreme Court fight. For that matter, he had scarcely heard of the controversy over the Court and seemed surprised to learn that it might have important repercussions on American political life. Understandably, it had made no impact on the world in which Sir Ronald Lindsay lived.

The confines of that world were rudely shattered by an event that occurred in the spring of 1939. King George and Queen Elizabeth were to pay a long-heralded visit to the capital. No delicate seismograph was required to record the tremors that that announcement sent through political and social Washington. So much has happened in the intervening time, so many earth-shaking events, that it is difficult to realize the furor the royal visit caused.

If Sir Ronald and Lady Lindsay believed they could make it another and brighter occasion for their set, they were soon disillusioned. Not every year did Washington have a British king and queen.

Very early the pressure began. Senator's wives seemed to feel that they should be invited to the garden party at the Embassy. It was fantastic. Then, because it was gently intimated to them that they were not to be present on the history-making occasion, the women of the press began a vendetta with Lady Lindsay; they snarled and snapped and were generally rude and unkind. From other sources came other pressures. The walls of the great red fort began to crack under the cruel assault. Sir Ronald held a press conference and was photographed surrounded by thirty or forty newspaper men. The walls of Jericho had fallen down. There was nothing left to do but invite the town and that was very nearly what happened.

The rancor that survived the storming of the Bastille was forgotten in the great success of the royal visit. The queen was beautiful and gracious and queenly, with a special humanity of her own that could not be concealed by the royal trappings. And the king was living up to a difficult situation that he had not foreseen and had not wanted. All, or nearly all, was forgotten and forgiven in the warm afterglow of the royal departure.

There were those of course who cherished a grudge against the king and queen for having come at all, counting it as part of the sinister plot to link isolated America to corrupt and decadent Europe. I remember that after the garden party one of those tireless Washington hostesses had assembled for dinner some of the guests who had come down from New York for the occasion; some of "the names" on Lady Lindsay's own special list. Into this gathering the hostess had, by way of providing a shocker for the evening, thrown John L. Lewis. On both sides of the social abyss there was a certain constraint which was not relieved when one of the ladies from New York, thinking to make a little light conversation, asked Mr. Lewis how he had enjoyed the garden party. Leveling his leonine gaze on her he said in a voice cold with reproach, "I do not know. Mrs. Lewis and I were not present at the occasion."

The Embassy had hardly been restored to its regular routine when the blow of the war fell and Sir Ronald was recalled to London to be replaced by the astute and very unshy Lord Lothian.

In one of those long timeless periods, when things as they are seem destined to last forever, the ritual of career diplomacy might have sufficed. For those who were conditioned to it early, it provided a pleasant enough existence. Having little to do with modern life, it was nevertheless an innocuous preoccupation, adding a decorative note to the gray monotone of most present-day capitals. The number of people who chose to live by the Almanach de Gotha and the Diplomatic List was, after all, small.

It was rather like the game children call "dressing up," digging out of the trunks in the attic the gayer and more brilliant costumes of the past. The actual cost was comparatively slight and the game might have gone on forever if one side had not suddenly decided to ignore all the old and established rules.

Germany's career diplomats did not differ essentially from their British or French counterparts. In accord with the much-vaunted German efficiency, they may have been a little better trained; but seen together in a room you would hardly have distinguished them one from the other. They were part of an international caste, consorting exclusively with each other whenever possible in the capitals to which they were assigned; presented at their worst by Marcel Proust and at their best by Harold Nicholson.

The Nazis did not suddenly destroy the system of career diplomacy that stemmed from the Wilhelmstrasse. Quite the contrary. It was left as a false façade to deceive the world, while behind that façade the Germans in virtually every country in the world plotted for conquest. They did attempt of course to bring the careerists under their influence, and here and there honest men resigned and others committed suicide. But in each capital they allowed the Embassy and its staff to continue to function very much as before, while Gestapo men and undercover agents carried out the really important assignments. The latter were not troubled by the need to go through "diplomatic channels." They created channels of their own, reaching down to sources of knowledge undreamed of by the careerists; conspiring with all the elements in the population that would do their bidding.

The deception worked almost too well. In the moldy old German Embassy in Washington the accredited ambassador was first Doctor Hans Luther, who enjoyed an honorable reputation in America, and then later Hans Dieckhoff, a career diplomat of respectable status. They were the front for the ex-gangster who was the real power. This was arrogantly handsome Herbert Scholz who had at one time been a protégé of the scandalous Roehm; Roehm who was cut down in the bloody Nazi purge of 1934. Scholz could play the career diplomat too. He and his slender blonde wife managed to make themselves something of a vogue in social Washington. They were so charming, it was said by authorities in that line. For reasons, having to do, one may be sure, with the needs of whatever conspiracy he was furthering, Scholz was assigned as consul general at Boston. There too those charming Scholzes captivated certain of Boston's oldest families. On the opposite coast, in San Francisco, Hitler's personal friend, Captain Fritz Weidemann, was using the same technique.

This was the Fifth Column, the Trojan Horse. We in America were considered worthy of hardly more than a sample. London got Von Ribbentrop, the master dissembler, who did his work consummately well. Within the hollow framework of the old diplomacy he sought to undermine Britain's unity, beginning at the top.

If with the exposure of this treachery and concealment the empty structure of diplomacy had also come tumbling down, this would be history, and history written from far too short a perspective. But the slavery of habit is one of the strongest things in the world. Whole rooms and galleries were undermined but the structure survived the shock.

What was true of the British Foreign Office was true in only a lesser degree of our own State Department. At the top for the past nine years has been that grave saint from Tennessee, Cordell Hull. Mr. Hull has not, however, been primarily concerned with the workings of the career service. He has dealt in moral imperatives, with the broader issues of right and wrong that go inevitably to making up policy. In fact, almost his entire concentration has been in this field; toward furthering the Good Neighbor policy and in meeting the attacks of the Axis enemy.

Below this lofty level the career service in the field and the department in Washington continued to function more or less as usual by the inertia of habit. The inherited system was full of crotchets and quirks and for the most part inflexible. Many officers succumb to the system, or it would perhaps be more accurate to say that it serves as a convenient refuge for their own weariness and narrowness of spirit. Others, brilliant men keenly aware of the swift course of world events, struggle within its confines, spending not a little of their time and energy circumventing its rigid barriers. The cry of cookie-pusher is beside the point. Naturally the careerists wear the outward marks of their profession. But underneath, the average of alert minds is rather high.

Once caught within the system, escape is difficult or impossible, although now and then there are rebels. The method of admission, which by indirection filters out most candidates who lack certain class and family specifications, makes for a minimum of rebellion. Women, for example, are theoretically admitted to the foreign service and there are two or three who now hold career positions. By an interesting coincidence, however, women who apply for admission are invariably flunked out on their oral examinations, no matter how brilliantly they have done on the writtens. Wealth, or a wealthy wife, is important. Nevertheless occasionally a sinner falls from grace.

To pass the examinations the candidate must have a superlative background in history and foreign affairs, acquired preferably from one of the three or four eastern universities from which most of the foreign service roster is drawn. In addition to the ordinary education he must have advanced specialization. If he is really up to the mark, and not merely pushed through by virtue of cramming and family background, then he is as finely drawn as a race horse, ready to do an important job. But what happens to him? Ordinarily in the past he has been sent first to a post where there was a heavy burden of visa work; one of the consulates on the Canadian border. There for a year or two he was put to handling visa and immigration records; a sort of endless game of solitaire that any efficient clerk could do. Moreover, his superior intimated that, what with the crowding in the lower grades and the persistent penury of Congress with the Department, he might expect that type of work for quite a number of years to come.

Faced with this deadening prospect, the young man could lapse into the rhythm of five-course lunches, prolonged cocktails, and endless dinners. Or he could rebel and probably ultimately leave or be forced out of the service. I remember one such young rebel who came back from his novitiate to write endless memoranda of protest. As he had the requisite backing of family and money, nothing much was done about him until he finally resigned. His memoranda may still be in the files of the gray wedding cake of a building across from the White House.

They were intelligent memoranda. He pointed out that most men in the foreign service were completely out of touch with their own country. They were given leave, during which they could come back to America if they chose, for a month or two. Many spent these holidays in Europe. Those who returned came customarily to Washington or New York. They were almost totally unaware of what was happening out in the country which they undertook to represent abroad. Likewise the information they sent to Washington was accessible to only a handful of men in the State Department; their dispatches were marked confidential, carefully reserved for a few eyes. Officers long in the field acquire a broad and important background of the region in which they have lived but this background is put to too little use.

The young rebel had an idea that might change all that. Why not, he wrote, bring foreign service officers back to America at stated intervals for a stay of at least six months? Have them go back to the place of their origin; to the Middle West, to Ohio, to California, and there, first, get to know America, and, second, pass on the knowledge they had acquired abroad. Let them speak at Rotary clubs, Kiwanis clubs, high schools, women's clubs. Let them forget for a time the tight little sphere of diplomacy. It seemed to me to be an excellent idea, as did other ideas which this brash young man ventured to put down on paper. As I say, those memoranda may still be in the Department's vast files.

Between the men of the career service and the interlopers appointed to ambassadorial and ministerial posts for political reasons there has been an ancient feud. Career men may become ambassadors, and in fact in South America most chiefs of mission have come up through the service. To be an ambassador in Buenos Aires is, however, a very expensive business, as it was in London and Paris and Berlin before the war. The salary is $17,500 a year with a small entertainment allowance, as compared with the $90,000 which the British give their ambassador in Washington to do his job. Obviously only a man with an independent income could maintain the traditional standards.

The political angels named to the costly ambassadorial posts were the object of a great deal of kidding. But from what I had seen of our representation abroad I concluded it was a healthy thing to bring in from the outside men free of the delimiting prejudices of the careerist. True, they might have other prejudices, but at least they were more likely to bring to the foreign scene a fresh American point of view. Not, again, that any sweeping generalization was possible.

In Oslo I had watched our minister to Norway, Mrs. J. Borden Harriman, adjust herself to her new position. She was as American as corn on the cob, full of gusto and vigor, wanting to know everything about the new country in which she found herself. She would take a dispatch prepared by one of her aides in careful diplomatic language and read it with mounting impatience. "Now just listen to this! Now why do things have to be written this way? Why do you have to throw in all those words to say such a little bit?" With her grand sense of humor, she was able to laugh at the more absurd diplomatic niceties. And in ordering her life in the handsome legation on Nobelsgaade, she did not permit the narrow conventions to stand in the way of seeing whom she wanted to see and going where she wanted to go. She skiied in the winter and visited the popular bathing beaches in the summer. Tall and straight as a soldier, her presence became a familiar and a welcome one in that northern capital. When the barbarians came, Mrs.

Harriman left with the court and the diplomatic corps, pursued by German dive-bombers for nerve-racking days and nights.

At the other end of Europe our ambassador to Spain was another political appointee, Claude Bowers; a restless little man full of warm democratic enthusiasms. The outbreak of the rebellion in the summer of 1936 had found most of the *corps diplomatique* at the seaside resort of Santander. From there, as the fighting became intense, cutting off the capital, the diplomats fled to the near-by French resort of St. Jean de Luz. At St. Jean they established a sort of rump court from which, comfortably if remotely, they followed for three years the course of the civil war. The place was a nest of Franco agents, since they moved freely back and forth across the border into the part of Spain that the Franco forces controlled. Although the diplomats were accredited to distant Madrid and the Loyalist government, it was Franco's court.

In this stuffy atmosphere that smelled so strongly of the embalmed past, Bowers had constituted himself a rebellion of one. Other men finding themselves in disagreement with their colleagues might have kept silent but that was not the stuff Bowers was made of. He spoke his mind freely and frankly when the occasion seemed to call for it. This Connecticut Yankee at King Franco's court had a lean and Jacobin look, and many of the diplomatic corps secretly suspected him of helping "the Reds" by manufacturing bombs in the handsome villa he had taken for the duration.

With two or three of the careerists sent to serve the American ambassador at St. Jean he carried on a running warfare. They were Francoists, he discovered, or what amounted to Francoists. At his express request two secretaries were recalled. But his particular adversary was a professional diplomat over whom he could exercise no authority. Sir Henry Chiltern's long and honorable career in the British foreign service was to have been concluded in the ambassadorial post at Madrid, but the civil war intervened. Sir Henry was as ardent a Francoist as Bowers was a Loyalist and often between them when they met were thinly veiled passages at arms. In Sir Henry's view, the view of the professional, the Amer-

ican ambassador was everything that a diplomat should not be—
indiscreet, injudicious, indelicate, incautious.

They had many brushes, but St. Jean remembered one in particular that had begun innocently enough. The two ambassadors
had met at a cocktail party. Bowers had remarked to Sir Henry
that he noted the sinking of another British merchant vessel by a
German submarine. The Britisher in response gave the American
his best Wodehouse stare.

"But Berlin denies it," said Sir Henry in a bland, imperturbable
voice.

There were various versions of what happened next. Apparently
in his turn Bowers gave the Britisher a look of bold Yankee disdain. Sir Henry, turning scarlet with indignation, muttered something unintelligible about ". . . those damn ships . . . those
damn Reds. . . ."

"They are British ships you are speaking of," said the American
ambassador with a flourish, turning his back on his colleague.

Such encounters were not uncommon in St. Jean de Luz. Being
so far away from the scene of the strife was obviously an embarrassment for the American ambassador who felt so strongly about the
Loyalist cause. The Czech minister had returned to Madrid and
of course the Soviet ambassador was there. Bowers complained that
Washington would not let him go back. His embarrassment was
added to by such papers back home as the Chicago *Tribune* which
printed editorials charging that he was afraid to return to bombed
and shelled Madrid. For the spunky little ambassador it must have
been a period of great trial, particularly at the end when he saw
his cause degraded.

In Paris our ambassador was William C. Bullitt who fretfully
watched Europe charge down the Gadarene slope. Nothing was to
his liking. The Reds in Spain were a curse and so were the Nazis
in Germany. Bullitt's Moscow experience had colored all his judgments. He had gone to Russia in 1933 strongly prejudiced in favor
of the Soviet experiment. But his reports back to the State Department became steadily more acrimonious as one incident after another altered his prejudices. He sent back accounts of the abduc-

tion, yes abduction, of his cook, the best cook in Moscow. He described how soldiers in Leningrad had halted him and his party on the street with fixed bayonets. The illusions he had taken to Soviet Russia were swiftly dissipated.

By contrast, another political appointee, Joseph E. Davies, went as ambassador to Russia without any illusions and only a strong prejudice in favor of American democracy as he had known it. The service that he performed there is well known. He recognized where the strength of Russia lay. Without letting his personal prejudices get in the way, he understood the meaning of the Moscow trials. And he understood, too, the necessities which would force Germany ultimately into war with Russia. His book *Mission to Moscow* shows what intelligent use can be made of the dispatches that informed diplomats send back to Washington. His mission was proof, if further proof were needed, that no generalizations are possible about career and political appointees.

When you speak of the State Department, even when you limit it to the Foreign Service, you cover a motley company. Through most of the Roosevelt administration, Under Secretary of State Sumner Welles has carried the heaviest responsibility for keeping this company in order. Against almost overwhelming odds he struggled through the difficult period of the late 'thirties to keep a hold on realities. Appeaser is one of the tags pinned to him. Too often the blame has been put on him for failures of diplomacy that were inevitable in view of the revolution that had struck the world. He has not been credited with the benefits that have derived from the kind of delaying action American diplomacy fought in various parts of the world.

In South America, Welles has come up against almost insuperable difficulties since the beginning of the war crisis. From the left he has been charged with dealing with "Fascist dictators" instead of going to the people themselves. At the same time our own military have accused him of temporizing and coddling Latin sensitivities. Welles has had to stand firmly in the way of forces within our own government that would have ridden roughshod over Latin-American sovereignty.

"By God, it's our own money, and we'll have our bases where we want them and when we want them," these strong men have told him.

"You cannot do that," Welles has repeated over and over again, "because you will give Axis agents exactly the opportunity they are looking for to prove that we are indeed the imperialist Colossus of the North."

In dealing with the South American powers he naturally dealt with those groups in control of government. To have attempted to do otherwise, once the crisis had set in, would have been also to court the charge that we were exploiting the emergency for our own purposes. What might have been done in the pre-crisis years is another matter. Certainly the controls in Latin America, both of government and of wealth, are narrowly held. Through loans and even through direct subsidies we might have shown the way in Latin America in such elementary reforms as housing. This was the argument of keen-minded younger men in the Pan-American Union such as Ernest Galarza.

Welles has always realized, and it has been the basis of his approach to South America, that the Latin-American countries must be regarded as equals; equal in sovereignty and equal in stature. Too often in the furious barrage of good will that has been directed at our neighbors South of the Rio Grande the attitude has been one of condescension. Latins, with their long background of culture, the elaborate civilization of the Mayas and the Incas, the Spanish tradition, find that attitude intolerable.

Many who might otherwise have been sympathetic to Welles's struggles have found him cold and forbidding. He has what could be called, with a wide margin of understatement, a disciplined exterior. His thin, precise features are carved on a phenomenally large head. He speaks with a distant precision in a voice which is, with rare exceptions, kept in polite modulation. For all his external frostiness the Latins go for him. Welles's close personal friendship with Oswaldo Aranha, the foreign minister of Brazil, has been one of the useful working relationships behind the successful series of Latin-American conferences held since 1939.

Rio de Janeiro in 1942 was a close squeak. With shipping at a terrifying low, the South American foreign ministers demanded to know how they could be furnished from the United States with the industrial necessities that they require. It took all of Welles's skill and persuasion to hold to a common line, and Americans, who saw only that the declaration of Rio was not as forceful as had once been contemplated, failed to realize the scope of his achievement.

What American diplomacy has attempted during the critical years since 1939 is to maintain in those areas of the earth which have not succumbed to the Axis a status quo benevolent to the interests of the United Nations. That has been a minimum goal for the duration. Repeated reproaches have been directed at the arbiters of our foreign policy for failing to provide the dynamic drive that would seek and achieve far more than this minimum. But first there must come a revision of the method itself and the approach. New ideas and new forces must not be excluded.

The old tradition dies hard. Men conditioned early to the diplomacy of the past have, as it were, been subjected to a freezing process. They look very well while kept under glass at a certain temperature, but once taken out of their environment they tend to droop. As the war went on, Washington swarmed with diplomats in exile from the lands overrun by Hitler and the Japs. They were hard working, most of them, and very well intentioned, but they were a little like actors out of a formalized theater that had forever put up its blinds. And since no one had given them new roles, they continued to repeat the old parts.

There are signs of change. Younger men such as Dean Acheson and Adolf Berle are working within the confines of the State Department on economic problems, particularly in relation to the period immediately after the war. But the changes have come very slowly, the tempo retarded by the inevitable resistance of habit and tradition.

Chapter IX

The National Schizophrenia

THE habit of security had a strong hold on most of us. We sensed the doom that overhung Europe but we could not see, so powerful was the legend of our safe isolation, our invulnerable strength, how the fall of Europe would strip us of our defenses and leave us quite alone in a hostile world. There were a few who saw and understood, even before the fall of France, but understanding was of little avail in the face of the national preference for comfortable illusion. One who understood was Bernard M. Baruch, a key figure in the history of our time.

In the summer of 1938, Baruch went abroad for his annual cure at Vichy which was still what nature intended it to be, a well-run spa and not a seat of government. Having leisurely completed his cure, he stopped in Paris to see old friends among the ruling clique. His position in the last war, the weight of his wealth and prestige, to say nothing of the dynamic force of his personality, had long since put him on terms of intimacy with the elite of the *deux cents familles*, with military men, with high politicians, the small group that governed France.

It was not idle curiosity that led him to question these great men who were still for the most part sublimely unaware of the fate that lay before them. Baruch had begun to get a picture of German rearmament that was frightening. American military attachés in Berlin had begun to send out the facts with all their startling implications and a few men in high position had had access to those facts. The response from some was to say pro-Nazi. Anyone who reported that Germany could produce that many thousand planes must be pro-Nazi. This was the tag fastened on Colonel Truman Smith who, whatever his political predilections, had been permitted to see and report on the extent of the Nazis' air program. Baruch knew facts when he saw them and he knew, too, from the depths of his experience that no amount of rhetoric could exorcise them.

So he talked to the men of France who were responsible, if anyone was responsible, for armament production. There were shrugs, apologies, bitter references to Blum and labor, the forty-hour week and the Reds, and underneath all the conversation was the dismaying fact that little progress had been made in the face of the Nazi threat. Just how bad it was they were not quite prepared to disclose to a foreigner, but Baruch went on to London deeply disturbed in his mind over the fate of the country he knew and loved.

In London he went almost at once to see Lord X., one of the highest officers of the Chamberlain government who had long been a personal friend. To this great and powerful man he put the same searching questions as he had put to his Paris friends. Finally he put a question to which in France he had found no answer.

"Can the French make shells?"

The man behind the desk lowered his head in a gesture that had in it something of despair.

"I'm sorry to say," he replied, "that in that department they must rely on us."

For Baruch, knowing the vital importance of armament supply, knowing this from painful experiences of the last war, realizing that modern arms cannot be improvised when war has been declared, the answer was like a blow at the pit of the stomach. He saw suddenly that the outer bastions of our security were far weaker than anyone dreamed. If we could not rely on France and England, then our position was perilous indeed. For our security, our comfortable illusion of isolation, lay, in the last analysis, in our reliance on the friendship of the powerful democracies of Europe. Our orators did not say that on the Fourth of July, but the realists among us knew it. And if these democracies were no longer powerful, then our own pitifully small military establishment was all that stood between us and the aggressors who had boldly announced their intention to control the riches of the world.

All this Baruch understood behind the shrewd mask of his face. Having this knowledge, there was only one thing you could do if you were Baruch and that was to turn it and twist it in your mind, wondering how people in America could be awakened in time to the peril they faced. How they could be got ready for the ordeal that was almost certain to come. Moving on to Scotland for the grouse season, he sat in the butts with his gun across his knee but his thoughts were not on the sport. Various cables passed back and forth across the Atlantic, and finally there was a trans-Atlantic telephone call from the President who wanted to know when Baruch was returning and what he had learned. The two men arranged a conference at the White House for shortly after Baruch's return in mid-September.

Coming out of the President's private office at the end of that conference, Baruch was surrounded by the newspapermen who wait to entrap each visitor. This was no new experience for the tall, straight, silver-haired financier. His custom was to nod and smile affably and to say nothing. But not this time. He stopped in the big reception room and said that, yes, he did have a story. Coming from him it was a sensational story.

Baruch said that immediate preparedness was essential for national security. He urged an increase in the Army to not less than 400,000 effectives, with a high degree of mechanization, the Army eventually to have a total strength of 750,000. He urged the construction of airplanes and still more airplanes. He suggested the need for a two-ocean Navy. He recommended adoption of a plan of industrial mobilization to be worked out at once. He stressed the need for an immediate program for far closer cultural and economic collaboration with Latin America. And last, but not least, he urged a tax program to pay for it all in the shortest possible time. There were headlines in all the evening papers—Baruch Urges Nation Re-Arm.

To those aware of his background of knowledge this was obviously no hasty curbstone opinion. Ever since the last war Baruch has maintained close personal friendships with high-ranking officers of the Army and the Navy. Once a year he has delivered a lecture to the Army War College on industrial preparedness. One of his close friends was Assistant Secretary of War Louis Johnson. When he spoke to reporters in the White House, Baruch knew precisely the tragic lacks of the American military establishment.

The next day was Friday and President Roosevelt met the press at his regular Friday morning press conference. One of the first questions that came out of the crowd gathered in front of his desk was about the need for military preparedness. Without any reference to the Baruch interview, he replied that he believed the nation should begin to arm in view of the European threat to peace and security. His statement, too, caused a sensation throughout the country. It was fairly obvious that there must have been some relation between what Baruch had said on Thursday and what the President said on Friday. White House visitors who expect to come back again do not use the White House steps as a sounding board for their views without having had some indication that this will meet with the President's approval. What is probable is that the two men agreed on a plan to arouse the American people to the immediate need for rearmament.

What happened next was profoundly revealing. In Berlin, little Doctor Goebbels pushed all the propaganda buttons. Twenty-four hours later the German newspapers were filled with attacks on Baruch of the most virulent sort. "The Jew Baruch Smells Business Profits," said front-page headlines. Along with this venom went attacks on "the bellicose clique of Churchillians" in London. And, of course, these attacks were reflected all over the world.

The New York *Times* had a full column reporting, as news, the barrage that had been loosed against Baruch. Elsewhere, in less respectable quarters, it was more than news. In Father Coughlin's *Social Justice* and in numerous other sheets that were busily spreading the pro-Nazi line Goebbels's propaganda was displayed with the same virulent enthusiasm that the German press had shown. Thousands of copies of a vicious cartoon of Baruch, showing him with a great, fat paunch and a hooked nose, grasping his money bags, were circulated throughout the country.

That is a bit of significant history we dare not ignore. Those same papers that deliberately spread the attack on the rearmament proposal are, many of them, still, today, spreading the Goebbels line. They are filled with the venom of anti-Semitism even though this incident alone should have taught us what a powerful weapon in the hands of our enemies that poison is. The expert propaganda analysts would do a great service if they would dig into the Baruch episode, for it is a classic example of how our policy may be influenced by the pressure of enemy propaganda.

I wish that some sort of psychological scale existed by which could be measured the actual effect of that assault directed from across the water. The disturbing thought is that what followed might have followed if little Doctor Goebbels had preserved in the controlled German press a complete silence on the rearmament proposal. By almost everything that had happened after 1918 we were conditioned to consider the word armament as an evil word. That had been the chief effect of the Nye munitions investigation three years before; to re-enforce the national prejudice against war and the furnishers of war. There had been a spate of books from Dos Passos' *Three Soldiers* to Remarque's *All Quiet on the Western Front* in which writers had told with courage and honesty what they felt about the dirty, bloody business of war. Moreover, talk of rearmament suggested that there was some imperfection, some serious lack, in our safe, secure hemisphere and therefore we closed our minds to it.

The reaction to the President's statement was unfavorable. Politicians and editorial writers were critical. Little or no support was forthcoming. 1940 was on the horizon. There were congressional elections in November. The papers were aroused over the "purge campaign"; over the efforts of Harry Hopkins, Tommy Corcoran, and other New Dealers to unseat conservative senators. The rearmament statement proved to be a single skyrocket burning brightly for a moment against the darkening sky. Not for many months did Baruch visit the White House again. By that time people had forgotten the entire episode.

The name Baruch, as the semanticist would point out, has somewhat the same connotations as the word rearmament, along with other overtones that gave little Goebbels a perfect opportunity. Baruch is, of course, a legend. With his clear, penetrating mind, he himself is aware of the nature of that legend and the irony of its influence. Once he made a trip with Mrs. Roosevelt to West Virginia to inspect a housing project there in which she had interested him. They visited the housing development and then drove to the airport to wait for the plane that would take them back to Washington. As they waited, some townspeople whom Mrs. Roosevelt knew gathered around and she introduced them to Baruch. He noticed that one man, a schoolteacher, kept eyeing him intently.

"I can tell you what you're thinking," Baruch said finally with an ironic gleam in his eye. "You thought Baruch would be a little short fat man with a hooked nose. And now you see he isn't that at all."

He walks with a firm pride that belies his seventy-two years. It is the pride of an American who refuses to be anything but an American. Baruch was born on a plantation near Camden, South Carolina, and grew up there until he was twelve years old, a part of the free community of youth that hunted and fished and swam and fought in that simpler day. His father had been a surgeon in the Confederate Army, enlisting as a young man out of medical school. The Baruchs were poor, but so was everyone else in the South.

When the boy was twelve, they moved to New York, which meant opportunity for the father and later for the son. Of course, Baruch made money. He made money from the very beginning in the fiercest competition of a period when competitiveness and money-getting knew no limitations. He made money on the New York Stock Exchange with the Thomas Fortune Ryans and the Bet a Million Gateses. To the warfare of speculation he brought a fierce, self-reliant spirit, a resourceful mind and a tremendous capacity for knowledge, knowledge of people and of what was happening in the companies whose stocks he was trading in. I had to know, he has often said, because I lived by knowing more than the next fellow.

Out of the last war he emerged as chairman of the War Industries Board with a towering reputation. In this war the German radio now and then hints that Baruch is running the show again. Subtly it is suggested that he stands in the shadowy background directing in secret a war that he helped to make. This is, of course, of a piece with the attack that came at the time of his rearmament statement, and it has about as much foundation of truth.

In the critical years before 1939, Baruch was not one of those who called on America to go to war. On the few occasions when he was quoted, it was to speak, as he had spoken in his White House interview, of the need to build up America's armed forces for the defense of the Western Hemisphere. In fact, he had a habit of putting embarrassing questions to his ardently interventionist friends. "With what?" he would demand of those who called for immediate action in distant theaters of war. He dealt not in terms of ideas and ideals but in questions about shells and why we were, or were not, producing more torpedoes. Some people were annoyed by this habit, feeling that such troublesome details should be left to military men who were not concerned in any event with ideas. But Baruch would not be stopped. He had constituted himself a hair shirt for the new war, inflicting himself on the lax and the lackadaisical. A kind of Socrates, he began in 1940 to move about Washington, sharpening his questions for those who were responsible for production. How many? When? And if not, why not? These were the questions he asked.

Looking back from this present moment when all but the deliberately blind or the conscious traitors are united at least in an understanding of the peril the republic is in, it is difficult to re-create 1939 and 1940. Schizophrenia, split personality, is the psychiatric diagnosis. But that is merely a convenient tag with which to label a complicated condition.

On Capitol Hill the chairman of the Senate Naval Affairs Committee was ponderous David I. Walsh of Massachusetts whose complete isolationism was charged with a personal resentment of Roosevelt. His position was one of great importance for the navy. His naval friends were among those officers who believed as he did. The ranking Republican was sixty-nine-year-old "Puddler Jim" Davis of Pennsylvania and next in line was the die-hard isolationist, Hiram Johnson of California who was seventy-five years old. The chairman of the Senate Military Affairs Committee was aging Senator Sheppard of Texas whose death in the spring of 1941 elevated to that office Bob Reynolds of North Carolina. Reynolds was not only an isolationist but he preached in his paper, *The Vindicator*, a kind of Ku Kluxism which, while undoubtedly of purest native dye, was nevertheless a timid echo of Goebbels.

On the House side there was somewhat more hope of achieving unity in the general objective of rearmament. The chairman of the House Naval Affairs Committee, Carl Vinson of Georgia, is an able and a conscientious man. Likewise the ranking minority member, Melvin J. Maas of Minnesota, has worked hard to inform himself of the navy's needs and organization. While Andrew Jackson May of Kentucky, chairman of the House Military Affairs Committee, made the proper administration noise on the war issue at the proper time, he was to display a painful lack of knowledge of the military establishment and the direction its expansion should take.

What this reflected, of course, was a similar uncertainty in the country. The Committee to Defend America by Aiding the Allies was only formed in May of 1940. It was a small but highly articulate minority working against the indifference of the vast majority of the American people and the open hostility of another minority.

Within the President's own official family there was no real unity of purpose or any indication of an aggressive drive for rearmament. The charge of warmonger leveled against the President has always seemed to me to have been malicious and false. I think that he continued to hope America would not be involved in the war long after there was any real reason for hope, just as so many other millions of Americans continued to cling to a straw that wasn't there. Perhaps from the perspective of history Roosevelt will be blamed for cherishing this hope and encouraging others to cherish it rather than for having pushed the nation into war.

His secretary of the Navy until late spring, 1940, was Claude Swanson of Virginia, an infirm gentleman of the same tradition and background as Cordell Hull. Poor Mr. Swanson was not well enough to perform even the routine duties of his office, to say nothing of working aggressively for expansion and modernization of the Navy. As has been true so often in the past, the conduct of the huge department was left largely to the heads of the more or less autonomous bureaus who spent not a little of their time in jealously guarding a bureaucratic absolutism. At best the civilian head of a military establishment occupies a difficult and anomalous position. With energy and intelligence, however, he can serve a useful purpose as liaison between the world of the civilian and the world of the admirals. With a fresh mind he can look objectively at the ancient accumulation of bureaus, boards, commissions, and whatnot, put an end to the bickerings and the quarrels, and shear through the strangling confusion of red tape. All this was beyond Mr. Swanson, who needed the job and therefore would stay in office as long as he lived. At his death Charles Edison, who had been assistant Secretary of the Navy, slipped into the office until he was in turn absorbed by New Jersey politics.

The President's loyalty to those who have been associated with him, far from being modified by the intensity of the crisis in which he found himself, was if anything strengthened. It has been put down to the Dutch stubbornness in his nature and that may be in part an explanation. But it would also seem to have roots in Roosevelt's individual temperament, apart from any inheritance. So quick is the President to resent any criticism of his associates and subordinates that the surest way to stay in high office in the present administration has been to bring down outside attacks. The presidential ego is extended to cover high and low so that any criticism, even of the milder sort, is taken almost as a personal reflection. Partly, of course, this is natural and inevitable; one of the qualities that both the successful politician and the administrator must have. As the crisis deepened, however, this loyalty seemed strangely misguided.

In the War Department the President's reluctance to act had allowed an internecine feud to develop which had echoes throughout the country. On the death of Secretary of War George Dern in 1936, the President allowed the assistant secretary, Harry Woodring, to assume the duties of the office and finally, more or less by default, he appointed him as Dern's successor. Woodring had been governor of Kansas, and when that Republican state reverted to its normal condition and Woodring was defeated for re-election a job was found for him. He was put in the War Department as assistant secretary.

Woodring set out to make himself popular in the capital. Possessed of a sharp wit and an ingratiating manner, he rapidly established himself in a city where, in 1933, almost everyone was a stranger and willing and anxious to get on with the next fellow. The social ropes in Washington dangle temptingly within fairly easy reach of well-advantaged newcomers. Agile little Harry Woodring quickly skinned up to a place that suited him and there he enjoyed himself hugely. A few months after he came to Washington he married the beautiful daughter of the late Senator Marcus Coolidge of Massachusetts. They gave pleasant parties adorned with attractive representatives of the military. Woodring had many, many first-name friends, on the Hill, among newspaper men, all over town.

But he had an enemy, too, and that enemy was also powerful. With Assistant Secretary of War Louis Johnson, Woodring was to carry on a running exchange of hostilities. While he did not profess it openly, Woodring strongly leaned to the isolationist position. He believed that money spent on our military should go solely for defense of the hemisphere. Johnson on the other hand believed in offensive warfare as the best guarantee of American security. He was for a large air force with fleets of long-range bombers. At one time national commander of the American Legion, Johnson had influential friends in and out of the army and he also had his newspaper acquaintances who carried his banner.

It resolved itself into a battle by columnists. Charges and countercharges appeared with their inspiration only thinly concealed. For the most part Johnson was the aggressor. He believed that Woodring was unfitted to be Secretary of War and he was out to supplant him. With difficulty when meeting in the Department they maintained the bare amenities. Continuing month after month, reflected in miles of newsprint, this feud naturally affected the morale of the War Department and of the high-ranking officers within the Army.

At one point certain of the New Dealers, led by Corcoran, sought to effect Woodring's removal through the promotion of another candidate for the office, a compromise candidate, whose wisdom and strength would inevitably lead to his selection. Their candidate was Frank Murphy, then attorney general and already involved in serious administrative difficulties in the Department of Justice, later to be named to the Supreme Court. The plot was rumored in the press and after Cabinet meeting one day the Secretary of War confronted the Attorney General, demanding to know whether he had any part in a plan to get the war job. Murphy was all innocence. He had never heard of such a thing. In any event nothing came of the proposal and Woodring sat tight in his job.

The President in August of 1939 named a War Resources Board. It was such a board as had been contemplated a year before at the time that Baruch and Roosevelt pointed to the urgent necessity for rearmament. The members as announced by the White House included none of the men whom Baruch had recommended.

The chairman was Edward R. Stettinius, Jr., who at the age of thirty-seven pushed to the top of the United States Steel Company, thanks to a combination of his own obvious talents and the complicated inner politics of "big steel." The other members of this first War Board were Walter S. Gifford, head of the American Telephone and Telegraph Company; General Robert E. Wood, head of Sears-Roebuck and later to be chief of the America First movement; John M. Hancock, a partner in Lehman Brothers banking firm; John Lee Pratt, a director of General Motors Corporation; and Professor Karl T. Compton, the distinguished physicist, and Doctor Harold G. Moulton, the head of Brookings Institution in Washington.

This oddly assorted company held a formative meeting, but no one seemed to have any very clear idea of what the function of the Board was to be. The members complained a little in private that they had nothing to do. They all of course had their own important and absorbing jobs and their work on the Board was to be only part time at most. When they came to Washington they sat in limbo, discussing among themselves what they were to do. Inquiry of the President at press conference drew vague replies. The conclusion was difficult to escape that this was a political board, a board made up of front men.

The thunder clap of the Nazi attack on Poland echoed loud over Washington. In the first days it all had an ominously familiar ring. The *Athenia* was sunk and American lives were lost. Lights burned through the night in the White House, which had been closed to visitors, and in the State Department across the street. While the President's speech to the nation was reassuring, he nevertheless did not attempt to conceal the fact that American security was threatened.

On the statute books there was still the law which forbade the sending of arms to any warring nation; the law which had kept arms from Loyalist Spain while at the same time shipments of military supplies had gone to "nonbelligerent" Germany and Italy. The first move on the part of the administration was to modify this law in such a way that any and all belligerents could send their own ships to American shores to buy arms on a cash and carry basis. It was an ingenious formula intended to avoid any appearance of partiality. What it meant in reality was that so long as Britain controlled the seas only Britain and her allies could avail themselves of the cash-and-carry provision.

In the four weeks of debate in the Senate that followed, administration spokesmen insisted on the neutralness of the revision that was proposed. Germany could come too, if she was able, and buy whatever she could pay for. For hours on end the isolationists hammered away at this contention. It was a fiction, they said angrily, a fiction intended to align us on the side of Britain in a war that was just the same old European backyard quarrel all over again.

The leader of the isolationists was Senator Borah, the old Lion of Idaho. He had said in June that there would be no war. He had said that his advices from Europe were as good as those of the State Department, if not better. Nye, old Hi Johnson of California, Wheeler, La Follette, Bone of Washington, each had his turn. But the big moment was reserved for Borah.

The galleries were packed as he stood up in the Senate for what was to be his swan song. He was very old, almost pathetically old. His voice came out of the past so thinly that it was difficult to hear what he said. Through the whole afternoon in the dusk of the Senate chamber he talked on. His argument was legalistic rather than emotional. The fire was gone. It was a little like hearing a very old actor whose great reputation has been cherished by the past generation. This was Robert Mantell as Hamlet, a tired Hamlet with his leonine locks grown thin, his voice a little cracked.

The outcome had been of course more or less certain from the beginning. Sentiment for England was traditionally strong in the South. Administration pressure brought some doubting senators into line but no great effort was required to put the measure over. Doubters were mollified by provisions forbidding American vessels from going into war zones and forbidding American citizens from traveling on the ships of belligerents. The final vote was sixty-three to thirty.

What people in Congress and in the country wanted to believe was that now that this step had been taken we were insured against any further annoyance from the war in Europe. It was a safe umbrella which, like the foresighted people that we were, we had raised against the storm across the Atlantic. Senator Borah pronounced it a phony war. When you called him off the Senate floor to talk to him in the little entrance opposite the big old clock he would be full of reasons why neither side meant a word of it.

Britain was merely trying to involve the United States so that we should pull Britain's chestnuts out of the fire. That last was a convenient phrase that found its way into many speeches and many editorials.

Everything that occurred through the winter of the phony war tended to lull America back into a comfortable sense that wicked old Europe was fighting just another of its periodic wars; another family quarrel which this time we could ignore. In the meantime it might even be profitable to supply for a price, under the safe terms of the revised neutrality act, some of the expensive crockery that the principals would throw at each other. German propaganda funneled through American channels may have had something to do with this but more important was the attitude in American minds.

To say nothing, it should be quickly added, of British and French minds. Almost everything that got through the European censorship tended to confirm our isolation. France was isolated behind the Maginot Line. England was isolated across the Channel. It would be a long war, a war of attrition behind massive fixed fortifications. Of course, the British and the French would win in the end but only after long hardships and sacrifices. The British were not anxious to buy from us, under the new terms of the neutrality act. They were slowly building their own munitions and air industry to produce matériel which would be ready for a major offensive in 1943 or 1944. Dorothy Thompson went to France and was entertained at dinner, with champagne, in the Maginot Line. It was that kind of war, a war we understood.

Of course, here and there were disturbing signs. One was the awful gaffe that British military intelligence had made on Poland. Their men in G-2 had insisted to our G-2 officers in August of 1939 that Poland would last four months at least. The most optimistic American military attachés in Europe said six weeks at most. And poor Poland exploded with the hollow sound of a blownup paper bag in less than a month. The dust of the medieval walls as they fell under the charge of tanks and the rain of bombs made

the air full of an acrid, choking dust. But we were too far away
to see more than a distant cloud on an unreal horizon.

In the spring came Armageddon. The country was unprepared,
Washington was unprepared for the events of that nightmare
May. The dispatches came in, to the State Department, to the
War Department, to the White House, each one piling disaster
on disaster. It could not be true. This could not be happening.
Six hours or twelve hours later the ominous black headlines
shouted the same story. Hull, Welles, Berle all but lived at their
desks.

At three or four in the morning the switchboard operator at the
White House would ring the phone beside Marguerite LeHand's
bed. It would be Bullitt from Paris or Steinhardt from Moscow
or Kennedy from London. The ever-faithful Missy would listen
for a moment or two to the news and then decide whether she
should have the call passed on to the phone beside the President's
bed or whether the news could wait for him at breakfast. The
President needed sleep so badly. But usually the message was
urgent. Sometimes it called for an immediate decision from the
chief executive himself. In the dark hours of those grim May
mornings the President's sleep was broken by the high, excited
voice of Bullitt. ". . . only sixty miles from Paris . . . Reynaud
. . . the government about to flee. . . ."

It was like a newsreel of history which should have marched
at a sober pace so that men everywhere would know what was
happening, and instead it whirred crazily through the cosmic pro-
jector. Behind the horror of Dunkerque was the realization that
the British for the first time in more than a century had been
driven off the continent of Europe without a single ally. Then
what swiftly became apparent to the President and to the men
around him was that the isles themselves were all but defenseless.

So much had gone down. The sickening crash still reverberated
in every important office in Washington. And now was Britain to
go, too? That was the desperate fear that drove men on in July
and August of that summer. Men who had been only half awake
were jerked suddenly into the blinding, merciless light of day. I

know what my own thoughts were at that time. Like, I suppose, millions of other Americans I had never actually faced the reality of our dependence on Britain. I had never faced the meaning of victory by a resurgent Germany. The Washington atmosphere was especially lulling in the period immediately before, but the same illusion of invulnerability was general throughout the country.

In the prophetic phrase of Clare Boothe's little scrunchneck, Homer Lea, ours was "The Valor of Ignorance." Now suddenly in those months of 1940 it was like standing in a familiar house that has had one side blasted away. Everything is normal, or almost normal. Life goes on. Your routine is as it has always been. But nothing is the same nor ever can be again. The light falls in the familiar rooms in a new harsh way so that what has been safe and comfortable now looks naked and unprotected.

In this cold new light, steps were taken that had been long delayed. Harry Woodring was summoned to the White House and told that he must resign immediately. Sputtering hints that he might carry his case to the country, he sent that same afternoon a letter of formal resignation. One of the first moves after he had gone was to send whatever was available to the beleaguered English on their tight little isle. It was little enough but at least it was something that might help when the invasion, which everyone expected, should come. Out of armories and depots came the old Springfield rifles and other equipment that had survived the first World War. Nothing was said about this publicly, but officials worked with frantic haste in response to urgent appeals from Britain. Churchill, speaking in magnificent Elizabethan prose, captured the imagination of Washington and the country.

That bit of stage property, the War Resources Board, was relegated to the wings. In its place the President on June 24 named the National Defense Advisory Commission. The chairman was Stettinius, the white-haired boy of big steel. Other members were Harriet Elliott for consumers, Leon Henderson for prices, Chester C. Davis for the farmers, Ralph Budd of the Burlington Railroad for transportation, Sidney Hillman for labor. And for the first time William S. Knudsen stepped onto the national stage, as a member of the board, to be victimized almost immediately by a publicity build-up of such towering proportions as few men in public life have ever been embarrassed by. It was the first of many moves for Big Bill Knudsen who was to pass from one resounding title to another, each one more empty of authority than the last, until finally he was given the glittering stars and the brass hat of a lieutenant general and sent out to the production line where he had belonged all along.

The board was compartmentalized by interests and the members settled down each to work in his own field. Miss Elliott busied herself establishing a consumers' unit, drawing in eager people who wanted to protect and advise the consumer. Hillman, a dubious choice since he was the focus of so much animosity from various sections of organized labor, was on loan from his Amalgamated Clothing Workers. Budd came down from New York at fairly regular intervals but his assignment, he seemed to feel, was a nominal one that called for little immediate action. Knudsen and Stettinius were presumably the representatives of industry on this compartmentalized board. America had been shaken by the fall of France but not sufficiently to jar the rhythm of business and government as usual.

Far more important than the board itself was a change that occurred in the President's own family. On May 10, the date that marked the beginning of the fall of France, Harry Hopkins moved into the White House for the week end. He was still there in the summer of 1942, as permanent boarder and very possibly the most influential man in Washington next to the President himself.

A metamorphosis had taken place in Hopkins's life. He had been through a terrible ordeal. The job of relief administrator with all its political ramifications had drained his energy, leaving him tired and waspish. Then his second wife to whom he was devoted developed an incurable disease. Helplessly he watched as it destroyed her. And along with this torture went the constant worry about money. His salary had been increased to $12,500, but with a previous wife and three sons to support in addition to maintaining a smallish house in Georgetown and paying doctor and hospital bills this was inadequate. He usually drew his WPA check in advance and gratefully in this crisis he accepted the aid of the rich and powerful friends he had made.

Upon the death of his wife, he himself seemed to lose the desire to live. He was laid low with a serious stomach ailment and the doctors at the Mayo hospital in Rochester despaired of his life after a long and difficult operation. The problem was to find some diet on which he could sustain life. The man who had fed so many millions of Americans seemed about to die for lack of nourishment. Under the immediate eye of Admiral Ross Mc-Intire, the President's personal physician, Hopkins was made into a human guinea pig and every possible experimental mess was poured down him. But he only grew thinner and grayer. For long weeks through the spring of 1938 he sat in the sun in Florida, fretting sometimes at his enforced idleness but for the most part content to lie listlessly in a deck chair.

If there had been one thing needed to cement his relationship with the Roosevelts, it was the tragedy that had descended on him. Mrs. Roosevelt took his motherless daughter, Diana, into the White House to live. The President made it plain that he would always defend and protect his unfortunate friend. On Christmas Eve of 1938, Roosevelt as Santa Claus told Hopkins that he intended to appoint him Secretary of Commerce. He had rescued him from the WPA at a time when his congressional critics were out to slit his throat. Now he proposed to put him in a berth in which he could either continue comfortably his recuperation or, with his recovery, make a bid for greater honors; perhaps even for the Presidential nomination of 1940 that hung temptingly in sight.

Poor Hopkins seemed to have no health left in him. Through most of the summer of 1939 he moped on the terrace of a country house he had leased in near-by Maryland. At times he rallied. At the urging of Mrs. Roosevelt he came in to town to meet King George and Queen Elizabeth and tell them about the workings of the American relief system. For little Diana the visit of royalty was a memorable event. On the night of the great state dinner Mrs. Roosevelt took the little girl by the hand and led her down the corridor to the queen's suite where she was allowed to see Elizabeth in the full splendor of state costume. On the sunny afternoon that Hopkins talked with the royal couple on the White House lawn, neither royalty nor commoner could dream that they would next meet in bombed Buckingham Palace with the alert sounding full blast and antiaircraft shells bursting furiously overhead. Their roles would in a curious sense be reversed, with Hopkins the emissary of the only power in the world capable of trying to save the empire of George and Elizabeth.

The crisis of May 10 galvanized Hopkins into life. He would still be an ailing man but from that point on he was to ignore his health. Merely to conserve his energy, he had of course to spend about twice as many hours in bed as a normal man. And the doctors still tinkered with him when he would permit them. But the slight store of his energy he spent freely, as though he had made a sort of Faustian bargain which would grant him the right to live while he lived at the very center of perhaps the greatest drama in American history.

More than has been generally realized, Hopkins appears to have been influential in setting the pattern for the shifting war organization. He remained acutely conscious of the political significance of the New Deal. Suspicious of dollar-a-year men, he made no secret of his belief that the New Dealers were doing a better job in the war crisis than the industrialists who had come down from New York. Some of the New Dealers had been his protégés—Leon Henderson for example, and he pointed with pride to their rise. This war, he was heard to say, would be run by younger men, new men, and not by the old symbols out of the past. Baruch's friends blamed Hopkins for the fact that the financier was not called to a more active role.

At the same time he had his own friends among the rich and mighty whom he promoted in government. Catch 'em young and no matter how many millions of dollars they've got, you can convert 'em. That was Hopkins's philosophy. Youngish W. Averill

Harriman was one of the tame businessmen who had served on the Business Advisory Council in the Department of Commerce when Hopkins was secretary. Various assignments fell to Harriman's lot, leading up to his important mission abroad. Thirty-three-year-old Nelson Rockefeller was another Hopkins protégé. Full of a bouncing enthusiasm and with far more political oomph than the average politician, Rockefeller was given the resounding title of Co-ordinator of Commercial and Cultural Relations between the American Republics.

Harriman, Rockefeller, and others of the Hopkins gold-plated school of public administration were only the vanguard of a hoard of bankers, businessmen, advertising experts, and sundry and assorted other New Yorkers who were to migrate to Washington. Most of them approached government with a virginal innocence. They were to learn, and painfully, the mysteries of bureaucracy. All the pain was not of course on the side of the innocents. Settled and sedate officers of government, especially in the State Department, suffered from this invasion.

The newcomers were too ready to accept the outward signs of bureaucratic achievement. Rockefeller, for example, wrestling with the problems of his organization, as it grew in size with the mushroom swiftness that has characterized most of the war organizations, would get it all worked out on paper and assume happily that the particular job had been done. Needing shipping priorities in connection with his effort to improve Latin-American relations, he would get from the President a letter authorizing the proper priorities. Wreathed in smiles, he would show it to hardened old skeptics in the State Department, not realizing that such a letter was merely the first step forward in the great dismal swamp of government.

The feud was to grow sharper between the dollar-a-year wing and the New Deal wing of the defense organizations. Hopkins saw men on both sides of the great divide. They came to him for help in the White House, big and little, knowing that he saw the President every day; that the President trusted him. It was gall and wormwood to his enemies. Harold Ickes, who could find no niche or cranny in the new organization, ground his teeth and spoke contemptuously of the President's best friend as the little brother of the rich.

But Hopkins, even if he had known the whisperings of the envious, would not have cared. He was a man set apart, a man who had made a bargain. To see him you went in the porticoed north entrance of the White House. The usher took you up to the second floor and escorted you down the broad corridor to the next to the last door on the right. In the room where Lincoln signed the Emancipation Proclamation, the frail Hopkins lay in a huge four-poster bed telephoning interminably and seeing a stream of callers. Down below was the green of the White House lawn and, further off, the Potomac, grayish blue on the horizon. A dispatch case stuffed with documents lay beside the bed. Papers were spilling off of every chair. The emaciated man muttering into the telephone was to be compared with Woodrow Wilson's Colonel House. He was to be more than that. He would be an assistant President, the eyes and ears, yes, and the legs of his great friend and benefactor, Franklin Roosevelt.

Chapter X

Study in Frustration

ANYTHING went in this period of drift and uncertainty. The voice at the other end of the telephone said: "Don't you want to come over to the Mayflower and meet a German who's the chief undercover man in this hemisphere?" There had been a curious clicking in the phone at the beginning of the conversation. The connection seemed to be poor. "You know," said the voice, "I think this telephone is tapped." It was tapped, I was to learn later. That was May of 1940.

Little Joachim Hertslett was almost too good to be true. That is one thing about Washington; people are almost invariably caricatures of what they are meant to be. As Hertslett walked into the living room of the suite in the Mayflower, any Hollywood director would have recognized him instantly as the Nazi agent that he was. Not your arrogant, Prussian type at all, he was small, almost unobtrusive looking, hair en brosse, horn-rim spectacles and odd, sad eyes that never quite looked at you but that took in everything, you were sure. He was Hermann Goering's right-hand man in the business of economic warfare, and although he was young, considerably under thirty, it was quite apparent that he had what it took to carry out whatever assignments might come from Berlin. And you felt that he would be a pretty ruthless, effective operator on his own, too. I may have seen it there because I was looking for it, but there was a singular absence in his face of the qualities that we think of as human qualities. It was a face made to cover a mind from which had been sheared away everything kind, everything pleasantly superfluous.

Hertslett told me that he would cable the Foreign Office in Berlin and tell them that they were to release to me authentic figures on German oil reserves and German oil production. I said that would be dandy, knowing very well the figures would be useless, and went on my way, having seen Nazi Specimen A.

It was one of those days when Washington was more than ever a caricature of itself. As I went out the door, leaving Hertslett with his American business friends, I encountered a woman in the corridor who seemed to have no reason for being,there. She made for my benefit the idle gestures of having forgotten to lock her door or not having forgotten to lock it and then as I hesitated a moment, she went on down toward the elevator.

She was striking, handsome, with a handsome hat with veils. Hah, I thought, definitely a lady spy if I ever saw one. We walked to the elevator together and stood waiting what seemed an unconscionable time for an elevator. At that point, and just as the car stopped at our floor, little Herr Hertslett came round the corner. We three were in the elevator, the lady spy, the Nazi agent, and I. It was too much for my sense of the dramatic.

"Mr. Smith tells me you're going back to Germany very soon," I said by way of resuming the conversation with Herr Hertslett. "That's interesting. How do you propose to get back? The British'll grab you, won't they?"

He looked at me with something very like an emotion in his eye and a little color came into his pale face. Muttering something unintelligible, he got off at his own floor. And I thought as we continued down that the handsome lady spy gave me a smile intended to convey her warm, mysterious gratitude. It was Leslie Ford crossed with E. Phillips Oppenheim and if a corpse had tumbled on at the next stop, I should have behaved in a perfectly normal fashion.

Hertslett was one piece in a puzzle I had begun to try to put together nearly two years before. It was the puzzle of international oil and the obscure politics behind this commodity that is the essential X in the life equation of each great power. At times I seemed to be looking down into an undersea world where ordinary vision was of no use whatsoever; where ordinary values were strangely distorted. Beneath the calm, normal surface a titanic struggle was going on for the great prizes of our time. I worked at it hard, knowing always that at best I could see only halfway down into the murky depths. I thought it was important then, that nothing could be more important, and everything that has happened since has confirmed my conviction. After all, the Atlantic Charter declares that all nations shall have equal access to natural resources and natural resources must mean oil.

It began, my preoccupation with this puzzle, in the gaudy blue and gold presidential suite of the Hotel Reforma in Mexico City. Joseph Pulitzer had sent me to Mexico to do a series of articles on economic and social conditions there, following the expropriation by the Mexican government of the foreign oil properties. Just before I left Washington, he had phoned from Bar Harbor to suggest that I investigate a man named Davis, William Rhodes Davis, who seemed to have some connection with expropriation and the sale of oil by the Mexican government from expropriated wells which had once belonged to Standard Oil and Dutch Shell.

Davis had some connection with it all right. I had not been in Mexico City twelve hours before I realized that he was the center of an intrigue which led God knows where—anywhere. After considerable telephoning back and forth with his efficient secretary, I was admitted to the presence itself. There followed one of the most difficult and at the same time one of the most fascinating interviews I have ever had in my life.

I wanted Davis to talk about oil; Mexican oil, shipments to Germany, Dutch Shell and Standard, and what he thought they might be up to in order to get back the fabulous black Golconda they had lost. Instead he insisted on talking about everything else under the sun. I rather flatter myself that I have some skill in leading interviews into channels in which I want the conversation to go. But with Davis it was no soap. He talked mostly about his plan to further world trade. It was gigantic, tremendous, colossal with Indians, and while the man talked the whole thing seemed perfectly plausible. Thousands of tons of coffee that he had in Brazil, and on the other side of the world rubber, and somewhere else cotton.

I thought back to Ivar Kreuger, the match king, with whom I had talked briefly once on a boat a long time before. Kreuger was cold and somehow unpleasant. This man had an American enthusiasm that was almost genuine. "Of course, I don't know, I'm just a boy from the country," he would say every now and then. That was an old one but he made it sound somehow authentic. Twice in the hour and a half I spent with him London called and once his secretary came in and announced, as I recall it, that the Mexican supreme court wanted to talk to him. Or it may have been just the chief justice. This extraordinary fellow, as I was to discover later, was perfectly capable of making up brilliant telephonic conversations with Secretary Hull, his old friend Cordell, for the benefit of the important visitor seated across his desk. If it was an act that he bothered to put on for me on the trans-Atlantic phone, it was a good one.

Briefly what had happened in Mexico was this. The oil workers' union, with the backing of the Cardenas government, had presented Standard and Dutch Shell with a series of stiff demands. Just how unreasonable they were I could scarcely judge. Some of the demands seemed fantastic; vacations with free travel in foreign lands, that sort of thing. But this had to be weighed against the stupid exploitation of previous years. Lengthy negotiations led to an impasse, with the foreign oil companies standing pat. They took this as a test of sovereignty, not believing, apparently, that the Mexican government would carry out its threat of expropriation.

Duly sanctified by a decision of the supreme court, the government proceeded to do just that. Not merely the derricks, pipe lines, and refineries above the soil, but, far more important, the vast subsurface wealth was seized and the foreign managers and technicians ordered to leave the property. The British company, Dutch Shell, lost far more than Standard, Shell's reserves of oil in the Poza Rica field being one of the important treasures of the earth.

Expropriation took place on March 18, 1938. It developed that on the preceding day Davis had, fortuitously, entered into a deal with the Mexican government for some three million dollars' worth of oil in exchange for necessary machinery which, fortuitously, Davis had in Mexico. It appeared as though he had been a party to expropriation, anticipating it to his own profit, particularly since for several years he had been busy greasing politicians and political parties on both sides of the Rio Grande. He protested his innocence, saying he had lost his big Sabalo claim through the general seizure of all foreign oil properties, but this had a hollow ring.

Buying oil from Mexico was one thing, selling it in the world market was another. Standard and Dutch Shell immediately closed every outlet that they controlled—which was practically every outlet everywhere. Steamship lines were warned that if their vessels refueled with the "stolen" oil from Mexican wells, they would risk being refused refuelling facilities in all the ports of the earth. To the unknowing eye it looked pretty tough. The answer, of course, was Germany. Remember that this was the spring of 1938 and the Nazis were working desperately hard to complete preparations for the campaign of conquest that was to begin in 1939. Oil was vital. They wanted every driblet of oil they could get from whatever corner of the globe.

Davis was an adventurer, yes, a rascal, bound to the Nazis by ties of mutual interest. Yet in the undersea jungle in which he operated his motives were perfectly understandable. It shocked me to find I had almost a kind of sympathy for him; for the underdog in a long relentless warfare. Given the corruption, the ruthlessness, of power politics, the power politics of oil, you will get Davises. Yes, you will get Hitlers.

The story, or rather the story behind the story, was not in Mexico City. The dynamite might explode there eventually. But the story was in Washington, New York, London, Berlin. In Mexico City in the fall of 1938 all was outwardly serene. Kind, gentle, old Josephus Daniels, the American ambassador, had no intention of troubling the waters. Cursed by oil men and the "colony" in Mexico, his gentle inaction may have saved a bad situation. A strong man, one of your bold talkers, might well have precipitated a nasty mess with dire implications for the war that was to come. Mr. Daniels, in the pleasant autumn of his life, was writing his memoirs, which is often the best thing an ambassador can do.

For more than a year after I left Mexico, I followed the oil story. I talked with innumerable people in Washington and New York. I visited time and again the Davis offices on the fifty-fourth floor of that citadel of oil, Rockefeller Center. In the Congressional Library I burrowed through the files of the *Times* of London and less distinguished papers. At one point, before the war overshadowed everything else, I contemplated taking the clipper Londonward for two or three weeks of intensive work on the other side. That, incidentally, is one advantage of working for a paper like the *Post-Dispatch*; you have leeway to follow down a story that seems to have real possibilities.

While I knew that I had hardly touched the surface, still I had a view of the whole landscape and I saw that Mexico was only one segment, the last in a sequence. You had to go way back. You had, in fact, to see the outline of oil in the history of Europe since 1918. The system had been put together in such a way that two powers, Germany and France, were dependent on Britain and the United States for oil, France somewhat less so than Germany but nevertheless dependent. Britain had Iran and Iraq and we had the huge reserves of the Western Hemisphere or all except what the British had.

There was, however, still another great prize—Baku, the oil of the Caucasus. After the Bolshevik revolution various clever gentlemen worked on schemes to divorce Russia of this treasure. With it went industrial strength and military might, and the powers in London and Paris were depressed at the thought that such a bonanza should fall to the Soviets. Long after the effort to put down the Bolsheviks with foreign armies had been abandoned, the schemes and plots for Baku continued. A Dutchman with a Napoleonic complex, Sir Henri Deterding, the head of Dutch Shell, was obsessed with the idea of separating the Russians from their oil. The answer lay, he came to believe, in turning the Germans against the Soviet Union. And as Hitler began his climb to power, Deterding thought he recognized the man for the job. That was what Hitler told you; all he wanted was a chance to fight those filthy Russians. At one point when the Nazi political fortunes were low, Sir Henri staged a rescue party and found four million guilders to tide the Nazis over.

It would be extremely interesting to know what Hitler really thought of Deterding and how seriously he considered his convenient little plan for sending the Germans against the Russians. In any event the Nazis had another bet in the oil game, even if it was a small one. In March of 1933, Davis had met Hitler, Goering, and other high-up Nazis in Berlin. He had a neat scheme for converting the blocked mark account of a bank in Boston, with which he had a connection, into an oil refinery he proposed to build at Hamburg. The Germans thought well of this scheme.

They knew Davis's background, of course. He had a deep grudge which they could turn to their own advantage. He saw himself as the persecuted victim of the big oil companies, "the international combine," he called it. Davis would tell you how Standard had tried to ruin him; had taken him into partnership in a pipeline company, and then when the line was built had refused to deliver the oil called for under the contract. So Davis had gone broke and eventually a Standard company had acquired the line. That was what he believed and believing it he had a drive, an ambition, a desire to get even, that forced him to tireless, fanatical extremes beyond those of any normal man. This was a kind of pathology that the Nazis could understand.

The Hamburg refinery was completed in 1934. But that was only the beginning. It became apparent that Davis was out to put together the essential elements of an international oil industry. Nothing less than that! You had to have oil reserves. Davis had the Sabalo claim in Mexico. You had to have large-scale outlets that you controlled yourself. Davis had a guarantee of some territory in Germany. He formed connections with a Danish com-

pany. And about this time he met the very rich Lord Inverforth
and an eminently respectable gentleman named T. C. J. Burgess
who was managing director and the dominant figure in the London and Thames Haven Oil Wharves, Ltd.

London and Thames Haven was one of those firms in which the
money of widows and orphans was invariably invested; it paid
such a high dividend, it was so safe. The company had an extensive oil storage reservoir at Mucking on the Thames, and as the
law of the land said that gasoline and oil could not be stored
nearer London than Mucking the company enjoyed a cozy monopoly, lightering up to the great industrial city oil and gasoline
brought to Mucking by the tankers of Standard and Dutch Shell.
Inverforth and Burgess provided most of a capital of $22,500,000
through flotation of the stock of a company called Parent Petroleum. Even more important, London and Thames Haven had
connections in France. French oil men had always bitterly resented
the domination of Standard and Shell and the quota system they
enforced. So in France guaranteed outlets could be found for this
new colossus that was taking shape. And in Ireland, through Burgess's connections, a deal was negotiated which would mean a monopoly of all sales in Eire.

Tankers were a requisite too. The Germans had a few and controlled others. You could see the pattern. It was a formidable one.
It is not difficult to imagine Davis's emotions at this point. He
was so close. He would be able to compete with the titans. He
could undersell them. He could force them to meet his terms.

One requisite was political influence, and Davis set about acquir-
ing that. His London partners provided a half-million dollars for
use in the 1936 presidential campaign in America. I came upon a
letter that Davis had written to a Wall Street broker with political ambitions, in which he described how he had "made available"
to the Democratic party and to various Democratic senators the
sum of $291,286.06. He told how he had talked with Mr. Roose-
velt in the White House and how Mr. Roosevelt had seemed to
approve his plans for world trade; for a three-corner barter, Ger-

man machinery for Mexican oil for American cotton. Davis believed that for his money he would get the aid and co-operation of the American embassy in Mexico City, acting at the instructions of his friend, F. D. R. In this, as he shortly discovered, he was to be bitterly disappointed.

In 1937 the attack began. Davis had gone too far. One of his Danish partners began a series of harassing lawsuits in the London courts. The Irish monopoly was broken. Old lawsuits were revived in American courts. But most important was the attack on London and Thames Haven.

Ten years before, the Anglo-American Oil Co., a Standard subsidiary, had made strenuous efforts to have the limiting line moved from Mucking farther up the Thames and nearer London to Purfleet, which would have meant the end of London and Thames Haven's comfortable monopoly. A royal commission was appointed and, after taking volumes of testimony and considering at length the safety of the great mass of the people in the London dock area, the commission found against the change. Now this effort was revived and shortly Sir Thomas Inskip, Minister of Defense, ordered the change made. And here you have poor Mr. Burgess trying to explain to his indignant directors and stockholders why it happened:

"It was a most extraordinary position. On the one side you have had a government department appointing a commission to look into the question from a safety point of view. You have an official report in the archives of that department pointing out the almost certain coming of a calamitous disaster should petroleum ships be allowed up the Thames River. In spite of this you now have another government department insisting upon the necessity of this danger being disregarded and of plums being handed out to a foreign-owned company. For what? For a mere trifle of supposed safely stored petrol in a region so close to the heart of the City of London that the government commissioners had already reported, in the event of an accident, the London docks and Woolwich Arsenal would probably be involved. . . .

"At Thames Haven there are no other interests involved in a disaster due to air raids, and the passage of ships to Purfleet is an incentive for enemy aircraft to drop their bombs in a thickly populated area. . . ."

His protests were of no avail. The dividend of London and Thames Haven shrank pitifully, the stock sagged. Davis's empire-in-construction began to crumble. Here a prop fell out, there a stone gave way. Inverforth and Burgess sent batteries of lawyers to New York and Washington. Finally all that Davis had left was his Mexican oil, that and his Nazi tie.

He still had, however, powerful friends in Washington. One of them was John L. Lewis, head of the CIO. Another was Walter Jones, a minor Pennsylvania politico who had close connections with Senator Guffey and the bosses of the Democratic machine in that state, if only, perhaps, because he had so generously distributed Davis's money. Guffey, a member of the Senate Foreign Relations Committee, and Jones made a trip to Mexico City in 1937, a year before expropriation, and there Guffey, from the vantage of his position, introduced Jones to Mexican officials as the agent of Davis. Later they were to meet in Washington several times with Eduardo Suarez, the Mexican minister of finance.

More important was the service that Lewis rendered. The blockade declared by Standard and Shell was a formidable one. It might well have throttled the oil industry the Mexican government had taken over from private interests. And if it had been throttled, and private managers, private technicians, and owners had been called back, then the State Department would have been rid of an acutely embarrassing problem. All the time, of course, Standard and Dutch Shell were pressing for action. The British after a sharp note went so far as to remove their minister from Mexico City. In every port where they could impound it, they seized the "stolen" oil and brought suit against the Davis companies.

What Lewis did was, in effect, to vouch for Davis with Mexican labor. Lewis was dreaming dreams. He was strengthening his ties with the Mexican Confederation of Labor and through the head

of the Confederation, Vicente Lombardo Toledano, with a federation of Latin-American workers extending all the way down the
continent. It was a dream of power and position; of the leading
strings that he would hold in his hand. In the late summer of
1938, he had gone to Mexico City for a Pan-American Labor
Congress organized by Lombardo Toledano. Lewis was at that
time the darling of the Communists who were influential in the
Mexican labor movement. John L. sat as an honor guest in the
presidential box in the bull ring to watch a Red Ballet while red
flags fluttered in the warm thin air.

Davis had convinced him that he had resources to move Mexico's oil. Lewis told Mexican labor leaders that Davis could command at least thirty tankers outside the Standard-Shell ring. Persuaded of the importance of Davis's international connections, he
scorned the suggestion that the oil man was no more than an agent
for the Nazis. That, said Lewis, was Standard Oil propaganda.

Several times during this period I went to see the great John L.
in all the imposing grandeur of his office in the old University
Club, which he had bought for the United Mine Workers and
remodeled from top to bottom. He sat at a desk that must have
been almost as broad as Mussolini's. Behind him were great arched
windows. You approached across one of those rugs in which you
waded knee-deep in velvet. As you came within recognizable distance, he stood up to receive you. It was intended to be impressive
and it was. These talks were off the record. John L. would rum-
ble out his indignation, the phrase "the Standard Oil-controlled
State Department" booming out like distant thunder.

Surely Lewis should have been able to recognize the technique
of Standard Oil, for essentially it is the technique he has used in
directing the destinies of his United Mine Workers with their
six hundred thousand members. Never at any time has he permitted interference from his board of directors or from the public.
The Lewis rule has been absolute. Board meetings are held but
their function is merely to ratify decisions Lewis has already
reached. As he rose to power, becoming the hero of the left wing,

the darker shadows in his past were painted out. I remembered the miners' warfare in Southern Illinois and the part Lewis had played there; bloody Herrin and the bark of the machine guns.

It was not difficult to see why he had been drawn to Davis. Lewis, too, has an insatiable appetite for power. What it is that he must compensate for I have never understood but he is as sensitive to slights as a prima donna. Consider the façade he presents to the world; the language and the attitudes of a Shakespearean ham. He pouts. The little mouth, the little eyes, lost in the big face, are screwed up more often than not in an expression of sullen declination. Mr. Lewis does not choose to smile. The wonder is not that he broke with the President but that their relationship endured so long after 1936 when Lewis was trying to collect on the half-million dollars of UMW funds he had paid over to the Democratic party. That was like big business too. You pay your money and you buy your man.

Davis's grudge against Standard Oil would have been almost enough in itself to have attracted Lewis. The Shakespearean actor with the stage eyebrows likewise has a grudge against the powers that be. It is behind his ambition and that ambition was behind the formation of the CIO. When Lewis broke with the left wing and the Communists over the issue of the war, he started out to enlarge his own empire. Under the broad wing of the UMW his personal organizers are garnering in Yale janitors, dairy farmers, chemical workers, any group that can be persuaded or coerced into paying dues; but particularly, it should be noted, workers in essential industries. Consider what power would be his if he should succeed in organizing any substantial number of dairy farmers. Milk is an essential food. Coal is an essential commodity. You have to give Lewis credit for trying. If he is stopped in one direction, he tries in another. At sixty-two he is still a force to be reckoned with.

In 1939 he came to Davis's aid again. Davis told the State Department that his friends in Germany had a peace plan. He wanted to go to Berlin with semiofficial status and bring it back. It would save the world, save humanity. The Department thought this sounded a bit queer. Lewis called the White House to say that he felt his good friend Davis should be given more consideration. The President, with Adolf Berle sitting in, listened and then cautiously replied that he would be interested to know on Mr. Davis's return what Mr. Davis learned in Germany. The British, who put the oil man at the head of their list of American friends of Nazi Germany, tried without avail at several points to catch up with him.

At Lisbon on his way back, after two weeks in Rome and Berlin, he had with him Joachim Hertslett who was traveling under a forged Swedish passport. The American consulate readily saw through that dodge and denied Hertslett a visa. Indignantly Davis cabled the State Department, cabled his friend Franklin Roosevelt. When the clipper departed Hertslett was left behind. For the Nazi agent this was an inconvenience but not a real obstacle, since a day or two afterward he sailed for Brazil and a few weeks later he entered the United States on his German diplomatic passport. The peace plan that Davis brought back with him was, of course, a Nazi propaganda document, designed to mislead and confuse the world about German intentions.

Primarily the Davis story is a study in frustration. The drive for power turned back on itself creates something fearsome and corrosive. Power naked and uncontrolled begets the desire for power. Davis was driven on by an inner torment until the end. He was still to try to play a part in national and international politics. From the men around him there were hints that he would appear before a Senate committee and tell everything that he knew about Standard Oil. He was a little fellow, his associates were fond of saying. Why not find out what the big fellows were up to? The real story, they implied, would show that Standard and Dutch Shell were Germany's big suppliers with Davis merely caught in their machinations.

At one point isolationist Senators hinted that Davis would be permitted to come before a special sub-committee investigating alien propaganda to tell his story. Leaders of the isolationist cause had met Davis through his friend, Lewis. That was when the isolationist bloc still believed, like King Canute, that the sea could be made to stand still.

It would in all probability have served the isolationists' purpose. Davis would have made a brilliant witness. He would have helped to re-enforce the isolationist impression that the British kettle was as black as the German pot. Standard Oil was playing the Nazi game, supplying Germany with oil. They were all bad, all corrupt. There was no reason for America to take sides. That was the dangerous fallacy which so many American isolationists had espoused. They wanted to believe that it was a choice between good and evil which America should make and since there was no absolute good, then there was no choice. It was the most persuasive of all the fallacies that filled the air in this time of unhappy uncertainty.

All sorts of Machiavellian motives were attributed to Wheeler. For the interventionists he was the villain of the piece, capable of every sort of intrigue. That, to my way of thinking, was too elaborate. All you had to know was the bitter sense of injustice that gnawed at him to understand everything he said and did. It was a bitterness that fed on itself; that had long since gone beyond any original causation. It could take him to such lengths as that shocking, "plow under every fourth boy" statement, which came out when he and the President were in the course of a fishwifely quarrel that served only to further confuse the country.

Wheeler all his life has fought "the company." His company was not Standard Oil but Anaconda Copper, a behemoth that exercised much the same kind of control over an essential metal that Standard exercised over oil. The company, for Wheeler, was the embodiment of evil. Anything the company was for, he was *ipso facto* against. An elementary measuring rod but it had served him well in the rough, tough school of Montana politics. He thought of himself as a self-made man; having raised himself by his bootstraps in defiance of everything the company could do.

With this went a suspicion of the industrial East, the effete East. That element is strong in the Wheelers, the LaFollettes, the Non-Partisan Leaguers, the Farmer-Laborites of Minnesota. It grows out of a sectional sense of injustice. I am a Middle Westerner and I recognize it in myself. We produce the raw materials which the East buys at a low price, to process and sell back to us at a high price. (That is almost explanation enough for the behavior of the farm bloc in the critical summer of 1942; industrialists were profiting from the war, from big contracts, and they meant to be compensated, too.) The East drains off the strength of our soil and draws away from us our youth of brains and talent who might otherwise help to put our region on an equal basis. This goes way back to the pattern of railroad finance with eastern capitalists owning the means by which the Middle Western wheat grower reached his market and thereby setting the price for his wheat. If it has not actually been the root cause, then it has been the convenient political bogey behind innumerable protest movements in the prairie states in the past. The Know Nothings came out of it, anti-Catholic, antiforeign, anti-East.

In the light of this background, think how easy it was for that clever Nazi agent, George Sylvester Viereck, to reach Senator Lundeen of Minnesota. The ground was prepared. From eastern bankers, you went to "international bankers" and it was only a small step to "international Jewish bankers." I can imagine the clever, persuasive Viereck talking to the simple, rather stupid Lundeen. He would have done it all by implication, so shrewdly that Lundeen may never have realized that he had aligned himself with the propagandists for a vicious tyranny which would have smashed first of all the simple, unradical, social-democracy of the Farmer-Labor party in Minnesota.

It may have been more involved, but the point is that it could have happened in just that way. Lundeen was prepared to believe

the Nazi propaganda line that we were being forced into the war
to save the international bankers; that America must remain isolated to save itself, to save democracy. That was the line which
best served the end of German conquest and therefore it was the
line the Nazis pushed hardest.

Wheeler has a keen mind, and a strong sense of practical politics. He could never have succumbed to the persuasions of a
Viereck. But he was prepared to believe that the pattern of this
war would be almost identical with the pattern of the last war.
The last war and its aftermath had fed his sense of injustice. He
was framed by the agents of Harry L. Daugherty and William
J. Burns. Department of Justice men had been sent to Montana
to pore over his record. They put together a flimsy case and a
federal grand jury at Helena indicted him for violation of the
statute that forbids senators from pressing private claims before
government departments. Wheeler overnight became a national
cause with liberals in the country, and at the end of a brief trial
in Helena it took a jury only ten minutes to return a verdict of
not guilty.

But this did not take away the rancor. Wheeler remembered
the war years when he was called a Bolshevik, the most dangerous man in America; when his opponent in a political campaign
used against him posters showing a bloody hand with a dagger,
and said he believed in free love. Add to this a sense that the
Roosevelt administration had treated him unfairly.

Two more different men than Roosevelt and Wheeler could
hardly be imagined; the former smiling and smooth-surfaced, the
latter as prickly as a porcupine and almost as suspicious. Yet in the
beginning they had pulled together amicably enough. As chairman
of the powerful interstate commerce committee, Wheeler was in
charge of the President's utility holding company legislation, working with Corcoran and Cohen, the President's lieutenants on Capitol Hill.

At one point Wheeler suspected that certain Southern Democrats, outwardly loyal, were plotting to eliminate the so-called

death sentence clause. Accused of this, they hinted it was the President's own wish. Immediately Burt Wheeler went down to the White House to put it up to Roosevelt. Was he for the death sentence or was he against it? Sitting up in bed propped up by pillows the President called for a pad of paper and a pencil and wrote out a statement which he authorized Wheeler to show to anyone who raised the question. Framed, this scribbled message still hangs on the wall of Wheeler's office:

"Dear Bert [the President's spelling]:
"To verify my talk with you this morning I am very clear in my own mind that while clarifying or minor amendments to Section 11 [the death sentence clause] cannot be objected to—nevertheless any amendment which goes to the heart or major objective of Section 11 would strike at the bill itself and is wholly contrary to the recommendations of my message."

This working relationship could not last. For one thing Wheeler heard that the then attorney general, Homer Cummings, still kept in the files the Wheeler dossier. And certain of Wheeler's Montana enemies, conspicuously the lawyer-lobbyist Bruce Kremer, walked familiarly in and out of the Department of Justice. The break came over the President's scheme to remake the Supreme Court, but if that had not been the cause something else would have. The man from Montana developed an appetite for opposition. He fought the President on the reorganization bill, which was an elemental measure for revising the cumbersome machinery of government. He was in opposition for the sake of opposition. Nineteen hundred and forty was at hand and the gossip said he had a chance for the Democratic nomination. His fanatically loyal wife saw him in the White House.

It was inevitable that he should oppose the President on the war issue. He read the mail that came to him and convinced himself that people were on his side. Gesturing with his long, loosely jointed, nervous hands, he would toss the letters across the desk at his doubting inquirers; letters that reflected his own bitterness, his own frustration.

Davis never came before Wheeler's committee. I have wondered often why he passed up that opportunity. I think he knew a great deal about his enemies, the "international combine," the "big companies." But perhaps it did not suit the Nazis' purpose to have it published just then. To have made it public might have interfered with a relationship that was still beneficial to Germany. The American public, if the facts had been known then, might have reacted the wrong way. It is entirely possible that Goebbels and the men around him may have weighed that question. Would it help to confirm American isolationism or would the American people rise up in wrath?

What Davis might have told—the facts about Standard's relations with Nazi Germany—did not come out until two years later. Thurman Arnold in testimony before the Truman committee was to put the shocking story in the record. Under the cartel agreement with I. G. Farbenindustrie, Standard had delivered over to the Nazis the secret of butyl rubber at the same time, as a memorandum plainly showed, that the details of the process were being kept from an officer of the United States Navy. In reply, Standard executives said that in compensation Standard had received many valuable patent secrets, but they could not make a convincing case. These disclosures came after Standard had finally entered into a consent decree to cease charging American firms high royalties for the right to make butyl rubber which was then in wide use by the German war machine.

These were revealing flashes in the Stygian depths of world oil politics. They were scarcely more than that. No one has ever descended there fully equipped with diving bell, oxygen tanks, lights, and camera. A great many pieces of the picture are still missing.

Shortly after the Mexican government had expropriated British and American oil properties, it became apparent that Germany intended to buy all of the "stolen" oil that could be carried across the Atlantic. This caused deep pain among the titans who direct the destinies of the big companies. It definitely was not cricket.

A pompous friend of Standard took it on himself to go to Germany to remonstrate with Hitler, Goering & Co. I would have given a great deal to have been present, as an invisible listener, at those interviews. They must have had a comic side. I can hear the large imposing director appealing to the better instincts of Hitler, Goering & Co. Surely, they must understand that such behavior is contrary to . . . well, contrary to orderly procedure. (That would have been a nice general phrase to use at that point.) Quotas? Quotas for Germany? Well, now that that subject had been raised, perhaps it could be gone into. Perhaps there had been some injustice in the past. Surely something could be worked out when men of good will sit down together around a table.

The brave words of the Atlantic Charter on natural resources are as follows: "They will endeavor, with due respect for their existing obligations, to further the enjoyment by all States, great or small, victor or vanquished, of access on equal terms, to the trade, and to the raw materials of the world which are needed for their economic prosperity." If that declaration is lived up to, it will mean almost a revolution in the department of oil alone. If it is not lived up to, or if some hypocritical rigmarole is gone through with, then it will have been worse than no declaration at all, for it will merely have fed the frustration that nurtures the political pathology of our time. It might almost be possible to work out an algebraic formula for this business of frustration. X-proliferating power plus Y-frustration equals Fascism or its equivalent.

You encounter it in unexpected places. I remember prowling through the record of a Senate investigating committee that had just revealed some horrendous facts about aluminum, or labor, or oil. What it was I can't now recall. Helping me find my way through the masses of evidence was one of those efficient young women who serve such committees. I said, rather naïvely I suppose, that now big things would undoubtedly happen.

"What!" she said, in a tone that plainly implied I was two times a simpleton. "You don't think anything's going to happen. Why this is just a Senate investigation. I've worked in four myself. And nothing ever happens."

Chapter XI

The Education of Wendell Willkie

IN THE whispering gallery that is Washington there was one
preoccupation in the spring of 1940 that almost overshadowed
the war in Europe. It was an election year and whether France
fell or whether England fell Americans would observe their in-
alienable right to choose a president. The question was the third
term. Only one man could answer that and those around the President said they honestly believed he did not know himself.

That an election should cut athwart the world crisis was one of
the ironies of the inflexible American system. But there it was and
it had to be got through with. The poisonous whisperers said that
the administration intended to suspend the elections and perpetuate
itself in power. That was part of the miasmal breath which all
through this period seemed to have its origin in the Axis swamp.

The wonder was that when the turmoil of the '40 election had
ended so little damage had been done. It was a proof, if any proof
had been needed, of the vigorous functioning of the American
political system even in a time of grave peril and uncertainty.

I had decided early, perhaps a year before the Democratic convention, that Roosevelt would run for re-election. The reasons, it
seemed to me, were obvious. Ruling out personal desires and the
exhilarating thought of the stature in history of the first third-
term president, you could imagine what was in the minds of
F.D.R. and those closest to him. They believed, as any reasonable
man must have believed at that point, that collaboration with Great
Britain was essential; not in the old isolationist, save-the-empire
sense at all; but with the realization that we were faced with the
most formidable foe in our entire history and that anything we
could do to hold off that foe we must do. If the Republicans were

193

to win, then isolationists, and isolationists in the narrowest sense of the word, would take over all the key positions in Congress.

No matter what the Republican President might believe with respect to the world crisis, he would have to cope with Hamilton Fish, for example, as chairman of the House Committee on Foreign Affairs; or should Fish decide to take instead the more powerful position of rules committee chairman, he would then have George Holden Tinkham on foreign affairs. In short, he would have two strikes on him before he got up to bat. You could call that a rationalization, but it happened to be the cold, hard fact. The Ham Fishes and the Tinkhams were aching to get into power. Incidentally it was at this time that Fish's office became a sort of congressional headquarters for the Nazi agent, George Sylvester Viereck.

Of course, there were also practical reasons why Roosevelt should run again. Politicians want to win elections. They are in politics to win. And there was apparently no other man in sight who could win. The third term was a risk, looking at it from the practical point of view of the bosses and politicos in the party, but it was not so great a risk as running one of the New Deal satellites.

It is just here, it seems to me, that the debate over the third term begins. If Roosevelt had not so completely dominated his own administration . . . If he had developed a man to succeed him . . . If he had been willing to step back . . . If . . . If . . . If . . . That is the way the argument will run, I believe.

There was no doubt that Roosevelt overshadowed the party just as he overshadows his time. But there were also men who might have been pushed forward if the President had been of a mind to push them. One of them was Robert H. Jackson who had seemed to me five years before to have a high political potential. I had watched him present the government's tax case against Andrew Mellon, as difficult and involved a legal action as could well be imagined, involving the vast structure of the Mellon empire and how it was put together and then taken apart.

Jackson, at that time counsel for the Bureau of Internal Revenue, was to rise rapidly. Along with a keen mind, he had a warm, pleasant personality; a disarming frankness and honesty. There had been reports in 1938 that Roosevelt wanted Jackson to run for governor of New York. This was to be part of the buildup. Then, so the New Dealers said, Jim Farley stepped in the way. Farley had his own ambitions. He was loyal to Roosevelt, dog loyal, but that same loyalty did not extend to the men whom the President had gathered around him. They were not the kind of men whom Farley understood or trusted. They were intellectuals, idea men, before they were politicians.

After a brief period as assistant attorney general in charge of antitrust prosecutions, during which time he brought Thurman Arnold into the government, Jackson became solicitor general. The solicitor general represents the government in the Supreme Court. He is the government's law specialist, in contrast with the attorney general who is primarily an administrative officer at the head of the big business that is the Department of Justice. In this office Jackson shone with such a luster that lawyers' lawyers could not remember his equal. Even the crusty conservatives on the Supreme Court respected his technical skill, the breadth of his law, even while they sniffed contemptuously at the New Deal arguments he presented.

In 1939, Jackson was appointed attorney general. The political gossip had it that this was a move to make him more conspicuous and therefore more eligible for the nomination in '40. While that may have been the intent, the effect was directly the opposite. The outstanding qualities that Jackson had were somehow lost in the vast administrative tangle of the D. J. with its twenty-four thousand lawyers, wardens, turnkeys, clerks, secretaries. True, he inherited the confusion left behind by his predecessor in office, Frank Murphy. But in any event he never got around to making the remedial changes he had talked about for so long. And he was unhappy in his complicated new job. He could be ticked off as a possible candidate.

Harry Hopkins had sent up a boomlet, going so far as to establish a residence in his home state of Iowa, returning to Grinnell, the old home town, to be photographed in homely simplicity. The

President, so Harry's friends said, had tapped him. Then there was Paul V. McNutt, he of the handsome visage and real, not make-believe, political past. You had to look hard to find any politics in the background of Jackson, Hopkins, or Henry Wallace, but McNutt had Indiana in his vest pocket. Unofficially McNutt launched his campaign when he flew back from the Philippines, where he was governor general, to give the Gargantuan cocktail party which he has never quite lived down. Thousands of guests, hogsheads of Martinis, tables groaning with those unhealthy little comestibles that are the sign of the mass cocktail party in Washington.

Jim Farley was the only candidate who without any stalling or fooling around told the world he wanted to run for President. He stuck to that all through the grim, grisly convention in Chicago. He was a candidate with a manager, a headquarters, two of everything. And only now and then did his smile crack a little at the edges. It was for "Big Jim" a heartbreaking ordeal. His was the simple logic of the professional politician. For all of his political life he had given Roosevelt complete and unswerving loyalty and now his friend owed him the same kind of loyalty. Instead his friend had decided to violate the rules and run for a third term. There were men around Farley who did him a distinct disservice by abetting his resentment and flattering his ambition.

Each morning in a room at the Stevens full of crystal chandeliers Farley received the press. Giving off wisecracks, as jaunty as ever, he knew nevertheless that while he still held the office of Democratic national chairman the real power was just across narrow Balboa Street in the Blackstone Hotel, where in a small bedroom opening off from a big living room done in sickly green and imperial purple Hopkins had a direct wire from the White House. Against overwhelming odds, Hopkins was trying to give a solemn, respectable look to a spectacle that could at best be counted a grim, inevitable choice in the face of a threatened world collapse.

The national schizophrenia was painfully evident in that convention. The New Dealers wanted to wind the whole thing up in two days or less and show the country that the Democratic party realized it was no time for bands and hoopla. But Farley was determined to go through with five days of conventioning and, if he could not have the nomination, at least he could dictate, as Democratic national chairman, the way the gathering should be run. And Mayor Kelly who was host had promised the hotels five days of business as part of the bargain that brought the Democrats to his city.

So for the better part of an uncomfortable week the motions were gone through with. The man who got all the dead cats and overripe tomatoes was Hopkins. I happened to be in his room when a delegation of indignant interventionists led by Herbert Agar came to call. They had heard that there was to be a compromise on the foreign affairs plank, an evasion of the issue of aid to Britain, and they railed at the slight, gray man who was the intermediary between the power a thousand miles away and the convention. Hopkins said little.

There was little that he could say. Once again it had been assumed that, in the face of a national election, the party would take on the neutral coloration that would make it possible for marchers of every shade of opinion to fall in.

Down the street at the Congress Hotel was a Wheeler-for-President headquarters. Three or four rooms were hung with photographs and posters. Pretty girls passed out Wheeler buttons. But the senator himself took all this with a certain cynicism. Publicly he insisted his name would go before the convention. When the time came for nominations, however, Montana was silent. Wheeler had stepped aside, unwilling for the sake of the record to go through with the form as Farley did.

Apparently he felt that the weak compromise plank on foreign affairs had been triumph enough. That plank contained empty rhetoric about not sending American boys to fight in foreign wars on foreign soil. Put in to appease Wheeler, Walsh, and the other isolationists in the party, this same obeisance to isolationist emotions was to recur throughout the campaign that followed.

On the night that Roosevelt was nominated a "demonstration" of sizable proportions was put on. In the hot, smoky atmosphere of the stadium, it had all the fine spontaneity of a parade ground formation. Mayor Kelly's director of sewers was discovered to have led the cheering from a master microphone concealed somewhere in the subterranean depths of the great hall. Banners emblazoned with huge photographs of Roosevelt were joggled up and down as sweaty demonstrators milled about in the viscous air.

It was not a pretty spectacle but undoubtedly it coincided with the desires of the great majority of delegates. Political commentators who wrote otherwise were merely indulging in wishful thinking. A large number of the delegates represented powerful state and city machines. These professionals were fairly certain of winning with Roosevelt. The President's choice of Wallace as a running mate did not please the pros. The boys from the Bronx had heard that he was an omphalos gazer who consulted the ghost of a Sioux Indian chief on difficult matters. But second place was merely a detail. They may have accepted the inevitable without enthusiasm, but the laborers in the Democratic vineyard went back home feeling fairly confident and relatively happy.

Chicago had been in painful contrast to the Republican get together at Philadelphia. A meteor had flashed across the political heavens in Philadelphia and the blaze of light had sent a quickening excitement across the country. Jealous Democrats said it had been rigged up, with Wall Street paying for the fireworks and directing their display. But no amount of carping could conceal the fact that an exciting new personality had jumped with both feet onto the national stage.

Willkie's reputation had been expanding for two or three years. The build-up had been carefully engineered, no doubt of that. When the moment arrived, however, the man himself burst through the trappings with the full force of his strong will. And if the convention was stage-managed to end in a close heat with victory for Willkie, as the Democrats were to whisper, Willkie himself gave no evidence of having heard about it.

During that week in Philadelphia he was sustained by coffee, cigarettes, and the tension that mounted as the hour of balloting drew near. I had not known Willkie before Philadelphia. Duke

Shoop of the Kansas City *Star* took me over to his headquarters in the Benjamin Franklin Hotel and we pushed our way through the eager hangers-on to find in the inner sanctum a big, square-jawed man with rumpled hair who looked as though he had not slept for thirty-six hours—as he had not.

"I don't know," he said in the warm, husky voice that was so appealing when you heard it at first hand, "how this thing is going to turn out. I think I've got a good chance but I don't want to say any more than that at this time."

An incident occurred while we were with him that was prophetic of the struggles Willkie was to have with the determined amateurs who surrounded him. Over the protests of one of these amateurs several news photographers came into the room to make some special shots of Willkie, an arrangement that had been previously agreed to. The debate became shrill and acrimonious as we tried to talk on the other side of the room with the defender of the great man plainly losing his temper, something you must never do with news photographers as Willkie himself well knew. After two or three minutes he stepped over to end the dispute. "Now look, Joe," he said to his friend, "you're very tired. I want you to go down to your room and sleep for twelve hours. There's one thing we can't afford and that's to have anybody lose his temper." Sheepishly the valiant amateur retired and the news photographers went to work.

In spite of the efforts of his eager champions, or it may have been because of them, Willkie won the horse race at Philadelphia. Certainly that was one of his assets. He was as fresh as paint with no color of professionalism. Americans who spoke disparagingly of "politics" and "politicians" could now vote for a man who was as innocent as a babe of any political background.

In the thrill of Philadelphia you could almost forget momentarily the horrors across the Atlantic. The station wagon set had come down from New York for the big show. The town was gay with the right hats. There were good parties all over the place.

A convention of politicians is also a convention of newspaper men. The talk never ends, good talk, full of loud, ribald laughter.

We saw each other at closer range than in Washington. Each convention time, I came to have a new respect for the judgment of Raymond P. Brandt of the *Post-Dispatch* Washington bureau for whom and with whom I worked. His is a judgment formed on twenty years of Washington and it is merciless and sure. Then there is that veteran of veterans, Henry Hyde of the Baltimore *Evening Sun* who for nearly fifty years has been chasing political fires with the same miraculous enthusiasm. With him always is round, owlish-eyed H. L. Mencken who collects conventions with the zeal of an antiquarian. Someone always has a new story, a new rumor, a tender new canard. There are feverish and futile expeditions to smoke-filled rooms where great things are allegedly afoot. Sleep is forsworn. And when there is nothing else to do, the convention itself offers a mild entertainment.

Willkie appeared in person at the last session at Philadelphia. It was a good show. He had a dynamic youthful quality, a simple directness, that broke through the hackneyed pattern of the political convention. A high moment, indeed, it was perhaps *the* high moment of the entire Willkie campaign. The Democratic performance that followed in Chicago seemed by contrast even more stale and empty than it was.

The relentless surge of events across the Atlantic inevitably pushed politics aside. President Roosevelt called on Congress to pass the draft act. Even though it was an election year, this could not wait. Nor was there any inclination, except on the part of the die-hard minority, to make the draft a political issue. Willkie approved its passage as did most other responsible Republican leaders.

There were reasons other than political for opposing the draft act. A military critic of the rank of Hanson Baldwin of the New York *Times* pointed to the need for a highly trained mechanized force rather than for a mass army. He pointed out that the building of cantonments throughout the country would take men and materials that might be better used in immediately equipping a smaller force. It was a cogent argument, the force of which was not entirely obvious until the draftees were installed in the raw new camps with little or nothing to do and little or nothing to do it with.

The draft act was adopted on September 16, 1940. While it had been debated for a considerable time, not then or for many months later were its implications faced. We took this step by indirection. The word defense came to be the key word in our vocabulary. At the same time that the slow machinery of the draft was being put in motion and the training centers were being planned, the campaign orators had begun to talk about "foreign wars" and the American boys who must never be allowed to jeopardize their lives on foreign soil. We wanted to go on believing that virtuous, isolated America could have no part in the vile world's quarrel.

In a political year there were not alone military considerations in the steps the administration took to prepare for "defense." Part of the propaganda was that Roosevelt and the New Dealers wanted to take the country into a war of their own making. It would be a New Deal war and under the false threat of that war Roosevelt would perpetuate the New Deal in office for another four years; a powerful propaganda line, the weight of which was to be felt long after the election.

When little Harry Woodring was summoned to the White House and told that he must resign, his adversary, Assistant Secretary of War Louis Johnson, assumed he would succeed to the office. The President had told him that he would get it, if and when Woodring stepped down. But the President had other plans.

He had asked Henry L. Stimson to be secretary of war. Stimson at seventy-three was an eminently respectable Republican who had been the head and front of the group in America that opposed Axis aggression. His moral imperative was as clear and as certain as that of Cordell Hull. It had in fact been enunciated in 1931 when Stimson, as secretary of state, sought to persuade the British to stand up against the Japanese who were then on the first lap of their avowed world conquest. Stimson had taken a strong stand on the Japanese invasion of Manchukuo and it was a galling and humiliating experience to have the British let him down. Sir John Simon in the Foreign Office in London was making the same old

moves on the same old chess board of power politics. Ever since
that failure and humiliation Stimson had followed with growing
anger and indignation the Axis successes. He was to come into the
Roosevelt cabinet out of a sense of patriotic duty, aware perhaps
of the political implications of his appointment but convinced too
that in such a crisis political considerations were decidedly secondary.

To the vacant post of Secretary of the Navy the President named
another eminently respectable Republican, Colonel Frank L. Knox
who had been the G.O.P. candidate for Vice-President four years
before. There were reports that several other Republicans had
first been offered this post. But Knox, if he knew this, harbored
no minor resentments. He too was happy to accept. It would give
him not only an opportunity to exercise his strenuous patriotism,
modeled after that of his patron saint, Theodore Roosevelt, but it
would also bring him into the larger sphere for which he had long
felt himself suited. At sixty-six the good colonel was full of a
jaunty optimism that soon took within its broad compass the Navy
and all its symbols and accouterments. It was a job to his liking
and he made the most of it. In a short time he had far more
grizzled and seagoing a mien than even the veteran admirals.

With that cunning sense of timing which he has displayed
throughout his political career, the President announced Knox's
appointment on the second day of the Republican convention in
Philadelphia when tempers and temperatures were running high.
The news was received in Philadelphia with loud and angry cries.
Knox was guilty of treachery and he was roundly denounced by
all the right-thinking in convention assembled. While this was
going on, the doughty colonel far from the strife and sweat of
Philadelphia was playing golf in New Hampshire. He enjoyed
the joke almost as much as the President.

No matter what the Republicans might say about the inclusion
of these decoys in the Cabinet, the fact was that they gave to the
Roosevelt administration a different coloration. As Secretary of
War, Stimson took some of the curse off the draft act. It was an
unprecedented thing to do in peace time—to conscript the youth of

the nation. With Stimson and Knox in office this seemed more nearly the act of a national, rather than a partisan, administration. This impression was of course carefully fostered as the election drew nearer.

In the summer, before the fury of the campaign had begun, the President took one of those bold steps which now and then he executes with such masterly skill. While there had been printed rumors in advance, the exchange of fifty destroyers for bases in the Atlantic burst with dramatic suddenness on the public. It was a transaction that satisfied almost every public desire. While England was given material aid in her struggle against desperate odds, this could not be accounted the principal motive for the transaction, since in exchange we were granted the right to construct a chain of bases on English soil from Newfoundland south to British Guiana. Even the die-hard Chicago *Tribune* could approve the destroyer deal, going so far as to claim credit for its origin. It strengthened our sense of defensive security at the same time that it eased our conscience in the light of the terrible news that came from blitzed Britain. Seldom has the President's creative imagination found a more happy outlet.

Against this background the campaign of 1940 began. Willkie had gone to Elwood, Indiana, and there his acceptance speech had been something of a diminution from the high pinnacle of enthusiasm of Philadelphia. The qualities that he was to display throughout the campaign were already obvious. He had a supreme self-confidence in his own powers. It was a self-confidence that transcended all advice, but especially he was suspicious of professional politicians. His was to be a new kind of campaign. The American people were tired of politics, tired of the old political speeches.

This went for small things as well as big. While he was still at Elwood, a friend from Washington had tried to persuade the candidate to take some lessons in voice placement. It would save his energy in the ordeal that was to come, the friend argued, and make it possible to speak oftener and with greater ease. Willkie would have none of this. It was sissy stuff, he said. The American people were tired of a smooth voice and a Groton-Harvard accent.

That was just before the start of the long swing to the West coast. In Chicago Willkie's voice grew rasping. Roaring like the bull of Bashan all through downstate Illinois the next day, his voice grew hoarser and hoarser. At Rock Island it was only a pathetic croak and panic seized his advisers as they feared that his throat had been so strained that he might be unable to speak for days to come. Without Willkie's knowledge telegrams were hastily dispatched to famous throat physicians in various parts of the country. The first to reach the ailing candidate was a noted specialist from Chicago. Considerable persuasion was required before Willkie would even see the man. He didn't need a doctor, he croaked. When the famous physician was finally admitted he was treated by the patient with scant courtesy. Departing indignantly, he muttered that what that man needed was not a doctor but a policeman.

From Hollywood another specialist had been summoned. Doctor Harold Gray Barnard of Beverly Hills, accustomed to treating the throats of radio and motion-picture stars, was better equipped to handle the temperamental Willkie. The energetic Doctor Barnard became a fixture on the train, fussing over Willkie like a mother hen charged with responsibility for a bold and astonishing duck. After he became reconciled to the idea of a doctor, a symbol of weakness and softness, as Willkie had first interpreted it, the candidate even welcomed the attentions of the throat specialist.

Willkie is an incorrigible talker. He would campaign all day, often speaking from street corner to street corner like an aldermanic candidate, yet at eleven-thirty or midnight he would go on talking so long as he had an audience of one in his private car. Little Doctor Barnard would stand unhappily at the edge of a knot of people while Willkie's hoarse voice rasped on. "My God, I can't make him stop," he would moan pitifully. "He goes right on night and day."

Willkie is a man of tremendous force of will. In a small way, this was demonstrated when, after a brief rest in Kansas City, he overcame what had been almost a paralysis of the muscles of his throat and went on to make on schedule one of the most important speeches of his campaign. He is also a man of tremendous partisanship. With Willkie there are no shadings of gray. You are either for him or against him and he simply cannot understand it, if, granted you are a fairly normal human being, you are not with him.

This is of course the mark of the amateur in politics. The professional takes his opposition with far more philosophy and understanding. Very early Willkie had begun to alienate the professional Republicans. They simply did not speak the same language. Joe Martin, Republican leader in the House and soundly grounded in the politics of his native New England, would come away from a conference with Willkie troubled and unhappy, divided in his loyalty between this new and startling apparition and the familiar politics of the past. Among Martin's flock in the House an antipathy toward Willkie grew up which was almost greater than their hatred of Roosevelt. In the Republican cloakroom they cursed that so-and-so whom they had been duped into accepting at Philadelphia. Such reactionary isolationists as Dewey Short, aptly described as the Ham Fish of the Ozarks, could hardly be restrained by Martin from expressing openly their resentment and bitterness.

Thus between the amateurs and zealots who guided the Willkie campaign and the professionals a widening gulf was created. On the train was a good-natured, tame professional, Representative Charlie Halleck of Indiana, but he was largely window dressing. Smiling Charlie sat in on the conferences with the publishers and the high-powered publicists who were constantly advising Willkie, but he readily confessed that his voice in the councils was a small one. That, incidentally, is one minor conclusion which seems fairly obvious on the basis of Willkie's experience. Publishers make poor political advisers. They were always hopping on and off the campaign train, ready to pour out torrents of advice. They were working as hard as they could for Willkie and he was naturally inclined to take their advice.

His intense partisanship was to lead him into paths that might well have proved destructive. There was the dickering that led up to John L. Lewis's support on which Willkie himself pinned so much hope. Out of his relationship with Lewis in the course of his venture in Mexican oil, William Rhodes Davis had developed a friendship with the massive leader of the miners. Now Davis came forward and let it be known that he would put up the money to pay for a nation-wide radio hookup in which Lewis would declare for Willkie.

Although no definite assurances had come from the labor leader, Davis seemed supremely confident that he could deliver his friend. Delilah was confident that her Samson, who in the days when he organized the CIO had been a very great Samson indeed, would appear at the barber shop at the proper time. In New York was a very off-the-record meeting at which the terms of the deal were discussed. This followed earlier negotiations carried on by a go-between concerning Willkie's labor speech in Pittsburgh. Davis, whose Nazi connections had by that time been widely advertised, agreed to pay for the broadcast which would cost about fifty-five thousand dollars. The Hatch clean politics act was in force and to get around it the oil adventurer and his associates set up a kind of political black bourse, exchanging checks at a furious rate to insure that no one individual would be listed as giving more than five thousand dollars. Shrewd Republican lawyers scanned all these transactions, scrutinizing the checks with almost microscopic care to make sure that there was no technical violation of the law. Finally the money was siphoned through the Democrats-for-Willkie Club which was publicly listed as the sponsor of the Lewis broadcast.

The net effect of that broadcast appears to have been almost nil. Willkie's middle-class following was disturbed that the mahatma of labor should proclaim in such a Jovian voice his support of their man. But this was not sufficient to drive them out of the Willkie camp. On the other hand it is highly doubtful if any considerable number of labor votes were gained for the Republicans by Lewis's lurid performance. A small group personally loyal and others financially dependent on the big boy may have followed his lead but the number was small.

Willkie told me after it was all over that he had never heard of Davis before Sam Pryor, Republican National Committeeman for Connecticut, told him of the oil man's willingness to pay for the Lewis broadcast. It had simply appeared to him as a fortunate windfall. If it had been known to the Democrats at the time they might well have exploited the episode to Willkie's ruin. My feeling was that a candidate whose managers were about to accept so substantial a gift under such circumstances should have known more about the giver.

By that time Willkie was so passionately bent on winning that he did not want to ask any questions. In the same way, in the passionate heat of the moment he was led into saying things that later he would regret. Departing from his prepared manuscript again and again or ignoring it altogether, he would say to his audiences in the closing weeks—"You mothers, you fathers"—that Roosevelt if re-elected would have the boys on the transports on the way to a foreign war within three months. In the year that followed Willkie was to go a long way beyond this fiery partisanship. His education was to progress rapidly in the throes of a crisis which would brush aside all but the blindest or the meanest partisanship.

What struck me all through the campaign was that only a very little bit in the way of a positive, constructive program might have won for the Republicans. There were reports that Willkie was about to espouse the cause of the small business man; that he would take a strong stand for breaking up the big monopolies. This, so the report went, would have brought into his camp that volatile trust buster Thurman Arnold. I believe that such a move might have gone a long way toward turning the trick. People all over the country seemed to be waiting for something positive, something to hope for in the future.

Yet Willkie remained supremely confident that he could win by the very force of his personality. I remember a half a dozen of us had a session with him in his private car somewhere in Iowa on the way back from the West coast. Bob Sherrod of *Time* asked him, with respect to his pro-British foreign policy, what he would do once he were in the White House with such recalcitrants as

Ham Fish and the incredible Tinkham. Willkie brushed this aside impatiently, saying that once he was elected, with the power of the presidency behind him, such details could easily be taken care of. And I am sure he believed that. We from Washington looked skeptical.

That campaign swing was a rare experience. In the first place there was a grand crowd on the train. Dick Wilson of the Des Moines *Register-Tribune*, Bill Lawrence, then with the United Press, Jim Wright of the Buffalo *Evening News*, Tom Stokes for Scripps-Howard, Doris Fleeson of the New York *Daily News*, Shoop of the Kansas City *Star*—you could not ask for a better crowd. Four or five of us would meet in Jim Wright's drawing room for dinner about nine or nine-thirty to review the events of the day with a running commentary that was scarcely flattering to the principals. Talk in the dining car, or in someone's compartment lasted until four or five in the morning as we rolled across the vastness of America. I remember Henry Suydam of the Newark *Evening News* in a lyrical description of one of Ambassador Bullitt's fancier dinner parties in Moscow. It was at this same predawn session that a solemn editor from New York warned us that if Roosevelt were re-elected all land would be nationalized three months after his inauguration. Moreover, he believed it.

The drama of Willkie in action against the broad sweep of the American land was irresistible. Washington is at best an artificial city, divorced from the deeper realities of American life. It is like Hollywood in that all the inhabitants live on a single industry and that industry depends on the caprice of the public throughout the country. Washington is a state of mind and most newspaper men as well as most politicians welcome the chance to escape it occasionally. We were, of course, traveling at the end of a meteor at the speed of light, but nevertheless the strength of the land and of the people was borne in on us. "Only the strong can be free," Willkie said again and again, "and only the productive can be strong." You could not help but feel the productive strength of America, real or latent, and the man on the back platform with the raucous voice and the free gestures seemed to symbolize that strength.

Willkie seemed to be speaking in a moment of pause between two worlds, a moment of deliberate hesitation between one world and another. He said at the end of his Western tour that he saw the light of a spiritual hunger in the thousands of faces turned up to him and this was no mere political figure of speech. The people were puzzled and uncertain. They listened earnestly, hopeful, to what this big man from the East had to say.

When I got back to Washington, I tried to put something of this in a piece for the paper, something of the beauty and strength and loneliness of the great country I had seen again; in the mood of autumn, the mood of pause before change; the warm September sun that never once failed to shine on the crowds. Willkie weather, said the Republicans.

In the stockyards of Chicago men sat on fence rails along the sorting pens, men in leather jackets. They gave no sign of what they thought of the speaker who roared at them. They listened but without any expression whatsoever. Here was Carl Sandburg's hog butcher to the world, the air full of an acrid stench, a faint haze of smoke. Men in bloody aprons standing on the sidewalk to see the procession go by, grinning good-naturedly, turning back into the great cavernous plants. Downstate Illinois was a blaze of sunlight, the last full glow of summer shining on the comfortable-looking towns, Joliet, Galesburg, Peoria. Missouri was like that, too, and Kansas, comfortable and contented looking in this pause.

At Tulsa there had been drama, the kind of drama Willkie rises to; a huge outdoor stadium, a full moon, a vast crowd, and Willkie grown eloquent, carried along on the tide of his own free-flowing oratory. Amarillo was the morning heat of Texas and little boys jeering. In the small hill towns of New Mexico the people had a lost and lonely look. They had come from miles around for this rare event, a presidential candidate in search of their scattered votes. It was hard to believe that this quick-talking stranger from the East could know what they needed and wanted. Washington, and New York, too, were very far away. Albuquerque was drama again; "Viva Villkie!" splitting the air, the largest political meeting in the history of the state, the chairman said with pride; the floodlights, the crowd yipping and whooping with good-natured abandon.

In the early morning the gray sky was low over the Albuquerque airport and everyone, even amazingly enough Willkie, was in a subdued mood. The airport is a plateau above the brown, smoothed-off mountains, above the town. The three planes were ready, the take-off perfectly timed, at ten-minute intervals, one, two, three. Phoenix was a brief pause in flight. A rush from the airport in a long file of cars. Willkie under the fierce Arizona sun was sweating like a truck horse. Around the speaker's platform built before the big bank of bleachers they had massed the products of the region—bales of cotton, mounds of grapefruit and oranges, sides of beef, jars of honey. Professionals on the train grumbled because Willkie was wasting his time in a state with only three electoral votes. But such an argument would not make a dent on Willkie. This was America and he wanted to campaign in every corner of it.

March Field came with a rush through bumpy air, down into the heat, gray and brown hangars and burnished silver planes in ranks along the edge of the smooth carpet we landed on. You can never remember what Southern California is like, the waxy green of the orange groves, the endless highways lined with filling stations and cheeseburger stands, women in slacks, old women, young women, children in sun suits. The people in California seem somehow almost as luxuriant as the vegetation, filled to bursting with a kind of energy and enthusiasm that the visitor cannot cope with. We paraded for miles through the environs of Los Angeles, a nerve-racking assignment with near crashes at every main intersection.

At Fresno in the San Joaquin Valley, John Steinbeck's valley, the air was dry and full of a powder of dust, the sky blue and immense. Willkie spoke in a park in the center of town. People who had followed the parade, mostly children let out of school, spilled into the green, shaded area and clustered around the bandstand. Here and there men were lying on the grass, itinerant workers in ragged overalls, lying in a state of such indifference or exhaustion that they gave no sign they knew the crowd was there or the voice was speaking, lying with closed eyes while the scurrying youngsters dodged around them.

It was as though they had been barred from the normal, prosperous American world that Willkie addressed. They had accepted, it seemed, a kind of exile. And was that true, less dramatically, elsewhere? Was it only the decently dressed, middle class that came out to the train or the auditorium? Is there a class in America in economic and political exile? These were some of the questions that came to mind seeing the lifeless men there on the dusty grass.

San Francisco is another California. Arriving at night, the hills terraced with light and the pungent smell of low tide in the air, you have a sense of exhilaration that no other town in the country can give. At the end of every street is a breath-taking vista, the bay, the bridges, an expanse of sky at the top of one of San Francisco's hills. This was real drama, inherent drama, and the San Franciscans seemed to walk with conscious pride, knowing the quality of their city and not too excited about a presidential candidate campaigning on their street corners. In the late afternoon sun, the hills that roll back from the Golden Gate were tawny colored, the red of the bridge a warm terra cotta. And the wind blows strong off seven thousand miles of ocean.

Seen from a car window, sleepily, Lake Crescent in Oregon was incredibly blue with the dark pine slopes going up from it. Although the railway passes so close, it has an untouched look. Over Portland there was a smoke haze from the fires that came at the end of a dry summer and the great mountains, Rainier and Hood, were obscured in the blue haze. The Northwest has grown accustomed to visits of Presidents and presidential candidates. Tacoma was indifferent, the workers in a millyard stony cold. At Seattle the crowd was warmer, cheering wildly in a packed stadium. Crowds and crowd reaction, it is evident, mean little. So much depends on whether the crowd is hand-picked, what time of day it is, what day of the week. A candidate touring a city on Saturday afternoon, for example, will draw twice the crowd he would get on Monday morning.

The way back East by the northern route had seemed endless. There is so much empty space. Small things are remembered. Standing on the station platform at Missoula, Montana, I watched a girl come toward me, her eyes looking straight into mine with a look that had something of candor, something of contempt. "You can go on wearing that if you want to," she said, her eyes on the official Willkie badge on my lapel, "but it isn't going to do you any good." She hadn't even paused, saying this in a measured, deliberate voice full of youthful confidence, and pride, too, perhaps.

North Dakota was one long horizon, the waving grass stretching from sky to sky. By a curious inverse ratio like one of those laws in high school physics, more politicians climb on the candidate's train in sparsely settled country than in populous regions. There are few jobs that pay as much as the jobs in politics. Along the railroad right of way the ring-necked pheasants flew up into the light as the train rushed by. The progenitors of these pheasants were brought from Mongolia to settle down in perfect ease in the Dakotas.

No one could miss the richness of Iowa. The fall-plowed earth was black and soft under a gentle haze. Iowa is a much-maligned state, not flat, not dull, but rolling and lovely. The sun sets in Iowa with a long, lingering beauty, seen across fields in which the corn shocks march row on irregular row. Willkie spoke at noon in Iowa Falls, a peaceful town with a green square. Mrs. Sabra Calkins, aged ninety-four, who has seen most Presidents since Buchanan, had been brought out to hear him.

After Chicago it was a wild dash against time. The long special train thundered down through the Mohawk Valley in the late afternoon, faster than the Century, faster than the Broadway. Then the change to a plane, with minutes counting. The lights of Schenectady below. They are waiting, a national network, millions of listeners. And Willkie made it, to the rising and falling scream of the motorcycle sirens, made it with two and a half minutes to spare.

When it was over, I tried to write something of what I felt about that swing around America. Newspapers are pretty formalized and the tendency always is to keep what you write within the formal pattern. Breaking over with impressions that were highly personal, I was apprehensive. But a wire of warm congratulation from my managing editor, Ben Reese, was my reward. He said he thought it was the best piece of writing in the *Post-Dispatch* in a long time and that was praise from St. Hubert. Dour Fitzpatrick, whose Scottish skepticism goes into so many of his brilliant cartoons, wrote that I seemed to be taking a last lingering look at the corpse and I could see what he meant. I felt that the country was on the verge of a profound change. I think the people sensed it, too, that fall. Much in the America we had known was to go. A greater, richer, stronger America might come out of the ordeal ahead of us. Or we might forfeit our birthright, the wonderful heritage of spirit, of earth, of people. But nothing would be quite the same again. The high wind of change was in the air.

The election was a hurdle to be got over. And when it was over, a thankful sigh went up from Washington and from the country. Not in a day, however, would the bitter words spoken in that contest be forgotten. The dark cloud of rhetoric would linger on, blurring and confusing the issues. President Roosevelt took his campaign statements more seriously than his interventionist backers believed he would. It was one reason why the Axis could strike in its own time.

In the interval between election and inauguration I went on a lecture tour that extended across western Canada to Victoria. My wife and I soon discovered that Canadians were assuming that the pattern would be the same as in 1916 and 1917. They seemed to feel that we would be actively in the war by April or May of 1941 at the latest. In turn I tried to be as realistic as possible. I said everywhere I spoke that I felt there would be no change of status before June 30 at the earliest. I pointed out that Wheeler of Montana had been elected by a larger majority than he had ever received before, several times larger than that given the President in Montana; that Walsh of Massachusetts and other isolationists who had been re-elected would come back doubly determined "to keep us out of war."

The President and his frail friend and adviser, Harry Hopkins, had gone away together for a cruise. On deck, under the warm sun of the Caribbean, they evolved the lease-lend concept. By sustaining Britain with planes, guns, and tanks, meanwhile guarding our own shores, we should not have to fight abroad. This theme the President sounded again and again in the weeks that followed. The British were fighting our battle and it was up to us to furnish them with the sinews of war. It was a clever line, a disarming line, but those who accepted it literally were scarcely prepared for the grim realities to come.

Willkie went to England. It was the most brilliant stroke he had made since Philadelphia, and without knowing anything about what led up to the decision, I guessed that he had broken away from the advisers who had pulled and hauled at him all through the campaign and had stepped out on his own. His journey captured the imagination of people on both sides of the Atlantic. And it was the perfect answer to the ugly whispering campaign that implied he had pro-Nazi sympathies. In the factories and in the pubs Willkie met the defenders of Britain, a meeting which neither will soon forget.

Straight off the return clipper, he came to Washington for such a carefully staged drama as the capital delights in. The marble and crystal caucus room in the Senate Office building was crowded as it had never been crowded before. Even veteran senators who waited until near the hour set for Willkie's appearance found it difficult or impossible to break through the crowd at every entrance. Wizened little Carter Glass of Virginia was literally pulled through by guards to whom he had appealed.

For Willkie it was the perfect entrance and he made the most of it. He seemed to radiate assurance and determination as a lane was made for him into the packed hearing chamber. And he read his prepared statement in a warm, confident voice. Britain could

not have had a better advocate. There was only one embarrassment. That came when Bennett Clark and one or two other isolationists on the foreign affairs committee questioned Willkie about
statements he had made during the campaign: that Roosevelt's
re-election, for example, would mean sending American boys into
foreign wars. For a moment the witness appeared discomfited. He
ran his big hands through his rumpled hair.

"Why, senator," he said, "that was just a bit of campaign rhetoric
and you know it as well as I do."

For a moment he looked a little shamefaced, like a small boy
who has been made to confess to teacher. But this could not daunt
his exuberant assurance for long. If nothing else, a strong sense of
righteousness would have sustained him. He had learned a great
deal in a short space of time.

A few nights later some of us who had been on the campaign
train with him gave him a dinner. In the reunion was something
of the excitement and the humor of that barn-storming tour. On
such an occasion Willkie is at his best. His talk is frank and unin-
hibited, salted with his convictions and prejudices freely and
bluntly expressed. He loves it, talking with men in a room through
a long, convivial evening. His trip to England had made him
more serious, more convinced of America's duty and responsibility.

"It's all right to talk about collaboration with Great Britain
now," said Jay Hayden of the Detroit *News*, shrewdly drawing
him out. "But don't you think that when this war is over the Republican party is going back to isolation. They always have and
they always will."

Without a moment's hesitation Willkie came back with an
answer for that one.

"Look," he said, his index finger raised in the familiar admoni-
tory gesture, "if we go back, it will be so far back that neither you
nor I nor anyone in this room can be a party to it. It will be way
back. We can never let that happen."

Yes, he had learned. He had learned that the conservative
party under a two-party system cannot afford the luxury of reaction. It must offer a positive policy as an alternative to the policies

of the party in power. That was the lesson which the parties on the right in Germany never learned—and the result was Hitler. Thenceforward Willkie was to wrestle manfully with the Republican party, seeking to convert the more bigoted and stubborn elements in the great lump of the G.O.P. to enlightenment. Whether he will succeed is still a question. And on the answer depends not a little the future of Americans everywhere.

Chapter XII

Politics and Prices

YOU could write off 1940. That was an election year. What happened, or rather failed to happen, in 1941 is more difficult to explain. A classic newspaper story is about the cub reporter sent out to cover a train wreck. Arriving at the scene of action, he was so overwhelmed by what he saw that he sent back the following laconic message to his managing editor, "Sorry all is confusion. Will be unable to file story."

It was a little the way we felt in Washington in 1941. Almost every story reflected the uncertainty in the capital. A fog of confusion lay as thick as a blanket over everything. Here and there you could dig in and get a particular set of facts, but they seemed unrelated to anything else that was going on. No one seemed to have the power or the will to bring form and substance out of this void.

The tempo was incredibly slow; like a slow-motion picture taken in a friendly lunatic asylum. The debate over lend-lease aid for Great Britain was in large part a repetition of the debate over the revision of the neutrality act. Sitting in the Senate press gallery, you had the feeling that this was where you had come in once a long time before. Not until March 11 was the first lend-lease administration for Britain established after final authorization by Congress.

Even with formal approval by Congress and the President, myriad obstacles seemed to stand in the way. On the basis of their experience in the war, the British wanted certain types of military equipment. They wanted antiaircraft guns of 3.7 inches with a ceiling six thousand feet higher than the American gun. In the tanks which we proposed to build for them they wanted guns of not less than fifty millimeters.

Based on actual experience in modern warfare, these requests seemed reasonable enough, yet members of the British military mission that was quickly established in Washington found themselves involved in a long-drawn-out controversy with the officers of our ordnance division. The latter insisted upon thirty-seven millimeter tank guns. If on British persuasion they finally agreed to follow British specifications, it was only on condition that they first proceed with pilot models and go through routine tests, a ponderous, lengthy process meaning months of delay before mass production.

Keen young British experts were tremendously disturbed over this time wasting. Appeal to their superiors was of little avail since the men at the top wanted at that point to do everything possible to avoid giving offense to their opposite numbers in the War Department. So the irritating debate went on month after month. Into the first tanks produced for the British went thirty-seven-millimeter guns. In the big offensive on the Libyan front in September of 1941 it was plainly demonstrated that these tanks lacked sufficient fire power and while the loss was somewhat made up for by their great maneuverability and by the skill of the men who handled them, it was not enough. Slowly, painfully, Washington was learning that every act has its consequence and that that consequence may be deadly.

The British fumed angrily at armchair colonels who debated practical knowledge acquired in combat experience. But their behavior was perfectly normal and natural in the light of their conditioning and background. Starved for funds, moving up slowly by the inevitable process of seniority, they had had an infinity of time for testing and experimenting and designing new models to supplant old models. It was unreasonable to expect them to develop overnight into bold pioneers, able to shear through the swaddling of red tape in which their official lives had been confined.

Yet the urgency of the crisis made itself felt like a consuming fire, the breath of the flames coming ever closer. The result was sometimes pitiful. I remember an unhappy armchair colonel squirming under a House military affairs inquisition. He had been in charge of some phase of the vast program of expansion, and moving in his customary way and at his customary tempo he had made glaring mistakes. The poor man was all but unnerved. He had been transferred to an innocuous position in the Quartermaster Corps but this did not save him from having to try to explain away his mistakes before the committee.

Not by any means was it the military alone that stood suddenly and pitifully exposed as deficient in the superlative qualities called for by the revolution raging in the rest of the world. The same painful deficiencies developed everywhere one looked.

The spring of 1941 marked the real beginning of the mushroom expansion of wartime Washington. With astonishing rapidity the members of the National Defense Advisory Council put together their staffs, already beginning the duplication and overlapping of effort which were to be such an unhappy feature of the wartime landscape in the capital. Within the Council the Office of Production Management was created to be a sort of board of overseers at the top.

At the head of OPM were those curious twins, Director General William S. Knudsen and Associate Director General Sidney Hillman. Knudsen, despite his resounding title and the munificent authority vested in him, was plagued by a sense of uncertainty. He was a production man, a brilliant production man. All his life he had worked for a board of directors, a boss. From his boss he had taken orders. In the field of high policy he was completely at a loss and it was cruel to force him into that role.

Knudsen would go to the White House with his hat in his hand. He would say to the President in his pleasant crotchety accent that made him sound more like Jean Hersholt than Jean Hersholt, "Now look, Boss, I wonder if we shouldn't do so-and-so. I want to give the orders but first I wanted to talk with you." The President would thereupon take the responsibility for whatever decision had been batted up to him. He would tell Bill Knudsen that in a few days or a week he would let him know. Thus would important decisions be deferred and delays accumulate. A different type of man might have assumed authority and thereby have carved for himself a commanding position. But this was not in the Knudsen temperament.

As though to compensate for the authority he failed to exercise, he took to making speeches. The trick was to be turned by words. High and low, they were all making speeches. The enemy was to be exorcised by rhetoric. Many of the men closest to the President, Felix Frankfurter, Archibald MacLeish, Robert Sherwood, were word men, brilliant word men. There was no lack of words. The deficiencies were all on the practical, production side.

Director General Knudsen's associate director general, Sidney Hillman, also behaved according to form. For thirty years or more he had been involved in the intricacies of labor politics and that was what he knew. His appointment had been an effort to strike a compromise between the A. F. of L. and the C.I.O., but as it turned out neither side had any very deep trust in the harried Mr. Hillman. Over one small dispute after another he fidgeted, succeeding usually in alienating both sides to the controversy. Achieving a succession of compromises that may have been inevitable, he nevertheless weakened his already insecure position. Aware of his insecurity, he struggled to aggrandize his power. The spectacle was an unhappy one. In the light of all this it was not surprising that when a director of man power mobilization was finally named it was not Hillman, part of whose job this had presumably been, but Paul McNutt who got it, McNutt having demonstrated that in a pinch he could do a job. That appointment did not come until April of 1942 at the end of a prolonged rivalry for the place.

Meanwhile in the summer of 1941 war production levels moved up, when they moved at all, by infinitesimal degrees. Shipments to Britain were a thin trickle that threatened to cease altogether. Only one commodity, food, was shipped in large quantities to England and that was thanks to the heroic efforts of Milo Perkins, then surplus marketing administrator. In a remarkably short time he had accumulated stocks of butter, cheese, eggs, pork, and vegetables for shipment abroad. Taking both price levels and domestic

whole of American life. Out of increased government spending was developing the greatest of all American booms; more motor cars, more refrigerators, more typewriters, more of everything than ever before. Here was the urgency. Sensing the long winter of war closing down, business worked at high pressure to produce for a market that seemed insatiable.

Within the defense organization a faction had grown up opposed to this orgy of civilian production. Ironically enough, its principals were in Leon Henderson's division; men such as Joseph Weiner, head of civilian supply, who argued not for more for the civil population but for less. This was the major difference between the New Dealers and their kind and the dollar-a-year men who overflowed the vast new Social Security building. The feud grew in bitterness as the boom developed. Each curtailment order represented a long and painful struggle.

Aluminum was first. Edward Stettinius had announced, on the basis of a report by the industry, that there would be ample aluminum. The New Deal economists said no. Internecine warfare went on for weeks. Stettinius revised his original opinion and the use of aluminum by civilians was at first curtailed and then abolished. The same little drama raged over steel with the same outcome. The New Dealers said bitterly that the dollar-a-year men were only in government to protect the special interests they represented. And the dollar-a-year boys replied that the New Dealers were out to destroy private enterprise.

Around the auto industry the Indians and the cowboys fought a new campaign. Each order was preceded by a major battle. While chromium was increasingly tight, over a proposal to ban brightwork the tug-of-war went on for days. Knudsen, said the New Dealers, was protecting the industry, and the industry wanted to go on just as usual regardless of the threat of war. Poor Knudsen was increasingly unhappy.

On the one side were his former bosses who *did* want to go on producing automobiles. And on the other side was his present boss, F.D.R., and what he wanted, Knudsen was never sure.

The order banning brightwork did not come until late October.

A similar struggle occurred over a series of curtailment orders. When representatives of the motor manufacturers met at the end of December under a fiat of complete conversion within thirty days, they had no plans ready. At the end of the road it was necessary to improvise hastily to meet an imperative necessity that had been there all the time.

In the quarrel between the New Dealers and the dollar-a-year men Hopkins was a kind of umpire. Given his predilections and background, his decisions were usually for the New Deal team. But he could defend business men, too, particularly those he had adopted. Taking Stettinius under his wing, he had him made lease-lend administrator, and with a salary. That last was one point Hopkins had insisted on. You're too blankety-blank good to be a dollar-a-year man, Ed, he told him, half laughing, half serious. With this account of his initiation into the New Deal tribe, Stettinius shocked and amused his fellow business men in Washington.

It came down to a quarrel over production figures. Knudsen presented the President with one set. Not long afterward Senator Byrd of Virginia gave out another set that showed a pathetic lag in almost every department. The President was naturally inclined to believe his own man. At that point Wayne Coy, an uncompromising realist who bossed the Office of Emergency Management, Robert Nathan, a tough-minded figure hound, and two or three others saw to it that the President got no estimates or allocations or dizzy contract figures but the real production totals. The ugly truth was that Byrd had been much nearer right than Knudsen. Out of this discovery came the Victory Program which called for sixty thousand planes and forty-five thousand tanks in 1942 and double that in 1943. At least the sights were raised even though the fumbling continued.

With the boom went increasing concentration in those great industrial firms that were already self-sufficient empires. This may have been inevitable. Certainly it was the simplest way; to feed out contracts to Bethlehem Steel, United States Steel, American Car and Foundry, the giants of American industry with the engineering and the technical skill immediately at hand. At the same time they were supplied with funds from a subsidiary of the Reconstruction Finance Corporation for plant expansion. Orders on the books of these companies, as the billions were allocated, extended one, two, three years in advance.

Within the defense organization, however, were men who believed that the job could not be done merely by piling orders on the big firms. Morris L. Cooke, an industrial engineer with a liberal slant, insisted that only by bringing in thousands of small firms through a carefully worked out system of subcontracting could sufficient production be obtained in time. He cited British experience in pushing a "bits and pieces" program under which prime contractors farmed out literally hundreds of small jobs. Of course, it was harder and it was less profitable. But the British had been driven to it after Dunkerque when they had had to re-equip an entire army. Within the defense organization Cooke was an evangel for farming out contracts so that all machines and all men everywhere would be put to work. In the special branch finally created to push this objective Cooke was ignored and somewhere within an overorganized organization the move for farming out came to little.

The concentration was to continue. Figures released by the War Production Board in April, 1942, showed that about 350 firms held 85 per cent of the $100,000,000,000 in contracts which had been awarded up to that point. These firms, among them all the industrial giants, have some 900 contracts calling for $85,000,000,000 of war materiel. There are an additional 5,100 prime contracts for planes, ships, tanks, guns, and munitions, but these contracts cover only about 15 per cent of the hundred billion. Between 40,000 and 60,000 subcontracts have been let by prime contract holders, thereby bringing in another 186,000 manufacturing plants. At least 125,000 plants were left without any war contracts whatsoever. And Donald Nelson said at that time that industrial casualties were inevitable, just as inevitable as casualties in the field. But perhaps if there had been really thorough energetic direction a year before, or a year and a half before, the casualty rate would not have been so high.

Statistics tell nothing of what this concentration means in terms of human beings. On the one hand it means communities drained of their economic sustenance, stripped, perhaps, of vital machine tools; stagnation, decay, followed by collapse into complete government dependence, ghost towns. And on the other hand it means hideous overcrowding in present industrial areas with emergency housing never able to catch up to the demand. It means a complete unbalance of the labor supply as between one region and another and one industry and another. It means a postwar problem of supercolossal dimensions.

A useful House committee, formed originally to study agricultural migration resulting from the factory farm system, has tried to show what centralization of war work will mean to American life. Under the chairmanship of Representative John H. Tolan of California, the committee held hearings in widely separated areas on what the vast dislocation caused by defense billions had begun to mean. Men were being drained off the land all over the country. Men and their families were moving from one coast to the other. Old roots were being torn up. Raw new communities were springing up overnight. Thousands upon thousands of words put into the committee's record gave this picture of America in upheaval.

As far-reaching as were the effects of this new industrial revolution, a still more profound force was at work. The upward movement of prices, gradual at first, subtle and unseen, measured only by the economist's measuring rod, then gaining swift momentum, threatened to destroy the very fabric of American life. Here was a force that touched every man, woman, and child. The very, very rich might hope to escape, at least until the political consequences of inflation should catch up with them. The middle class would certainly be destroyed. And the great mass of the American people would know grinding hardship and terrible insecurity. Here was a force as destructive as war itself; as complicated, as charged with prejudice and fear.

In 1940 the rise in the cost of living was comparatively small.

Not until the defense boom got going in July and August of 1941 did the barometer of prices begin to rise so sharply that no housewife could fail to observe it. On July 30 the President asked Congress for price-control legislation. He wanted selective price control; control of certain commodities that entered into the cost of living as opposed to an over-all price ceiling that would fix wages and prices as of a date chosen arbitrarily from the period immediately preceding.

The President's request precipitated a political wrangle that lasted for more than six months. And during that six months the cost of living inched up until in February of 1942 it was nearly 15 per cent higher than it had been in August of 1939. Moreover, this percentage figure of the Bureau of Labor Statistics only partially reflected what the housewife discovered each time she went to market.

Within the administration it was taken for granted that it was politically impossible to put through Congress an over-all price ceiling. Organized labor would never tolerate the freezing of wages at a fixed level. In any event, New Deal economists such as Isador Lubin didn't want an over-all ceiling. They argued that such a ceiling would work a hardship on labor. Labor costs, so their argument went, were not the cause of price increases. Prices went up before wages increased while at the same time, with industrial expansion, the cost of the amount of labor going into each individual unit went down. Wage increases, it was argued, could come out of increased profits or high salaries. "By fixing prices," said Lubin, "we shall in fact fix some sort of maximum wage levels, by limiting the amount the employer can pay."

This became the official administration line. In the marathon hearings that began before the House Banking and Currency Committee all administration witnesses took substantially the same point of view. And it had a persuasive sound with the financial pages of the newspapers reporting from day to day new profit peaks, new high dividends, and new salary increases.

What this thesis overlooked was the political explosive inherent in anything less than an over-all ceiling. The powerful farm bloc promptly took the attitude that if wages were not to be covered in, then major concessions would have to be made to farm prices. Not parity but 110 per cent of parity prices was the demand of the organized farm group in Congress. Organized labor might be able to protect itself in the race between wages and prices, although it was doubtful whether wages could ever move up fast enough. Under the pressure of wage demands, the employer would press for price increases and the government price controller would have to have the strength of Hercules and the patience of Job to be able equitably to end the race. And what about the millions of unorganized workers with no bargaining power? What about white-collar workers, teachers, firemen, policemen? They could not press for those maximum wage levels fixed by the limit the employer could pay.

The witness to voice most powerfully the need for an over-all ceiling which would leave little to the discretion of an administrator was Bernard M. Baruch. Like another Moses, tall, silver-haired, he appeared before the committee to say in clear, unmistakable language why he favored over-all control. It would, he said, be fair to all men. It would be simple to administer. It would control prices which anything less could not do. Answering his critics, he said that it was not inflexible; wages that were too low could be adjusted beneath the ceiling; regional adjustments would be possible. And along with this ceiling, he stated plainly, went other controls; most important of all, high taxes that would mop up excess profits and excess purchasing power.

This was irreducible logic etched on tablets of stone. When Leon Henderson was asked about the "Baruch plan," his answer was that it was sound in theory but that in actual practice it would be all but impossible to administer. What made it harder to say this was that Baruch had endorsed Henderson personally. The older man admired the younger man's tenacity and courage. He told the committee that Henderson was the man to administer prices, knowing, of course, that the conservative majority on the committee and in Congress would have liked to hear another opinion.

Henderson was strangely suspect. The committee put him

through an ordeal comparable to the Ojibway Indians' trial by torture. Day after day after day it went on. Under it the victim, who
had the reputation of being a mercurial, hot-tempered fellow,
showed unflagging patience and fortitude.

The committee members took the victim in turn, each one developing his or her specialty. Miss Jessie Sumner, a Republican
from Illinois, a long time before had had an elementary course in
economics at Smith College from which she has never entirely
recovered. Miss Sumner proceeded to put Henderson through that
course. Now Mr. Henderson, she said, shaking her finger at him
in the manner of a schoolteacher, I want you to define the law of
supply and demand. The witness allowed that that might be
rather difficult and time-killing. But isn't it true, she persisted, that
the law of supply and demand is just as good as the law of gravity?
The witness, solemn-faced, went on to make a few well-chosen
remarks about the law of supply and demand as compared to the
law of gravity.

This was merely comic. The way in which Henderson's racial
background was pried into was not comic. On the floor of the
House, Representative Cox of Georgia had given currency to a
persistent rumor when he referred to the price administrator as
"that man who goes under the alias of Leon Henderson." A whispering campaign, with origins that might well have been traced
back to the Axis, had it that Henderson, a Jew, had changed his
name to conceal his religion.

At some length Henderson was interrogated on this by the committee. He said that his father's name had been Henderson and
his grandfather's. He had seen his grandfather's tombstone and
it said on it Leon Henderson. His grandfather had fought on the
Union side in the Civil War. If the name had ever been changed,
he knew nothing about it. These questions he answered with the
same patience and courtesy that marked his entire appearance
before the committee. It might have been a Nazi racial court, so
shameful was this performance.

The truth is that whatever his religious or racial origins Henderson's story is straight out of the American tradition. He was

born forty-seven years ago in Millville, New Jersey, into a family so poor that it was a question whether he should quit school after the eighth grade and go to work to help augment the household income. The deciding voice was that of his Grandmother Beebe, a determined old lady who saw things in the young Leon that no one else discerned.

Of course, he would have to work his way through high school and after that, if he was so bold as to try, through college. But nothing daunted, the lad with the shock of black hair and the ready grin got himself three jobs to begin with. At dawn he delivered the Millville *Republican*. Two hours later he collected the neighborhood children and drove them to school. At noon he took down the telephoned United Press report in the Millville *Republican* office. At 2:20 he dashed from school for another ten minutes with the United Press. Then, when school was out, he collected the kids from his neighborhood. And finally when that job was done, he bicycled back to town to play, depending on the season, basketball, baseball, football, or track.

At Swarthmore College he worked at every kind of job from baby-tending to secretary to earn his way. Swarthmore was for Henderson the first taste of something like ease and luxury and he flourished there. In 1917, a junior, he enlisted in the Ordnance Corps. His rise in the army was almost as rapid as his upward climb at Swarthmore had been. In January, 1918, he was made a second lieutenant and, upon transfer to the War Department's property-accounting division in Washington, a captain. Returning to Swarthmore, he combined his senior year with teaching at the University of Pennsylvania.

Economics was Henderson's field and for two years after graduation he taught at Swarthmore and Pennsylvania. From there he went to Carnegie Tech at Pittsburgh. Believing that economics should be taught not from textbook theory so much as through direct experience with living, he used Pittsburgh with its vast steel industry as a laboratory for his students. When his methods became too unorthodox for conservative Tech, Henderson resigned. For a time he went with the Russell Sage Foundation. Later he served in Gifford Pinchot's enlightened administration in Pennsylvania. And from there he went to Washington and the New Deal. His brilliant analytical mind quickly won him recognition. Predicting the slump of 1938, he gained a reputation as a seer and he underwrote that reputation in his prodigal feats of research and analysis for the Temporary National Economic Committee.

Roosevelt had named him price administrator and had instructed him to try to obtain voluntary price regulation until legislation should be adopted. It was as though he had been asked in to do a few easy sleight-of-hand tricks at a children's party; just a diversion until the main performance began. Then swiftly he found himself forced to juggle the furniture, the house itself, the earth, the universe, in an imitation of Hercules that was decidedly difficult to sustain. Price control by the voluntary method was an all but impossible assignment, and that prices rose no higher than they did was a tribute at the same time to Henderson's toughness and skill and to the willingness of most segments of American business to co-operate.

The hearings continued, broken by an interval in which the House was permitted to vote on the Baruch over-all price ceiling. This plan had been espoused by Representative Albert Gore of Tennessee, one of the keenest young Democrats in the House. Baruch's testimony had made a deep impression on Gore and he embodied the financier's major recommendations in a bill which the administration opposed. It was voted down, and the price-control measure was thereupon sent back to committee for still further hearings.

Even when a selective price-control act was at last adopted, and signed by the President, in January of 1942, it was plain that Henderson was to continue to have his troubles. Reluctant to move into a retail field, Price Administrator Henderson, his appointment finally confirmed by the Senate, sought to check the upward spiral by controlling commodity and wholesale prices. He had yielded to the demand for 110 per cent of parity of farm prices and this proved an irrepressible yeast. Steadily, with the effect of flood water creeping up a levee, the level of prices rose.

It reached the point at which confident New Deal economists had expected a natural wage maximum would be arrived at. The slack of lowered labor costs due to the expansion of industry had been taken up. In the spring of 1941 there had been a 10 per cent wage increase in steel and everyone had expected a corresponding increase in the price of steel. Administrator Henderson had held steel prices down to the previous level. Yet at the end of a six-month period Lubin could point to operating profits in the industry greater than in 1940. This was the slack. Further wage increases would have to be passed on in the form of higher prices.

And labor was pressing insistently for a further rise. What the economists had ignored was the political potential. In November of 1941, John L. Lewis had put on his Me-or-the-Nation strike in the captive coal mines. Sullenly he had refused to consider anything less than outright victory, even though the nation's steel mills should be shut down for lack of coal. And he won. Now he was prepared to destroy Phil Murray and replace him as head of the C.I.O. if Murray got less for his steel workers than Lewis had got for his captive miners.

That was the political dynamite and it was directed at Henderson. The War Labor Board, faced with seemingly irresistible wage demands, turned to the price administrator in the hope that he would agree to price increases in the affected industries. Steadfastly Henderson said no. And thereby he became the target of the politicians who lead labor. Roundly denouncing him, William Green of the A. F. of L. went so far as to blame him for the price rise. He had failed, said Green pontifically, to enforce effective price ceilings on consumer goods and to institute fair and democratic rationing. What both Green and Murray were in fact asking of Henderson was that single-handed he establish a new egalitarian economy with goods rationed on the basis of need rather than capacity to pay. Even for so stout a public servant this was rather a large order.

The flood water was creeping up the levee. Methods of control were quite obviously inadequate. First hint of a change came in Mrs. Roosevelt's column which the President has now and then used as a field for sending up trial balloons. Mrs. Roosevelt reported that a group of triple-dome thinkers had met at the White House to consider anew the issue of prices and their control. It was a good strong hint and when the President was asked about it at his press conference, he admitted that consideration was being given to the subject.

What followed was a Niagara of leaks from every conceivable source. That was how Dexter Keezer of Leon Henderson's staff described the plague of rumors which issued forth from Washington. There would be a rigid price ceiling. The President had gone overboard for the "Baruch plan." There would be no ceiling. Instead, all goods would be rationed by the price administrator. A great many of these rumors found their way into print.

They reflected, of course, the divided counsels within the White House circle. Henderson favored a ceiling that would include wages. So did Marriner Eccles, the chairman of the Federal Reserve Board. So did Budget Director Harold Smith. Henderson also favored compulsory savings in the face of Henry Morgenthau's insistence that the voluntary method be given a further trial. The planners could not agree on a plan, which may be the reason that so many days and weeks passed before action came from the White House.

It came in the form of a curious compromise that was a step forward but not the whole way that the President had been expected to go. In a message to Congress, President Roosevelt announced that a ceiling would be put over virtually all prices under the new powers conferred on the price administrator in the already existing law. This, he said, would work to establish a maximum beyond which wages could not go. What he asked Congress to do was to restore parity farm prices instead of 110 per cent of parity which had been a concession when the price-control measure was passed. He called also for higher taxes and for a twenty-five thousand dollar limit on incomes, the last a gesture which he must have known Congress would reject.

Following the message was a fireside talk and in the talk the President told labor that wage increases could not be granted under the price ceiling he had called for. There could be no more wage rises. Buckets of ink were spilled over the message and the speech and it was broadcast and rebroadcast to every corner of the earth. But when the last echo had died away, it was difficult to see what had been altered. The steel workers were asking for a raise of a dollar a day. Phil Murray, with the shadow of John L. Lewis at his back, was pleading that to say no would be fatal. The big bad wolf would break into the C.I.O. sheepfold and where the trouble would end then no man could say.

It was a little like one of those nursery tales in which a chain of disastrous events grows out of a single small circumstance. Whether you did or you didn't you were asking for trouble. Certainly poor Phil Murray was in an unhappy plight. Lewis was ready to try to destroy him if he failed to get as much for the steel workers as Lewis had got for his captive coal miners (captive in more ways than one) in his Me-or-the-Nation strike in November of 1941. Before a meeting of his old United Mine Workers' local Murray tried to talk and words would not come. Tears ran down his cheeks. The miners and their wives stood and cheered him. But that was sentiment and it would hardly count against the dollars in the pay envelope at the end of the week. ". . . water won't put out fire, fire won't burn stick, stick won't beat dog, dog won't bite pig, and I can't get to market."

Once again Henderson stepped forth as Sisyphus. He could never agree to a wage increase. One aperture in the dike and soon the whole structure would give away. Yet dammed up behind it was the same old pressure.

In his bearing, when he met the assembled press to announce the price ceiling, was a new humility. Gone was the cocky self-confidence of the past. The scene was the auditorium of the new Social Security building. More than a hundred correspondents had gathered to learn the details of one of the most far-reaching economic controls ever to be adopted in the United States; and also to see and hear Henderson in the most important moment of his career.

His manner was almost apologetic. Talking, he conceded, was

the sword that he lived by, as it would probably also be the sword
that he would die by. The time had come to stop talking. There
it was, in the sheaf of printed and mimeographed announcements
that had been handed to every newspaper man. It went a long
way. They had worked on it for weeks, he and the members of
his staff who stood near him. And they looked as though they
had been through an ordeal, with the gray weariness that signifies
the long hours of wartime Washington.

Wage ceiling? No, there was no ceiling on wages. Yes, under
the Canadian system wages were put under a ceiling. Would he
guarantee to prevent inflation with the new price controls? No,
nothing could do that, no one. Experience in Europe had shown
that in spite of the best efforts that could be exerted prices did
move upward under the pressure of vast streams of purchasing
power in a market arid of goods. Food not included? That wasn't
true; of the foods used by the average household 65 per cent were
covered by the price ceiling.

This reticent, reluctant Henderson undoubtedly saw the perils
on the road before him; the dangerous curves, the precipitous
cliffs below. He is far too wise not to know those dangers. In the
driver's seat, he could only use the road map he had been furnished, having failed to get the more specific one he had requested.
And we were with him, all of us, passengers or innocent by-
standers. "Hang onto your hats when the dips come!" That was
what solemn Leon Henderson seemed to be trying to say. In his
mind must have been the thought that the responsibility would
be his, his the blame for failure, if price control failed, no matter
who was really at fault.

That contemplative hour, looking forward and back, was a luxury Henderson would not soon enjoy again. With almost every
other executive in Washington, he had reached out for new duties
and responsibilities. Not only price control but rationing was in his
province. To ration scarce commodities among 130,000,000 Americans was in itself a job of no mean proportions. It began with sugar,
but plainly that was only a beginning. You could see behind the
door the piles dwindling and the time drawing nearer when tickets

would be necessary for many of the things that are necessary for everyday life.

To one paragraph in the President's message to Congress Stephen Early had called particular attention. "I assure the Congress," it said, "that if the required objectives are not attained, and if the cost of living should continue to rise substantially, I shall so advise the Congress, and shall ask for any additional legislation which may be necessary." Those who had been disappointed in the limited objectives sought by the President could draw some consolation from this assurance. It was Mr. Roosevelt, the gradualist, speaking. And perhaps even under the impact of war Mr. Roosevelt, the gradualist, knew how far the American people could be taken at one leap. Possibly he knew better than anyone else how to resolve that difficult political triangle of which John L. Lewis was the stubborn hypotenuse.

SECTION III
THE WAR

Chapter XIII

The Military Take Over

WE WERE slipping swiftly down the shelf of Time into another era in the soft fall days in 1941, but we had little or no awareness of it. The exact date has gone out of mind but some time about the middle of November a cabinet member described for me the cabinet meeting at which the President had for the first time spoken in unmistakable warning of the war with Japan which was coming.

Cabinet meetings under Roosevelt have ordinarily an easy first-name informality. This one was different. After a very brief preamble the President told his official family that in his view war with Japan was inevitable. Moreover, it would come soon, he said; perhaps when the long-drawn-out negotiations with the smiling, so-sorry Mr. Kurusu and the phlegmatic, stolid Ambassador Nomura could be prolonged no further. Then the President did an almost unprecedented thing. He polled his cabinet, asking two questions. First, he wanted to know whether in the opinion of each member the country was ready for war in the Pacific; and, second, he wanted to know how the country could be got ready.

I understood clearly that this information had been passed along to me for a purpose. After talking with another member of the cabinet, getting further background, I wrote a story which appeared in the *Post-Dispatch* on November 13. It said, without reference to sources, that war with Japan was just over the horizon; that the negotiations with the Japanese were getting nowhere; and that the President was concerned over how the country could be made to realize this inevitability.

In the light of what was to happen scarcely a fortnight later that cabinet meeting has a grim irony. The President expected war but he expected it on our own terms. It would come when the conversations with Kurusu and Nomura, which were now being deliberately prolonged, had finally broken down. It would come when the Japanese diplomats with their suites had solemnly departed. It would come on our ultimatum.

All this was in accord with our experience of the past. The diplomatic farrago might be extended for weeks. That was the hope, you learned at the State Department, of the military, both British and American. While the details could not be known, military preparations were far from completed. Considerable work was still to be done at Singapore before that great base would be ready for war. This was the word that was brought to distracted Mr. Hull in those last uncertain weeks.

Moreover, Mr. Hull's ambassador in Tokyo, Joseph Grew, took a somewhat less gloomy view of the situation. Career men within the Department had held the traditional belief that after a sufficient number of ritualistic diplomatic gestures Japan must be converted, by physical exhaustion if not by persuasion, to a reasonable course. Back of this was the long finagling over how much oil, how much aviation gasoline, how much scrap iron, should be shipped from America to Japan. Henry Morgenthau in the Treasury had argued for months the importance of shutting down entirely on such shipments. Likewise a group of younger men in the State Department had long since concluded that appeasing Japan with essential war matériel was a futile business which could only postpone, to Japan's advantage, an inevitable clash. Yet the final embargo had not come until August, thereby creating the "incident" which led to the "conversations."

In the warm sunny days of late November the conversations continued in Washington. From Mr. Grew in Tokyo, ending an honorable career in a post of the highest responsibility, came lengthy reports. All this was perfectly normal. Yet in the soft, familiar atmosphere was an uneasiness which somehow communicated itself. The conversations were like an endless dance of the seven veils. What was behind it or where it was going one could only guess. Washington was full of uneasy surmises.

In a futile search for some clue I went out to see little Wakasugi, minister-counselor of the Japanese Embassy. That must have been in the first week in December, on Wednesday or Thursday. I had met him in the spring at the University of Missouri's Journalism Week. There Jimmy Young and other correspondents from the Pacific had described him as "one of the good Japanese," entirely out of sympathy with the clique of war lords who were consolidating their power in Japan. He had seemed then an unhappy monosyllabic little man with downcast eyes and an extreme reluctance to talk about anything except the weather.

Now his reluctance and his unhappiness were if anything greater. He had been very hesitant about seeing me at all. My questions seemed to fall into a bottomless pit of Oriental melancholy. Yes, the conversations were continuing. Nothing more could be said. Hopeful? Oh, of course he was hopeful as long as the conversations continued, his voice trailing off into a faint mutter. He sat silent, looking sadly into space. The gilt and crystal clock on his mantel ticked loudly. Our conversation appeared to be at an end, yet I had the disturbing sense of vast stores of secret knowledge locked away in Wakasugi's small head. I dropped two or three more questions into the Oriental prayer wheel and reluctantly took my leave, passing down a long corridor through the Chancery where occasionally from an open door busy little Japanese looked up.

No American who lived through that Sunday will ever forget it. It seared deeply into the national consciousness, shearing away illusions that had been fostered for generations. And with the first shock came a sort of panic. This struck at our deepest pride. It tore at the myth of our invulnerability. Striking at the precious legend of our might, it seemed to leave us suddenly naked and defenseless. That was true at least in Washington.

The peace of that gentle, sunny Sunday was profoundly shattered by the first dispatch from Honolulu. In country houses in Virginia and Maryland men were summoned and sped away toward Washington. Orders began to go out. The city stirred to unexpected life. Kurusu and Nomura, who had been engaged in one of those interminable conversations, were shown out of Mr.

Hull's office to the accompaniment of a shattering fire of Tennessee invective which I only hope they could understand. A crowd of newspapermen moved between the State Department and the White House. But there was little that could be added to the tragic news flooding in over the radio from the Pacific.

All through the night, lights burned in the White House and in the State Department. Generals, admirals, diplomats, came and went. With his cabinet ministers the President was phrasing the message with which he would go before Congress to ask for a declaration of war. That was a heartbreaking night as official confirmation of the disaster came on the heels of the news. And if it was a humiliation to Americans everywhere, how much greater humiliation it was to the President, to the admirals, to Secretary Knox, to those men charged with responsibility for the Navy; those men who had believed in the Navy's invincibility. The heartbreak was that it came against the long summer of optimism which now seemed so brash and mistaken. The trumpetings of Secretary Knox had in echo a hollow and unhappy sound.

The overwhelming fact was that everyone had been wrong. The boldest interventionists had pitifully underestimated Japan's striking power. The isolationists had their chief argument—that no foreign power wanted to assail us in our own sphere—completely knocked out from under them. No matter what they said for the record on December 8, the blindest and the stubbornest would continue to believe that Pearl Harbor was no more than America deserved for not having remained pure and isolated as such wise men had counseled. This was a line that would verge on treason in the months to come; the bitter haters skulking in the shadows attempting to do a work of destruction within that the enemy could not do.

Monday was almost worse than Sunday. A merciful kind of shock had prevailed under the first impact and now as that wore off, the truth was inescapable. The order had gone out for all Navy and Army men to report on the following day in uniform, and Washington overnight became a city of blue and olive drab. The rumors had begun to fly, inspired God knows how, and they

were much worse than the news on the radio and in the big, star-
ing black headlines in the newspapers. Mrs. Roosevelt came to her
staff conference at the Office of Civilian Defense and, in a voice
high with suppressed excitement, told her aides that a great
disaster had occurred, a catastrophe narrowly averted, and that
now civilian defense must work to offset this terrible blow at
morale.

The Capitol was guarded by men in trench helmets with fixed
bayonets. They were at the doors, in the corridors, everywhere.
To get from the Senate entrance to the House press gallery you
had to show your credentials a dozen times. As the workrooms
of the gallery filled up, the hum of talk grew louder. Each arriving correspondent had some contribution to make. He had just
talked to Senator So-and-so. It was five battleships sunk, not two,
and the number of civilian dead . . . The tension of waiting
mounted as the hands of the clock drew near to twelve. On the
House floor the members were assembling and from them came
the same burble of talk. This was history and history of an uncomfortable sort.

When the President came, his face was more drawn and solemn
than I had ever seen it. He spoke gravely, without any of the
deliberate oratorical gravity that in the past he consciously put into
a line or a phrase. Gone was the histrionism. He spoke out of a
realization of the ordeal that was ahead. The tension of the preceding twenty-four hours was in his voice. But at the end of his
speech his anger and indignation burned through. A wave of
cheering burst over the crowded chamber that just before had
been so silent.

This was war and as the President left the Capitol senators and
representatives moved quickly to comply with the request of the
Chief Executive. The endless debate was over. No longer was
evasion possible. The Axis had at last settled the issue. When the
time for voting came, there were still men who wrestled with the
old prejudices, the old convictions and illusions. It was painful to
move from the illusion of peace and security to the terrible reality
of war. We had lived so long in a state of indecision that we suf-

fered now from a kind of invalidism of the mind, clinging to our schizophrenia. But this hurdle could not be balked.

I had ridden up on the elevator that morning with one of the recalcitrant isolationists who grumbled bitterly about the President and what a plight he had brought us to. With this went dark hints that he would never vote for a declaration of war. When the clerk came to his name in the course of the roll call, his aye was almost as loud as those of his neighbors. While that moment carried all before it, there were those who were to show later that their conversion had been only temporary.

Only one member dared to vote no. That was white-haired Jeannette Rankin of Montana. Word of what she intended to do got about among her friends on the House floor and they gathered round her in an effort to dissuade her from this rash step. Obviously under a great emotional strain, she shook her head firmly and waited for the fatal moment when the clerk should reach the R's. It seemed to me that those who tried to coerce her into voting aye were foolish. A solitary no was a demonstration to the world that even in the critical moment of attack we do not compel the false *Ja* vote of dictatorship. Miss Rankin had been elected to Congress in 1916 just in time to vote her pacifist no against American entry into the last war. After twenty-four years she was elected again in 1940 to perform the same symbolic office in America's second world conflict.

On Tuesday the Army began installation of anti-aircraft and machine guns on top of the Senate and House Office buildings. Tuesday was a bad day. The rumors of the damage at Pearl Harbor hovered like a low-hanging gas, spreading the panic fear that seemed to infect the capital. On the previous evening Chairmen Walsh and Vinson of the Senate and House Naval Affairs Committees had gone down to the Navy Department to hear from Admiral Stark, chief of naval operations, the extent of the damage in Hawaii. Walsh called a meeting of his committee that morning and "off the record" told them what he had learned. They came out of the committee room with set faces, grim-lipped.

As the Senate assembled at noon other senators gathered around

Walsh and the effect of the tale he whispered was visible as they turned away. What this did, of course, was to fan the fire of rumor into a fierce blaze. Each senator by nightfall had told ten other persons and they had told ten others, the story losing nothing in the telling. In midafternoon came the false rumor that enemy planes were over New York and might soon be over Washington. The atmosphere in the Capitol was on the narrow edge of hysteria. The air in the Senate chamber was full of gray foreboding. This could not be true. It was a cruel dream, a sadistic joke, and the comfortable reality of yesterday must still be somewhere around the corner.

The President's first wartime fireside chat was a sharp disappointment. Not only in Washington but in the country people were ready for a frank avowal of tragedy and disaster. They were ready to face the worst. They were prepared to accept a part of the blame for what had happened. The President's speech was an effort to gloss it over, encouraging the belief that Pearl Harbor had made no essential difference. While following the report of the official commission of inquiry a franker statement of losses was made, with only the details and time of reconstruction withheld, Roosevelt continued to insist that nothing would have been very much different in the Pacific if there had been no sneak attack on Hawaii.

If you accept the President's thesis, then the long roll of Pacific defeats—the Philippines, Singapore, Java—would have occurred just as they did occur even though there had been no Pearl Harbor. But surely the thousands of man-boat hours required to re-garrison and reconstruct the Hawaiian naval base must have made some slight difference; to say nothing of the fleet units that were destroyed or put out of action on December 7. One result of the President's insistence has been to put all the burden of blame for the blows in the southwest Pacific on our allies, the British and the Dutch. That is a rank injustice in the light of the long-time assumption that the American fleet in the Pacific would be ready to operate in the Singapore area in the event of an attack by Japan. Moreover, it contributed toward the anti-British feeling which grew up in 1942 and which was complemented in London by a distrust of America. Where were those damn' British, some Americans said, forgetting American responsibility in the far Pacific.

Something had happened in the six months that preceded Pearl Harbor. What it was we shall not know with any certainty or with any detail until after all the documents are available. In the aftermath of the attack, however, I thought back to a certain June evening and a cruise down the Potomac with one of the men responsible for framing our military and diplomatic policy. War with Japan? No one, said the great man, expected war with Japan, least of all the Japanese. The distances were too great. It was foolish to talk about making war across such great areas of ocean. This coincided, I am convinced, with the movement of units of the Pacific fleet into the Atlantic. Perhaps it was only the expression of a hope. Some of us after that cruise wrote inspired stories about the remoteness of any Pacific war. But we were doubtful about those stories and we continued to be doubtful, knowing there was so very much we did not know.

I suppose it will be impossible to tell the story of Pearl Harbor alone, short of a small library of books. Stories began to drift back to Washington, some true, some false. The best account I heard was from a naval officer who had been on shore leave in Honolulu the night of December 6. Commander of a destroyer squadron, he lost his gear when the commanding destroyer was sunk and he went through the next three days in a blood-stained Palm Beach suit, hunting the Japs on one of the destroyers of his squadron that had not been knocked out. He said that the Japanese in one of their own harbors had apparently done a complete construction of the Pearl Harbor installations—like a movie set. Then they had practiced on this target. Otherwise it was impossible to explain the accuracy of their bombing.

He was tremendously impressed by the immediacy of their information. At least twice during the raid they had bombed a certain spot in the harbor. Twenty-four hours before a cruiser had been moored on that spot. It had been unexpectedly moved in the night. The Japs had had the location of that vessel just before their attack. What is more, if the Japanese general staff had risked all of their battle fleet in the attack on Hawaii, our naval force in the Pacific would have been totally destroyed and our coast left undefended.

The Pearl Harbor disaster made perfectly clear the need for sweeping changes in the armed services. From Congress came an immediate outcry for heads to roll. Some senators demanded openly that Secretary Knox resign. Others muttered angrily but did not speak out in public. From politicians and the press there was a rising demand for a court martial of Admiral Kimmel and General Short, although even their attackers recognized that they were merely a part of a system that had been faulty.

The outcry was understandable. Our unpreparedness had been shamefully exposed. We had lost our best planes and three thousand trained men. Yet if President Roosevelt had yielded to the outcries following Pearl Harbor, he would probably only have fed the hysteria of the moment. To have dismissed some officials would have merely whetted the appetite of Congress. Other heads would have been demanded and no one could have foretold where the purge would end.

Instead, the President set about quietly making some of the necessary changes. A complex human institution with the sensitivities of the Navy might easily, under such a shock as Pearl Harbor, have become demoralized by abrupt and sudden change. It was essential above all to preserve the esprit de corps.

The way was prepared for the departure of the chief of naval operations, Admiral Harold Stark, who had been intimidated by Congress and who was never entirely in sympathy with administration policy. He was put in charge of naval units in European waters and since there were comparatively few American naval vessels operating on the other side of the Atlantic this was a more or less nominal position. Stark was replaced by Admiral Ernest J. King who, a flier himself, had long been an advocate of greater naval air power.

These and other changes were made after the hysteria over Pearl Harbor had subsided. They were made to seem routine

changes rather than in response to any demand from outside.
Under Secretary of the Navy James Forrestal, who had previously
been overawed by the atmosphere of gold braid, gathered up his
courage and pushed a reorganization within the department. En-
joying autonomous powers, the Navy bureaus had spent not a
little of their time in internecine warfare. Intense jealousies prevailed. The irony was, as Richard Stokes of the *Post-Dispatch* staff
discovered, that an effective plan of reorganization had long mol-
dered in the files. This was the work of Admiral Joseph K. Taussig, but he had not been allowed to carry it out before his retirement. Having earned the displeasure of President Roosevelt in a
dispute going back to the last war, Taussig was one of the few
retired admirals who was not recalled to active service after December 7, as he was also one of the few who might have made a
contribution of an exceptional nature.

Meanwhile the American public had found something to cheer
for. Even though it had not occurred against the gloomy background of the defeats in the Southwest Pacific, the heroic stand
of the men on Bataan would have captured the American imagination. This was in the long American tradition of heroism; fighting
against overwhelming odds with native skill and resourcefulness
matched against brute force.

Given the American temperament, it was probably inevitable
that the story of Bataan should focus on a single individual. The
legend of MacArthur and the way in which it grew out of the
green hell of the Bataan Peninsula, with the magic of a djinn, was
a peculiarly American phenomenon. This, too, was something
Americans could understand; a hero who had prepared his defenses and then stood his ground with the frank picturesqueness of
a man not afraid to be a hero.

Washington joined in the hero worship, forgetting the long
years of neglect. As chief of staff, first under Herbert Hoover and
then for two years under Franklin Roosevelt, MacArthur had
argued for funds for mechanization. Taken out of ancient committee hearings, his words had a prescient sound. They forecast
Adolf Hitler's blitz warfare and warned in unmistakable language

of the dangers of continuing on in the twentieth century with a muleback army hardly large enough for an Indian campaign.

Washington remembered him from further back. He was recalled as a young colonel on a tour of duty in the War Department in 1917. Then he had spoken prescient words, too. He had talked about his father, General Arthur MacArthur, who had not been chief of staff, because, said his son, he had not been a political general. Douglas MacArthur let his friends know that he would not permit modesty to stand in his way. He would be chief of staff and more than chief of staff. The young colonel clearly recognized the star of his destiny. And his faith in that star was unshakable.

He had been the youngest chief of staff in the history of the nation. There had been the episode in 1932 of the bonus marchers fired on by the army with General MacArthur in an immaculate uniform at its head. But the blame for that had fallen on Hoover. Stepping down as chief of staff at fifty-five, he seemed to have conquered all visible worlds. His enemies, and he had enemies, hoped that oblivion would swiftly overtake him. President Manuel Quezon asked him to organize the defense of the Philippines. That seemed remote enough and obscure enough. Washington prepared to forget about the showy general.

Manila was another Washington. The story was the same. The general argued, persuaded, cajoled, and yet from the Philippine assembly he could not obtain the funds that had been promised him for the army he was building up. MacArthur was convinced that the Philippines could be defended against an attack by Japan. But no one in Manila or in Washington could be made to share this conviction. Or, rather, they blew hot and cold from month to month and year to year. The general did all that he could with the resources given him and when the test came, he could stand up to it. Singapore fell with a great crashing, rending sound. Java followed. Yet Bataan held out.

As the MacArthur legend swelled, the demand grew in Washington that somehow he be got out. His old friends on Capitol Hill hinted that they were in communication with the general. He approved what they said and did. Bring him back to Washington, was the demand heard from various quarters. He should come back and tell the country how the war should be conducted. But how to get him back without having it seem that he had abandoned his men? This question was debated endlessly among the general's friends in Congress and he had many friends there.

In one of the last columns that he wrote, old Ironpants Hugh Johnson said, God save MacArthur from his friends! It was the plea of another soldier who knew what he was talking about. In the first place, the MacArthur legend had grown to such proportions that no man could live up to it even if all the odds were with him. It was scarcely a service to General MacArthur to make him appear as a superman. Then, too, the political implications that his friends had begun to read into the MacArthur cult could hardly help the general and must have been embarrassing to him.

His rescue from Bataan and his introduction into a larger sphere of action were managed with consummate skill. A task of overwhelming proportions was put on him, but so great was the country's confidence in this soldier that no one doubted he could carry it off eventually. What was scarcely realized either in Washington or in the country was the vastness of the area over which MacArthur would have to fight. He was in Australia, which was only one theater of action, and there was the strong possibility in the spring of 1942 that forces assembled there might be thousands of miles from the center of the Pacific war. He had not been in Melbourne long, when differences developed over the extent of his command and innumerable cables passed back and forth in the course of what might have become an unpleasant public controversy.

The Pacific assignment did not altogether satisfy MacArthur's ardent backers. The demand persisted that he be brought back to Washington and put in direction of the entire war organization. Wendell Willkie in a speech in February, before MacArthur had been flown out of the Philippines, urged that the hero of Bataan be given full power to direct the war.

A man as conscious of his destiny could not miss the significance of all this. He was a soldier first of all, yet his language was not that of a soldier. His speeches were pure rococo. When President Quezon presented him with the gold baton of the first field marshal of the Philippines, MacArthur poured out such a spate of purple rhetoric as had rarely been heard even in the islands where a Latin floridity has flourished. On the fall of Bataan the news dispatches brought MacArthur's tribute to the heroes of that desperate siege. The news story from Melbourne said that he came out of his hotel suite with a ruled sheet of paper from which he read a statement that contained language charged with extraordinary emotion.

"To the weeping mothers of its dead," he said of the men who had fallen on Bataan, "I only say that the sacrifice and halo of Jesus of Nazareth has descended upon their sons and that God will take them unto himself."

The restless, driving energy of the man may sweep all before it in the far Pacific. He has daring, imagination, resourcefulness. On the other hand, the very scope of the war across thousands of miles of lonely water may frustrate even MacArthur's military genius. One thing is certain and that is that Washington will watch this figure that looms so large on the Far Eastern horizon.

Quietly, without any dramatics and with few newspaper headlines, another general had proved his worth in the fire of the crisis. The chief of staff, General George C. Marshall, had begun long before Pearl Harbor to modernize the army. He had begun to break down the barriers of tradition, the obstacles of seniority. General Marshall was fully aware of the need to move younger men to the fore; to discover and exploit men with brains and imagination. But he knew, too, out of his years of experience in the institution that is the army that abrupt and sweeping changes in the midst of a general world upheaval might destroy the assurance and the solidarity that are so important in any fighting force. As rapidly as possible he moved down promotion age limits and with this, of course, the retirement limit, so that the sixty-four-year-old colonels would go. At the same time he moved up new men.

New brigadier and major generals were created by the score. One of Marshall's shrewdest moves was to revise G-2—Army Intelligence. Intelligence, both in the Army and Navy, had been one of the unhappy failures that Pearl Harbor had revealed. Now Marshall worked out an extensive revision of this nerve center. All down the line there were changes. Marshall's ultimate objective was a streamlined organization with only three principal components. The fumbling and the friction were being eliminated as fast as possible.

Marshall has the temperament for a crisis. He moves with a quiet steadfastness that inspires confidence in the men around him. His experience, in the Philippines from 1902 to 1903, in charge of operations in France from 1917 to 1919; his close association with Pershing, his three years in China; the military mission he led to Brazil in 1939; all this and much more equipped him for the long, grueling task that he faced in the spring of 1942. He had made mistakes, of course. Not even generals are infallible. But men who had known him over the years appraised him at very close to 100 per cent. America was fortunate to have two such soldiers as Marshall and MacArthur; a piece of luck we scarcely deserved in the light of our long years of military neglect.

Under the fierce erosion of the moment other men stood up, too, towering out of the confusion and uncertainty around them. One was Under Secretary of War Robert P. Patterson. Ever since he had come to Washington, with his chief, Stimson, giving up a federal judgeship, Patterson had slaved to break through the confines of routine and red tape. Primarily his had been the job of procurement—getting the stuff to equip the vast new army. From early morning until late into the night he toiled like a troglodyte to make the wheels move faster. The rewards were few, chiefly those of knowing that procurement schedules were advancing; that the deadly confinement of "routine procedure" was being sheared away.

He had little to say when you saw him in his office. His job was doing and not talking. A look of grim resolution was his constant expresison. He had given up his farm at Cold Spring, New

York, and the sober, orderly life of the Circuit Court of Appeals
for the harassments of Washington; the morning-to-night wrangle
to get more guns and more ammunition from the industrial plant
to the men who were now on the firing line or soon to be there.

In a related field another man had shone conspicuously. Brigadier General Brehon B. Somervell had got the camps built.
Stepping into as messy and confused a situation as you could have
asked for, in a remarkably short time he had straightened it out.
This army engineer who had had the tough job of WPA administrator in New York, kicked out the laggards and scuttled the
chiselers. He cut through devious real-estate deals, and through
the mud and muck of winter and early spring he pushed the camp
construction to completion. As a reward he was made assistant
chief of staff in charge of the services of supply.

The military was beginning to roll with a million horse power
harnessed to the machines of modern war. We were passing out
of the muleback and Indian campaign era. There might still be
time to protect our liberties and our great rich land.

Many believed that this new, powerful machine should be
directed by a military man who would have full authority to
conduct the war. That implication was in Willkie's "suggestion"
that MacArthur be put in charge of the armed forces of the
United States. But the Constitution of the United States designates
as commander in chief the President of the United States. And
anyone who knew anything about Franklin Roosevelt knew that
he would be commander in chief not merely in name but in fact.
In many respects he was better equipped for the role, thanks to
his experience, training, and temperament, than any other American. Knowing him in the long years of peace, as a reformer and
a brilliant politician, most Americans had forgotten how much war
was in the President's background. But he had not forgotten.

Not many weeks after the shock of Pearl Harbor, Stephen Early
paid the President his usual early morning call. Sitting on the
edge of the bath tub as the President shaved, he told "the boss"
about the reaction of commentators and correspondents to the
resolute calm which the man in the White House had shown

under the impact of war begun in stealth and treachery. Almost without exception, Steve reported, they had commented on the President's iron nerves.

For a moment the President considered this. Well, why not, he said, why shouldn't we have reacted in just that way? He reminded his friend and secretary of two things. First, he had seen the long shadow of war and had written and talked about the threat to America years before. Second, he had had personal experience of war—its perils and uncertainties both on land and on sea—more than most men. A day or two later Early sat down with him and the President recalled the details of that experience.

When he became assistant secretary of the Navy in 1913, Roosevelt was thirty-one years old. His chief was Josephus Daniels, a North Carolina newspaper editor and a loyal supporter of Woodrow Wilson. Daniels had little knowledge of ships or the sea and he inclined from the first to entrust the lion's share of the job to his young and vigorous assistant, who had from childhood taken to the water and the lore of the water. It was an excellent working partnership and the beginning of a lifelong friendship. Roosevelt has ever since called Daniels, whom he appointed ambassador to Mexico in 1933, "Chief." The "Chief" shaped policy and his alert young assistant carried it out.

As the crisis of that other war drew on, the assistant secretary of the Navy was more and more absorbed in problems of supply and procurement, transportation and construction. He visited almost every important Navy Yard and defense center in the country. Personally the active boss of the Navy inspected war plants and yards where battleships and cruisers were under construction. He paid an official visit to the West Indies and in Panama he had a good searching look at the new canal which another Roosevelt, his distant cousin, T. R., had initiated.

All this was leading up to the first World War. Roosevelt in 1917 was impatient for a more active role, restive under the demands that kept him at his desk in crowded Washington. Not until the spring of 1918 was he able to get away. With U-boats ranging the Atlantic like wolf packs, preying, as they are preying today, or any unwary ship, he departed on a destroyer for Europe. His was a roving inspection commission that took him first to the Azores and then to United States destroyer bases in Ireland.

From Ireland he went to England to inspect American destroyer, sub-chaser, and air bases there. While in London, he worked in close touch with the British Admiralty and American Naval Headquarters. It was a bad time, with the Germans making their big push in France and the Allies in a state of gloom over the trend of the war. Pessimistic prophets said the conflict would last for years.

Leaving England, Roosevelt crossed the dangerous mine- and submarine-infested channel to visit Dunkerque where an American air base was under constant fire from German 15-inch guns. The commander of that base was a handsome, athletic young flier named Artemus Gates who had left Yale to go into naval aviation. The fliers out of the Dunkerque base maintained a submarine patrol in the channel. Few brass hats had gone up to Dunkerque, a hazardous post. The assistant secretary was the first important personage to chance it. He arrived at the seaplane base full of an eager curiosity, reviewed the Americans stationed there, talked briefly with the officers about their flying experiences, and then was driven off again.

Not until the winter of 1941 did Roosevelt and Gates renew their brief acquaintance. Then it was in the White House swimming pool. The commander at Dunkerque is now assistant secretary of the Navy for Air, appointed by Commander in Chief Roosevelt who is not only boss of the Navy in this war but boss of the whole show. They had a good talk about that other meeting under the threat of German guns and German bombs.

American Naval Headquarters in Paris was Roosevelt's next stop. With headquarters as a base, he visited the marines near Nancy and Verdun and for three days he was with the American-French offensive from Chateau-Thierry up to the Vesle River at the end of July. His next errand was a secret and confidential mission to Rome to try to persuade the Italian cabinet and admiralty to bring the Italian fleet out of Taranto Harbor where it had lain behind a boom for a whole year. Unsuccessful in this attempt, he next visited the Belgian army and following that came a detailed inspection trip of all the American aviation and antisubmarine bases on the Bay of Biscay from the Spanish border to Brest.

That was nearly a quarter of a century ago, but it is a safe guess that the President today has stored away in his extraordinary memory many of the details—tides, currents, depths—of that coastline. Especially for such facts is his memory prodigious. Once a naval aide referred to the approaches to a certain harbor as having such and such characteristics. The President gave it as his impression that there was twenty feet more water once you got beyond a certain shoal. A polite argument followed and Roosevelt called for the charts which proved him right.

After the Bay of Biscay, some point on which may well be the focus of an invasion of the continent in the present war, the assistant secretary spent the last two or three weeks of his European tour in an inspection of the Grand Fleet in the Firth of Forth, including the American Battleship Squadron. He took the same opportunity to inspect the laying of the North Sea mine barrage from northern Scotland to Norway, as perilous a venture as any he had embarked on, with sudden death always close at hand in the slate-gray sea. Returning, when he could not stretch out his visit another day, he contracted double pneumonia on the *Leviathan* on the way back. Carried off the ship on a stretcher, he put in a long convalescence and when he had finally recovered the war was over. This marked the end of one career, the beginning of another.

That first career, in the ways and means of war, Roosevelt was never to put out of mind. When he entered the White House in 1932, he resumed his Navy ties. It was, in fact, one of the charges his political opponents brought against him—that he was a "big Navy" man. The new commander in chief never lost an opportunity to participate in maneuvers or get off on a cruiser. On the cruiser *Houston* in 1939 he took part in the greatest maneuvers in the Navy's history in the Caribbean and the South Atlantic.

Under the eyes of Commander Roosevelt the problem of the defense of all the Americas, North and South, was worked out.

During the past eight years I have seen F. D. R. in many moods and many roles but none that seemed to suit him better than that of commander of the fleet. In 1938 in the course of a tour to the West Coast the President visited San Francisco and there reviewed, for the first time in any Pacific Coast port, the battle fleet. It was the kind of drama this sailor President enjoys. He had spoken briefly at a luncheon at the site of the San Francisco fair. Then he had been driven to the Oakland dock where he boarded the *Houston* for the grand review. In San Francisco harbor, with the clifflike city rising from the blue waters of the bay as a fitting backdrop, sixty-six ships of the line steamed in battle array past the commander in chief, each to fire a twenty-one gun salute. Hatless, a Navy cloak with velvet collar about his shoulders, he stood on the bridge with his head thrown back in the wind, the image of a seagoing man, a man knowing and delighting in the command of ships.

The transition to a war footing was for the President comparatively simple. Increasingly his time was spent in the map room which is the inner sanctum, the holy of holies, of wartime Washington. So closely guarded are the secrets of this room, that the President did not want the fact disclosed that it had been moved from the White House offices to the White House proper so that the President might have easier access to it. Here, with the strategic maps of each theater of war on the walls around him, with his military aides and the chiefs of staff, he helps to plot grand strategy. Here he gives range to his remarkable knowledge of geography and oceanography.

It means twenty-four hours a day on duty. Into the nerve center of the White House go lines from all the hush-hush offices in Washington. There is a direct line from Operations 37 of the Navy. Operations 37 is the brain that directs the movements of all American ships, naval and merchant vessels alike. At any moment of the day or night the President can ascertain the position of any ship flying the American flag by lifting the telephone which con-

nects with Operations 37. To Operations 37 come reports of sink-
ings long before the public is informed. From day to day the
President makes decisions which in this global warfare mean the
movement of men and matériel and ships in the Red Sea, in
Australia, in the Mediterranean, in Libya, in Ireland.

For the President, absorbed in directing this greatest war in
all history, the shift from armed neutrality to active conflict was
a minor one. For civilian Washington it was more difficult. Few
newspaper correspondents had concentrated on the military. We
had for the most part been preoccupied with the politics of peace
time. Now it seemed as though every civilian interest was to go
into the discard. The civilian suddenly found himself an embarrassing obstacle in the path of the military machine.

Men from the press gallery began leaving for the far-flung
fronts of the war. The orders came under seal of secrecy. Be
prepared to leave in ten hours from Norfolk or New York or
San Francisco. Destination unknown. Your family might guess, as
you could guess, that it would be Australia or Cairo or Belfast.
If you happened to talk to an old friend in the brief interval before departure, the story merely was that you were going on a
trip.

Many newspapermen, among them the most brilliant and aggressive, were drawn into the armed services. They too went off
to the far corners of the earth. In June before the outbreak of
the war Joseph Alsop and Robert Kintner had given up their column to go, Kintner with the Army, Alsop for a brief period with
the Navy and then later with Colonel Clair Chennault who directed
the American volunteer fliers for China. Both Alsop and Kintner
had been of draft age and as their vigorous and forceful column
had been strongly on the interventionist side, they felt under com-
pulsion to enter the services before they were called.

It was a shock to learn one day at the office of the Co-ordinator
of Information that Joe Alsop had been taken prisoner at the
fall of Hong Kong. I remembered so well his furious disappointment when he had been sent by Secretary Knox to India
instead of England where he had had his heart set on going.

Then word had come back that, on his way through Chungking, Colonel Chennault had persuaded him to take an administrative post in the organization directing the gallant young fliers who had gone out to fight for Chiang Kai-shek and the cause of China. From Bombay his release from his Navy assignment was negotiated by cable.

And now it was difficult to imagine imperious, fastidious Joe Alsop in the bloody horrors of Hong Kong. Remembering him in his elegant house, taking his cuisine so seriously, it was hard to imagine him existing on a handful of rice. He was for me a kind of symbol of the fall of the bastions of another era; bastions which with their glaring contrasts of wealth and poverty could never be restored in the new world destined to supplant the old.

We who stayed behind were to discover that we were not, as it had seemed at first, the last civilians left in America. Over the civilian and his care and feeding a violent storm was to break. We were to hear used and misused that dubious word morale.

Chapter XIV

The Battle of the Civilians

IF MRS. ROOSEVELT and her friends in the Office of Civilian Defense had any inkling of the storm that was to break, they gave no sign of it. OCD was a cozy affair, well meaning but almost entirely devoid of reality. Until the outbreak of the war no one really cared very much. It provided an opportunity for earnest men and women to do good works. Moreover, it furnished a suitable backdrop for little Mayor LaGuardia who was in the midst of a difficult campaign for re-election to a third term as mayor of New York. In any event, America was still living under the illusion of isolated security, and you could scarcely have persuaded the average citizen that the hocus-pocus of OCD was necessary.

In accepting an official position with OCD, Mrs. Roosevelt made one of the few political blunders since her rise to remarkable popularity. She had gone very far from the days of that unfortunate magazine, *Babies, Just Babies,* when she was a sort of national joke. Her great good will had overcome the animosity and resentment directed at a President's wife who proposed to have a career of her own. She moved in a warm, beneficent glow through a routine of daily activity that would have killed the average, able-bodied male. Her daily column, My Day, was only the smallest part of it. That was dictated to a secretary between trains or on a plane as the first lady whirled like a dervish from one side of the continent to the other.

Many people, and particularly rich Republicans, laughed condescendingly at Eleanor. But the fact was that she was a great political asset to her husband. She won friends and influenced people in spheres to which he had no valid access, and this was not out of any calculated sense of gain but out of the sheer goodness of her heart. Cynical critics sometimes said that Franklin and Eleanor deliberately worked opposite sides of the street. And there were curious coincidences. On one and the same evening Mrs. Roosevelt addressed the Women's International League for Peace and Freedom on peace, while the President sent a message to the Daughters of the American Revolution assuring them that a sizable Navy was dear to his heart.

More important even than the good will she engendered was the first lady's ability to bring to her husband's notice strata of American life and American opinion that he might otherwise have been wholly unaware of. The men around the President com-plained about the back door that Mrs. Roosevelt held open to all sorts of curious people with curious stories to tell. But Mr. Roose-velt gave every sign that he was grateful for the unofficial insight which accrued from his wife's tireless activity. For her judgment he has always shown the greatest respect even though he does not always follow her advice.

Her reason for taking an official position with OCD is said to have been directly related to the mayor's third-term campaign. In her column Mrs. Roosevelt criticized the conduct of Civilian Defense under LaGuardia. It was being neglected, she said; ob-viously something more was called for. This disturbed certain of the mayor's friends in New York. As the story goes, they sent an emissary to the President to say that these strictures had hurt LaGuardia, especially among trade-unionists who were loyal per-sonal followers of Mrs. Roosevelt. If the President's wife were to join LaGuardia in the direction of OCD, there would be a gain all around, it was suggested.

In any event, Mrs. R. consented to become assistant director in charge of Volunteer Participation in the Office of Civilian Defense. A woman of strong personality, deeply aware that in modern war-fare it is not merely a question of providing physical safety for civilians, air raid shelters and gas masks, she soon put her stamp on the organization. Total war strikes hard at the nerves of the civilian population. A sense of participation, confidence in the future, physical well-being and mental health—all these things, as Mrs. Roosevelt well knew, are of primary importance.

The catch came in executing her ideas. First, through the entire organization ran an unfortunate amateurishness. Partly this was because Washington and the country were indifferent. But also it came out of the well-meaning people whom Mrs. Roosevelt gathered around her. The tone was that of an earnest social work conference mixed up somehow with folk dancing and the artsie-craftsie movement. Some of the good ladies of the town brought hampers of dinner to those who had to work late. And they did work late and work hard. But they were working in a cozy little corner that was walled off from the main currents of American life.

In addition, of course, Mrs. Roosevelt made certain grievous mistakes. Even if the dancer, Mayris Chaney, had been ideally equipped by training and experience to have charge of a physical fitness program for children, she should never have been appointed to a $4,600 a year job. She was Mrs. Roosevelt's personal friend and this would inevitably have the look of personal patronage. Both in Washington and the country, even with billions being hung on every bush, $4,600 a year has a large sound. Civil service compensation begins very much lower than that. Physicians with full medical training are taken into the Public Health Service at a lower rate.

But the storm that burst over poor Miss Chaney was far out of proportion to the cause. Even the well-meaning muddling in OCD could hardly have justified the furious abuse that descended on the unsuspecting heads of Mrs. Roosevelt and her friends. It had in it something ugly, yes, to use that overworked phrase, something un-American.

What happened, I believe, was that Mrs. Roosevelt became the scapegoat for the pent-up resentment of the American people. One humiliation and defeat had followed on another after Pearl Harbor. The men of Bataan were in a hopeless siege. They were, however, still fighting, along with the American forces everywhere, and fighting desperately. No criticism could touch them or even, except by indirection, their military superiors. This was a war, a war for survival, and pending the perilous outcome criticism was stilled.

That did not mean, however, that there was any closed season on Mrs. Roosevelt and the civilians who had been trying to direct civilian defense. They were a convenient target and every disgruntled citizen in the land threw the overripe tomatoes he had been saving in the hope of just such an opportunity. It raged through the press. In Congress dangerous ranters of the type of the incredible Clare Hoffman of Michigan had a field day.

What accentuated the attack, I am convinced, is the fact that the folk dancing and the picnic hampers, innocent enough in themselves, continued against a background of grave danger. Moreover, the real necessities of civilian defense—arm bands, steel helmets, gas masks—were not being provided. This failure had little or nothing to do with Mrs. Roosevelt's effort or lack of effort but again she was a convenient target.

It became a witch hunt and once Miss Chaney's status on the pay roll was discovered decency was out the window. Even hitherto responsible newspapers went to scarifying lengths. For a time the President's wife tried to stand bravely against the storm. Those who watched it close-up believe she was less to blame than the mayor who waited off at one side, doing nothing to avert the stream of missiles aimed at the lady in the White House.

Between the mayor and his first assistant relations became, to put it mildly, strained. At one point when LaGuardia called at the White House to settle an internal controversy that had grown out of the attack on the OCD, Mrs. Roosevelt telephoned one of her women advisers in whom she places great confidence. "The mayor," she said, her voice rising to a pitch of excitement, "is down in the Red Room and I don't know what to do with him."

It is a picture ludicrous and yet pathetic; the little mayor sitting with his legs dangling on one of the solemn, stiff red chairs in the Red Room; the great lady upstairs reluctant to cope with his formidable temperament.

LaGuardia had extended himself far beyond the powers of any human being, even a LaGuardia. As mayor of New York City, he had done a superlative job, yes, a superhuman job. The desire to use his considerable talents in a larger field was understandable. And it was natural that the mayor should want to get into the national picture. He was first appointed a member of the Joint Permanent Board of Defense—United States-Canada. This should have taken a great deal of his time, but next he was made head of Civilian Defense, a post that might well have ranked with that of the cabinet officers responsible for the military departments of the government. LaGuardia was active enough but his activity seemed always to focus attention on his own volatile person. Flying from city to city like a latter-day Paul Revere, he left in his wake a sense of vague alarm which his organization did nothing to alleviate.

The force of the public attack finally compelled Mrs. Roosevelt to resign. Shocked by the violence of it she drew away from many of her public activities, displaying for the first time an open dislike of the continuing public interest in what she said and did. Her friends had been hurt too.

She had persuaded the Hollywood star, Melvyn Douglas, to be head of OCD's arts section. Before he left California for Washington, Douglas had been warned of the kind of reception that might await him. Knowing little of the background, he poohpoohed such fears. Arriving just as the storm broke, he was like a man who has been sideswiped by a hit-and-run driver. It happened so quickly that he hardly knew what had struck him. Rallying, he responded with dignity and a just resentment of the unfair attacks that had linked his name with that of Mayris Chaney as a time-waster and a boondoggler. Douglas had voluntarily interrupted a highly profitable career and he did not propose to be repaid in abuse. Nor did he apologize for his interest in New Deal measures to help the Okies in California which had been one of the sticks used by House reactionaries to beat him.

All in all, it was not a time to which we can look back with anything like pride. Not long after Mrs. Roosevelt's resignation, Mayor LaGuardia stepped out. Hastily Dean James Landis of the Harvard University law school was appointed in his place.

There were many, even including some of Landis's friends, who felt that he was scarcely the type of man for the job. An intellectual, inclined to precise and arbitrary intellectual judgments, his critics said that he lacked the necessary ability to mix with and understand ordinary people.

Landis had done an excellent job in organizing civilian defense in his own community, Cambridge. That was why he was chosen. Laboring under a fearful handicap, he started in to revise the organization he had inherited. Fortunately he was able to cast off the more fanciful appendages, such as the co-ordinators of mumblety-peg and table tennis. And fortunately, too, he succeeded in keeping OCD out of the headlines. Lacking the qualities of, say, a Jim Farley, who had been suggested for the job, Landis worked, as though to make up for these lacks, until it seemed that he would literally drop in his tracks.

All day long through his office in the Dupont apartment building trailed a stream of visitors, each one depositing on his desk some problem of horrendous dimensions. And Dean Landis, chainsmoking—he must smoke more than Willkie's three packs a day— unsnarled the snarls and struggled to bring order out of chaos. Progress was almost imperceptible. Nevertheless, there was progress in spite of showers of brickbats from Mayor LaGuardia who, ironically enough, blamed his successor for everything that was wrong with civilian defense. Imitating Patience on a monument Dean Landis labored to overcome manifold obstacles.

One of the major problems, as Mrs. Roosevelt had clearly understood, was to release the vast potential of American energy; to bring it to focus on the war effort. No one had begun to touch that one. There was a formal organization out throughout the country, state and county defense councils, but it remained largely on paper. This formal organization was in the hands of bigwigs in the local communities, men who already had too many responsibilities; men who thought about defense and the war, when they thought about it at all, in wholly conventional terms.

A young newspaperman named Fred Sweet went back to his home town of Mt. Gilead, Ohio, to try to help organize the people of Mt. Gilead into an organization to win the war. Mt. Gilead was America in little, as Fred Sweet discovered. At the head of the Mt. Gilead defense council was the town banker who was also the town patent medicine manufacturer and the town rich man. He was an honorable and patriotic citizen but the fact remained that members appointed to his committee had never been called for a meeting. Now, however, when this young interloper came in with the idea of a town meeting to arouse people to the need for action, the chairman of the defense council tried to step in the way. He wanted to keep the controls in his hands, among the half-dozen men who ruled the affairs of the community.

There was a good, hot fight and in the end Fred Sweet won. From all over the town and from the surrounding countryside came men and women who wanted to do something, something tangible and real, to win the war. In a hundred and one ways they went to work, doing the organized community jobs that civilians can do. They had been waiting for a sign, a signal, and the town meeting and the rebellion that had taken place there, the rebellion against inertia and things as they were, had been that signal. What OCD needed, perhaps, was more Fred Sweets.

If Washington was concerned about the attitude—the morale—of the country, the country was just as agitated about what was going on, or not going on, in Washington. Not merely the obvious targets were aimed at in the flood of criticism which rose early in 1942. The entire administration was raked over with slight regard for personal feelings. Especially the cabinet came in for abuse. This was no war cabinet, said angry editorials. It was government as usual by men too old or too opinionated to know the rules of total warfare.

The way in which the Roosevelt cabinet had come through nine years of peace and war was an astonishing phenomenon. My father, who had been in Republican politics in Iowa in a small way, used to say that men in public office seldom die and never resign. Secretaries Hull, Perkins, and Ickes had held their cabinet posts since March of 1933. Secretary Morgenthau had been at the head of the Treasury since January of 1934. Secretary Jones had been in the administration from the beginning, steadily accumulating powers and offices.

Not a little of the attack centered on Jones for his failure to build up stock piles of strategic materials. The nation's twenty-five million automobiles would within a foreseeable time be laid up for lack of rubber, and Americans wanted to know why. For two years there had been large talk of stock piles and yet, when Singapore fell, the amount of rubber on hand was hardly sufficient for expanding military needs.

Jones is a massive man who maintains what might almost be called a professional silence on all matters of state. The words drop out of his thin mouth sparingly. A great admirer of the late Will Rogers, his political manners are modeled after those of his homespun hero. While he is one of the richest men in Washington, his fortune being estimated at nearly thirty million dollars, he maintains what is for Washington a studied simplicity, living with his wife in an apartment at the Shoreham and rarely appearing at big, showy Washington parties. Off the record and with men he has as lurid a vocabulary of profanity as anyone I have ever heard.

Until the outcry over stock piles Jones had had an excellent press. While he had been a part of the Roosevelt administration, business and the conservative newspapers had exonerated him of all blame for the New Deal. Jones had seen to that. On Capitol Hill he had powerful friends and a judicious use of his lending powers had given him a wider influence than perhaps any man except the President.

Outwardly the Secretary of Commerce gives the impression of being a stolid and stoical fellow. Actually beneath this surface he is a trembling mass of nerves. Under the unprecedented attack directed at him Jones writhed. When Leon Henderson came before the Truman defense investigating committee to testify on the rubber shortage, Jones came, too. Sitting directly behind the chairman, he fixed a glassy eye on Henderson, only looking now and then down the committee table at his friend and protector, Senator Tom Connally of Texas. With unparalleled tact, Henderson avoided putting the blame for the rubber failure on any single individual and you could almost hear big Jesse heave an audible sigh of relief.

At the Alfalfa Dinner a little later his iron control cracked and he seized Eugene Meyer, the owner of the Washington *Post*, a fellow diner, and shook him violently while he let him have some choice samples of his store of profanity. Meyer, sadly outclassed in weight and in height, tried in vain to strike at the angry behemoth. The day before, the Washington *Post* had carried an editorial which rejected Jones's defense of his policy, insisting that he could not pass the blame off on the President or the Malayan rubber growers. The encounter was symptomatic of the nerves that beset harassed Washington.

To blame Jones for failing to put together stock piles of strategic materials was on the face of it unreasonable. How anyone could ever have expected him to carry out such an assignment is difficult to see. He is a Texas banker and real-estate operator of great shrewdness. A man must, after all, be exceedingly shrewd or exceedingly lucky or both to make thirty million dollars. Jones had come through the depression in possession of his Houston, Texas, properties while small equity holders had been washed out. All his life he has been a shrewd trader and how he could have been expected to have thrown overboard at sixty-eight the values of a lifetime is difficult to see. He thinks in terms of money and the amassing and saving of money. He will dicker over a loan or a purchase until he obtains what he considers the greatest advantage for the government.

In normal times his shrewdness might have been an important asset. But the war was not a war of money. It was a war of things, a revolution against the values of money. Undoubtedly representatives of the powerful Malayan rubber combine made representations to Jones about not buying too much rubber so as not to disturb the market price; naturally they would oppose the construction of synthetic rubber plants in this country. The point is, however, that Jones was conditioned, by all his background and

by-pass her office, putting on others the responsibilities that should logically have been hers. This has made for confusion and it has also furthered the internecine wars that have raged around Miss Perkins and her department. The argument of the critics who year after year have tried to dislodge her is that if the office had been filled by a strong man with the confidence of labor leaders the more acute phases of the labor controversy might have been avoided.

In the first months of 1942, with a concerted and highly organized attack on the forty-hour week, the situation was critical. Representative Howard Smith of Virginia had gained considerable support for a bill that would have outlawed the forty-hour week, thereby invalidating all management-union contracts in major war industries, creating a chaotic condition that would certainly have gravely hampered production. Actually, of course, the work week of the average man in war industry was nearer fifty than forty hours and the issue was one of overtime pay.

Sidney Hillman, spokesman for labor on the War Production Board, was busily conniving to obtain for himself the man power mobilization assignment. Miss Perkins, who has never had the real confidence of top labor leaders, was of little help. The burden of checking the disruptive legislation and establishing some sort of equitable stability fell on the President himself.

Nor, in this crisis, did the representatives of labor come forward with any statesmanlike contribution. The opportunity was wide open to show dramatically what organized workers in the war industries were doing for victory. A minimum of courage and imagination at that moment and the focus might have shifted from what the wartime administration proposed to do for labor to what labor proposed to do for the government.

Philip Murray of the C.I.O. and William Green of the A. F. of L. publicly buried the hatchet at a big rally in Pittsburgh. It was a gesture in the right direction but the time called for something more than that. I think that Murray, a man of character and capacity, wanted to do more. On his neck, however, he could feel the hot breath of John L. Lewis who at that critical point was threatening to withdraw the United Mine Workers from the C.I.O. and thereby create a great gap both in the power of the organization and in its finances. Murray, struggling hard, may eventually succeed in freeing himself from the nemesis of the past. Green has always been a kind of captive balloon for the reactionary and often corrupt forces that wield the actual authority within the A. F. of L.

Perhaps it was merely that men adequate for the functions of normal peacetime leadership were made to seem small by the terrible march of events. In the course of the attack on the Cabinet, Stimson and Knox came in for their share of criticism. It was said that they had demonstrated their unfitness for their respective offices; that advanced age alone disqualified them. But, as was aptly pointed out, if they had been removed, who to name in their places would have been a problem. New leaders with conspicuous talents had not yet risen out of the upheaval.

On still another department the attack centered. Francis Biddle had succeeded Robert H. Jackson as attorney general in September of 1941, just in time to inherit the host of troubles that inevitably arose out of the war crisis. Coming from more or less the same background as the President, an old family, a modest background of inherited money, Groton and Harvard, Biddle, like the President, held strong liberal convictions. He said immediately after Pearl Harbor that he would never permit a repetition of the wartime witch-hunting that occurred in 1918 and 1919. FBI agents had arrested in Los Angeles a notorious anti-Semite and pro-Fascist named Robert Noble for making inflammatory statements a day or two after the Japanese attack. Biddle promptly ordered his release, convinced that he was no more than a crackpot expressing lurid opinions shared by few Americans.

For this action he was roundly denounced. This was, however, as nothing to the storm of criticism that developed on the West Coast when the Attorney General was reluctant to accede to the demand to intern all Japanese, aliens and American-born as well. The trepidations of the Californians were understandable in view of what had happened on December 7. But, as Biddle pointed out, to segregate 125,000 men, women, and children in an area back from the coast would mean a tremendous drain on man power and materials at just the time that the war production program would begin to make its full demands; to say nothing of the disruption caused by removing so many Japanese from truck farms and other productive enterprises. For some time Biddle resisted the pressure and then when it became irresistible he left to the Army the decision as to what should be done with the Japanese.

At the same time the pressure grew to take action against those loud fomenters who were skirting the narrow margin of treason. One of the most conspicuous was Father Coughlin whose *Social Justice* was following a line closely approximating that of little Herr Goebbels in Berlin. It was anti-British, anti-Jewish, anti-Roosevelt, antidemocratic; against everything that the United Nations professed to stand for. After a long period of uncertainty, the Attorney General ordered *Social Justice* barred from the mails. Earlier he had had William Dudley Pelley, the Silver Shirt editor of another rabid, pro-Fascist sheet, arrested on a charge of violating the 1917 Espionage Act. Biddle's action, particularly in the case of Coughlin, raised an extremely difficult question for which no answer has as yet been found. The Detroit priest insisted that he was merely expressing his views and that his paper was not seditious. Obviously, of course, its whole effect was to nullify the war effort and to spread the poisons of dissension and disunity. But what about democratic rights? What about the right of free speech?

In Germany the Nazis had been permitted under the Weimar Republic to abuse the privileges of democracy until they were powerful enough to put an end to them entirely. We surely should not fall into the same error. Yet liberals such as Biddle are haunted by the thought that a conservative or reactionary administration in power might use the precedent established now to suppress all dissenting opinion. Some formula was necessary to bring an end to treason or near treason and yet preserve the precious right of freedom of speech that was at the very heart of the democratic tradition. Nor was this an academic question. Roscoe Drummond of the

Washington bureau of the *Christian Science Monitor* had discovered at least ninety-five publications that were in the narrow borderland between rabble-rousing demagoguery and outright treason.

Francis Biddle, possessed of the sanguine temperament of a man who has advanced swiftly and with not too much difficulty, is likely to find the road harder as the war continues. One or two unhappy mistakes, apparently slipped over by subordinates, have caused him to tighten up the administration of his vast domain. One of these mistakes was a bill he sent to Congress over his signature which would have made almost every government document, even an order for clerk hire, a confidential document and therefore sacrosanct. It provided severe penalties for anyone daring to disclose the contents of such confidential documents. Had it passed in the form in which it was sent to the Hill, government officials would have had a convenient closet in which to hide any and all mistakes. Criticism of the war effort would have been all but impossible. For this blunder Biddle was properly criticized.

One thing that fed the attack on the administration during this troubled time was the unfortunate habit of cabinet members of contradicting each other loudly in public. The result often was to confound the confusion. The classic example grew out of the air raid alarm in the Los Angeles area. Secretary Knox said it was a false alarm. Secretary Stimson, twenty-four hours later, said it was a real alarm, growing out of the presence of enemy planes in the area. And what it really was, if anyone actually knew, the public was never permitted to learn.

When the contradictions occurred in fields directly touching the ordinary citizen, they were even more devastating in their effect. Various conflicting statements were made about the sugar rationing scheme which was delayed weeks beyond the date when it was first announced. In the same way motorists on the Eastern seaboard were confused by contradictory statements about the amount of gasoline to be allowed each motorist under a rationing plan. An anonymous spokesman in the Office of the Price Administrator said the allotment would be only two and a half to five gallons a week for each family. The next day Mr. Ickes, the petroleum co-ordinator, said this was all nonsense and that at least twenty-five to thirty gallons a month would be available. People were prepared to give up peacetime comforts and luxuries but they want to know what, how much, and when, without having to follow a public debate between government departments.

So serious did these conflicts of opinion become that a handyman was told off to make sure that cabinet officers and other government officials hewed to the same line. The assignment was given to Archibald MacLeish, head of the Office of Facts and Figures. An order went out from the White House that all speeches were to be submitted to MacLeish for reading before delivery. Likewise members of the government were expected to check with the head of OFF before making statements to the press. This made sense on paper but in practice it failed to work out. High officials of the government did not relish the idea of submitting to a subordinate officer their precious words. At least one cabinet officer frankly informed the official censor that he had no intention of submitting his speeches for advanced reading.

MacLeish was in a peculiarly vulnerable position. As in the instance of his close friend, Francis Biddle, he had been born to success. Owning a department store in Chicago, his family had a comfortable, secure position. After Hotchkiss he went to Yale where to crown a brilliant career he made Skull and Bones. Through the twenties he successfully combined the careers of poet and editor. One of the fast horses in the Henry Luce stable, he produced as an editor of *Fortune* some very exceptional work. At the same time scarcely a year went by that he did not publish a volume of verse, including the poem that won the Pulitzer Prize in 1932, "Conquistador."

The same shimmer of success seemed destined to surround him in his career in government. After a year as curator of the Niemann Fellowship at Harvard he was appointed by President Roosevelt to be librarian of Congress. MacLeish has exactly the temperament to get on with Roosevelt. He talks well and fluently. Ideas are his stock in trade. He is alert, attractive, sanguine. Congressional committees were prepared to dislike this poet who had been given a librarian's job. But when MacLeish appeared before them, they were charmed by his quick, responsive manner. He set out to make the Library of Congress a center of the nation's culture rather than merely a repository of books.

As the war crisis became acute, it followed naturally that the President should turn to his friend MacLeish for help with the function of propaganda. The Office of Facts and Figures was presumably created to do a propaganda job. But the word propaganda had come to have an unhappy connotation, conjuring up the shade of George Creel and other ghosts of the last war. Carefully avoiding the implication of propaganda, the Office of Facts and Figures, it was repeatedly insisted, was set up to provide nothing more than the unvarnished truth. The result was an anomalous role for MacLeish in which neither fish nor fowl nor yet good red herring seemed to be his dish.

From New York, Philadelphia, Boston, he gathered brilliant young editors and writers. Experts in radio, too, were assembled. The staff of OFF grew at that formidable, Jack-and-the-Beanstalk rate which had by then become so familiar to wartime Washington. But definition was lacking. The brilliant young men MacLeish had gathered around him seemed to be groping without any directive. (That was a word which Washington used constantly—directive.) While they were not precisely sure of their objective, they worked terribly hard at it.

Their first important effort, "Report to the Nation," was most unfortunate. Through it ran a note of optimism that sounded forced and wrong. Moreover, it preceded by only a day or two a report by the Truman defense investigating committee containing a series of appalling revelations of the failure of government and business. The Truman report told the truth about the rubber crisis, which "Report to the Nation" had glossed over. It contained the truth about the failures in plane production which the MacLeish document had ignored. Other and equally glaring inconsistencies between the two unhappily timed reports were obvious to even casual readers of the newspapers.

With a second pamphlet published several weeks later, OFF seemed to be closer to a possible goal. "Divide and Rule" tells in unadorned language the story of Hitler's effort to set nation against nation and class against class. It deals specifically with the German propaganda intended to alienate Americans and British. Here was a tangible objective and OFF hit it hard. "Divide and Rule" found its public through the myriad channels of information that normally reach the American public—newspapers, magazines, the radio. That must inevitably, of course, be the aim of an information agency. The public can be informed only through existing means of news dissemination.

Zealous New Dealers find this irksome. Distrustful of the press, they would reach the public direct instead of through a suspect medium. Especially for Lowell Mellett the vagaries of the press are difficult to tolerate. If any man in Washington is a simon-pure New Dealer, it is Mellett. If any man has an unadulterated devotion to the President, it is this same Mellett. Small, frail looking, there is in Mellett a compact energy which he expends wholly for the cause.

For years he quarreled with Roy Howard over the editorial line which the Washington *Daily News* should take under his editorship. Later he gave up his position at a considerable personal loss and entered the service of F.D.R. Ever since there has burned within him the passion of a crusader. And he has enlisted in his pilgrimage many others.

Not only Robert W. Horton, the director, but many of the staff of the Division of Information of the War Production Board were recruited by Mellett from the ranks of Scripps-Howard. The Division of Information, just prior to reorganization under Elmer Davis, had a staff of 343 which included forty-five or fifty former newspaper men. In a number of instances they were former press agents in government departments. Their positions in the regular departments had been filled by younger and less experienced men or they had gone unfilled.

Conservatives such as Senator Byrd railed at the battalion of press agents attached to the mushrooming war agencies. But the fact was that most of them were working hard, working long hours. And if you wanted information, you got it, unless, that is, someone above the rank of press agent stepped in to prevent your getting it. Of course, there were drones and incompetents and show-offs, as there are in any large organization, but if you worked from day to day with these men you were of necessity impressed with the number who were hard-working, efficient in the face of great odds, and terribly in earnest.

Here, too, that ubiquitous word directive popped up. Measurements of production simply were not to be had except in the vaguest and most general terms. While speeches of top officials could reflect a general optimism or a guarded pessimism, this was not enough. The public was entitled to know more about the progress of the vast armament program. For many weeks MacLeish struggled to get approval for some form of production communiqué which should be at least as specific as the generalized announcement on military developments issued by the War and Navy Departments. It seemed impossible to arrive at any agreement among those responsible for the production program. This had a disturbing connotation of France where behind a blank wall of official silence failures had been carefully concealed.

Disturbing, too, was the long delay in bringing together under a centralized direction the scattered information services. Through four or five agencies duplication and overlapping of effort went on. The Bureau of the Budget had drawn up an order for the President consolidating the various phases of press agentry under a single director who would fix a uniform policy. The order—it was an excellent subject for speculative news stories—had been placed on the President's desk. There it stayed for an indefinite period.

With the weight of the war on his shoulders, it could be argued, F.D.R. had no time for details. Yet on Mellett's word it was the President who personally ordered the information center which was built in a record forty days' time on the little triangular park on Pennsylvania Avenue opposite the Willard and the Washington Hotels. For carrying out the presidential order Mellett was roundly denounced both on Capitol Hill and in the press. The egregious name of Mellett's Madhouse was applied to the well-proportioned building that took form in one of the last remaining green spots in the gray, toil-worn capital. To the death, Mellett defended the decision of his chief and hero. It was necessary, he insisted, to create an information center where confused business men could be steered in the proper direction. When Senator Byrd took to calling names, Mellett called names back. For a hero-worshiper in the service of the man he reveres above all others this was no hardship.

What it came down to, in part at least, was that this Washington efflorescence was taking place against a background of perilous uncertainty punctuated by defeats and reverses. Burma and Corregidor were in the headlines as the United States Information Center opened for business. Leaving to one side the determined foes of the President, who could be expected to oppose anything he asked for, people failed to consider the complications and necessities of a huge organization such as had been assembled in the capital. They wanted not information centers nor government reports. They wanted news of production, news of progress in the war; something tangible that they could hold to.

Chapter XV

The War of Production

THE first task before Elmer Davis's new Office of War Information was to correct the unreal optimism which was the prevailing climate through the spring of 1942. How to do that was another matter, raising the question of the sources of this persistent illusion. It came seemingly out of newspaper headlines but the war organization must have furnished some substance.

Even though headline writers are ingenious with words that sell newspapers, they cannot actually invent the news they put in big, bold type.

Now and then the military departments seemed to catch themselves up short, as though with a twinge of conscience. Confidential warnings went out to editors while Bataan Peninsula still held. The action was heroic, it was a classic example of American heroism, but nevertheless it was no more than a desperate holding action and it should not be interpreted to the public as anything other than that. Yet when Bataan fell and then Corregidor, there was little realization that this was the culmination of the gravest military defeat the nation had suffered since the war of 1812. Nor did there seem to be any effort to bring about an understanding of what it meant for the immediate future to have the Japs in possession of Manila Bay and able to release a force of seasoned fighters for other theaters of war.

On the production front there was reason for at least a ray of optimism, and guns were moving off the assembly lines in what the military conceded to be battle production. A trumpeting of hope came from Donald M. Nelson in late April. We were, he said, over the hump. We were beginning to outproduce the Axis. Naturally this made the headlines, accelerating the warm optimistic glow that seemed to emanate from the capital. Other men high in the war organization reproached Nelson for his statement. They scolded him a little for having contributed to a state of mind which was unhealthy because it was unreal.

You could hardly blame the old bull elephant for that solitary trumpet blast. For so long he had been pushing his way through the enmeshed blackness of the jungle that when he saw even a glimmer of light ahead, the impulse to let the rest of the herd know about it must have been irresistible.

With poor old SPAB about to fall in public ruin of its own dead weight, the President on January 6 had made Nelson head of the new War Production Board. For the first time authority and responsibility were concentrated in one man. Nelson was the man. His would be the blame for failure, his the glory for success.

While he had the new authority—he had seen to that, crossing out, and interlining and working over the executive order creating WPB—he inherited the old organization with all that that meant in complicated human emotions, jealousies, frictions. The bull elephant had of necessity to tread softly; to reassure his restless, uneasy herd, to convince them that he knew the way out. This is Nelson's tempo: slow, cautious, deliberate, but sure. Some of the men around him were inclined to be impatient. They said he was not moving fast enough. But the bull elephant knew what he knew. He would cross no bridges without testing them with that deliberate forefoot, even though behind him the herd pushed impatiently, muttering, grumbling.

It was a disjointed organization that Nelson had fallen heir to. Layer on layer it had been added to in the troubled past. In the middle were difficult complications. For example, Nelson's old boss, Lessing Rosenwald, chairman of the board of Sears, Roebuck & Company, was head of the division of conservation. Out of this division could have come a program for saving enormous quantities of vital materials both in industry and in private consumption. The way had clearly been shown under the War Industries Board in the last war to standardization of styles and elimination of frills and waste. But little or no real progress had been made.

Then there were men in important positions who were not production men and who did not think in terms of production. One was Philip Reed, a lawyer who at forty-three had been made chairman of the board of the vast General Electric Corporation. Around Reed had grown up a whole series of feuds with New Dealers under the wing of Leon Henderson who accused him of thinking in terms of business as usual.

Revelatory was the row over medical supplies in the health branch of the War Production Board. From the British had come a request for one hundred and ninety different drugs and chemicals badly needed in the Middle East. The health supplies branch drastically pared one hundred and eighty items. This came at a time when an internecine warfare was raging over priorities for pharmaceuticals—Lydia Pinkham's, Father John's medicine, and the like. One faction was working for adoption of a standardized list of drugs that would provide everything necessary for safeguarding the health of the public and the armed forces but without any expensive frills and variations. On the other side William M. Bristol, Jr., head of the health supplies branch, was out to get an A-1 priority for the drugs essential for patent medicines.

Bristol, head of a firm manufacturing important patent medicines, was backed by Reed. While his request for top priority rating for the patent medicine industry was rejected, he was nevertheless kept on as head of his branch, although Nelson had announced that no dollar-a-year man would be allowed to serve in a post where he could make decisions affecting his own industry. Some little time after the controversy he retired, on condition that he be allowed to name his successor, another representative of the drug industry. The outcome was typical of this transition period when men who had obviously failed were supplemented, but by a gradual and presumably painless process. Often they were left with empty honors while more aggressive men went on to do the job.

That was Nelson's method as it was also the method of the President. He listened to those who wanted the whole thing stirred up and the bad spots cut out without benefit of ether, but it was not the way he operated. If he can avoid trouble, he avoids it. When the question of large-scale rationing came up, he said, a shrewd smile on his face, "We'll let Leon handle that one." Unlike so many other executives within the war organization, he does not reach out for added powers, especially if they bristle with public dangers and difficulties as does rationing.

He wanted to believe, as spring gave way to summer in the critical year of 1942, that all was well with the production program. And when the evidence was there before his eyes, he spoke. Now and then, however, he went too far.

One of his subordinates expressed doubt whether the ship program would be on schedule by the end of the year. A day or two later Nelson brushed this doubt aside with a bold assurance that shipping would be all right. Those who knew the actual situation were astonished. The word bottleneck like the word directive is triple-starred in the Washington lexicon. But if ever it could be used legitimately, it was with respect to shipping.

Shipping was the key in the perilous spring of 1942. It was the key on every front from Alaska to Libya. Months before, I had talked with a British general who had just come from a flight round all the principal theaters of the war. I recalled how seriously he had spoken about the matter of shipping. You are a continental power, he had said. You have thought in terms of transcontinental railroads and airlines. You have been very nearly self-sufficient or you thought of yourselves as self-sufficient. When you have considered shipping at all, it has been only incidentally, as a kind of good thing to have after you supplied yourselves with everything else. Now it seems to me that you've carried that attitude over into the war when you can scarcely afford to go on thinking that way.

That struck me as a shrewd analysis. And it was true, too, that in no other department was the dominance of business as usual and government as usual so strong. As chairman of the Maritime Commission, Admiral Land had been surrounded by shipping men —shipbuilders and the vice-presidents of shipping lines. They were working, with some progress, toward construction of a merchant marine on the traditional pattern, large, well-fitted ships to ply the trade routes of the world. When Land was made wartime shipping administrator, presumably with absolute powers over the shipping industry, these same men went along.

Quite understandably, they were not adequate to the new assignment which was to do the impossible; to create in record time small fast ships that would get through the submarine-infested waters of the North and South Atlantic. Land is a tough-talking Navy man who is inclined to be impatient with civilian interference. In fact, on several occasions when civilians from the War Production Board have attempted to criticize his program, he has flared up with a show of seagoing temper intended to discourage any such interference in the future.

The controversy over the small sea otter type of cargo vessel, built of reinforced concrete, with a speed up to twenty knots, is typical. Only by some such radical technique will the shipping bottleneck be broken, it was argued by those who saw the folly of continuing to lay down big, expensive vessels so slow, comparatively at least, as to be ideal targets for fast submarines and bombing planes. An experimental sea otter was built and put through a long series of tests. At the end, for singularly vague reasons, it was rejected by traditionally-minded naval officers and by the shipping men around Admiral Land. One of the reasons given, ironically enough, was that all the ways were taken up with standard-type cargo ships so that there was no room to construct sea otters. Finally, after word from Donald Nelson advising further experimentation, there was a hope that a modified sea otter might eventually be put into production.

Not alone on the construction side was the program inadequate. From a half-dozen sources reports came to me of the shocking misuse of available shipping space. Men not at the top but somewhere between the top and the bottom were furious, sick with a kind of despair, at what they saw and yet could do little or nothing about. Incidentally, that is one of the things that happens after you have been in Washington a certain number of years. You find friends and acquaintances in medium positions who know far more about what is going on in their own respective spheres than the men at the head of the organization. The top dog ordinarily has too much to do, too many responsibilities and duties, to see what is happening beneath the surface, the surface being made up of the official reports his immediate subordinates submit to him. But take a smart man operating more or less freely somewhere within an organization and he is likely to know the entire story. That was especially true in the war crisis as the big names spread themselves thinner and thinner.

In February of 1942 an allied shipping pool was created—on paper. Sir Arthur Salter was designated as the representative of the British Ministry of Shipping in Washington to collaborate with Admiral Land in pooling the tonnage of Great Britain and the United States. Dissimilar in temperament and background, they seemed unable to work out any practical arrangement. There had been notorious abuses, such as the ship that went off to the Netherlands East Indies in the Southwest Pacific with a cargo of empty beer bottles. That could be put down to the inevitable confusion following on the start of the war.

What was heartbreaking was that this continued long after it was reasonable to expect a system that would prevent such follies. In March of 1942 a British vessel left Brisbane, Australia, with three thousand tons of sugar, brought it across the vast Pacific, through the Panama Canal, touched briefly at an American port on the East coast and then proceeded on to Britain. This was at a time when Puerto Rico had a superabundance of sugar that might of necessity be used partly for fertilizer for the lack of ships to bring it to the mainland. Nor was this an isolated instance. At about the same time two vessels of American registry, belonging in fact to the Maritime Commission, brought sugar from Australia to Newfoundland.

It might have been argued that it was better to bring back sugar than nothing if it had not been for the fact that precious minerals —nickel and chrome, for example—were waiting transport to American mills which might be forced to close for lack of them. Here the Navy came in. There were vital supplies on the Vichy French island of New Caledonia, but merchant vessels were not allowed to put into ports under control of the United States Navy.

The only ships calling at New Caledonian ports were military vessels and the Navy does not concern itself over cargoes, even vital cargoes. That is a civilian detail. Ships came across the empty loneliness of the Pacific in ballast. To be sure, the demand for transport space to get men to Australia and India was urgent, desperate, but hardly more desperate than the need for those strategic materials which we had failed to accumulate in substantial amounts.

From February on through the spring I wrote about shipping in the *Post-Dispatch*, trying my damndest to make it sound as important and as urgent as I felt it to be. Almost the only visible result, as far as I could see, was a call at the office from the banana lobby. The banana lobby had had its feelings hurt by a story describing the politics of bananas, a devious bit of politics if ever there was one. The shipping section of the War Production Board had sent a letter to Admiral Land urging that for the duration there be no more imports of bananas. Through a government subsidy the banana crop in the banana republics would be bought up so that the economic repercussions would be cushioned in as far as that was possible. It was more important, the WPB letter pointed out, to bring back bauxite and other minerals than bananas. Through some curious circumstance a copy of this letter came into the possession of the government of Honduras and promptly there was a sharp protest at the State Department. In some mysterious way, too, it came into the possession of the United Fruit Co. which controls the highly profitable banana trade. United Fruit representatives also descended on the State Department.

Their argument was that conversion of the banana boats would be impractical, an economic waste, in view of the fact that they were partially refrigerated and equipped for this highly specialized trade. That argument had some validity. What it overlooked was that the banana boats might easily have been converted to carrying sugar from Puerto Rico. Then the larger vessels in the sugar trade could have been released and shifted to the run from Surinam in Dutch Guiana to bring back the bauxite that was in ever greater demand as the plane program expanded geometrically. Someone was needed who would shear through the special interests, cut through the thick cloud of tradition, end the fumbling and the hesitation.

Well over thirty boats continued in the banana trade as Honduras and the War Production Board and the United Fruit Co. and Admiral Land became more and more involved in the intricacies of the politics of bananas and sugar. Nazi submarines rarely wasted a torpedo on a banana boat. Versed in the economics as well as the tactics of warfare, they knew the value of a cargo of bananas, as compared, say, with a cargo of bauxite or manganese. They picked their ships with an uncanny intelligence which gave many men in Washington sleepless nights.

I was told of one cargo which was a key cargo. Nazi submarines pursued the vessel until it was sunk. If it had arrived safely at its destination, it might well have altered the tempo of an entire industry. Under the censorship I knew that I could not name that cargo or its significance. We had learned, intuitively for the most part, what we could and could not print. But the Germans knew about that cargo. That was why they sank it. Their intelligence service both in the United States and in Latin America was appallingly efficient.

Belatedly our own Navy set out to train officers, who would have the same strategic economic knowledge. On an aircraft carrier or a submarine they would be able to designate the German or the Japanese ship to go for; the one that might through its loss shut down an entire industry. The men recruited for this special administrative and economic school in Rhode Island were, as it happened, recruited almost entirely from the Racquet Club and from three or four brokerage firms employing young men with the right connections out of Harvard, Princeton, and Yale.

Certainly there are brains in the Racquet Club, brains as well as brawn. The point is, however, that not all the brains in the nation are concentrated in that institution, and an effort to bring in something more nearly approaching a cross section of the nation's intelligence might conceivably bring better results. Learning that J. P. Marquand's good old Jo-Jo, for whom adding two and two of a summer's afternoon is a bit of a trial, was to become a military economic strategist must have given even his fellow alumni a turn. When it comes to tweaking Britain's old school tie, we should be careful that our own school tie is not knotted too tightly. Men who go down to the sea in ships need more than the right school and the right background in the struggle for survival in which we are all involved.

We had undertaken, it was more and more clear, a task of superhuman proportions—arsenal to the United Nations. From every front the cry was the same—send us more and more and more. There could never be enough.

What failure meant, the immediate past had already taught us, or it should have. In late December and early January Lieutenant Governor Hubertus van Mook of the Netherlands East Indies was in Washington trying, trying so hard, to make officialdom realize the urgency of getting more planes to Java. This stout-hearted Dutchman had seen the shadow of coming events and he knew that each minute was precious. Yet he found it difficult to communicate his sense of urgency to people to whom he talked. He was thinking in hours and they were thinking in days. You could see him struggle, painfully, desperately, against the weight of inertia and confusion. He knew how many first-line planes were available in the Indies. How pitifully few the number against the Jap hordes!

I remember how he tried to convey to some of us his own realization of the lateness of the hour. He said that in the Gedeh Mountains, where the Dutch families went to escape the worst of Batavia's tropical heat, he had a pleasant summer house on Mt. Poentjak. During a dry spell grass fires would start far down the mountainside. The van Mooks would look down from their comfortable height and see the natives struggling to control the fires. Then one day a wind threatened to carry the flames within their own compound. Not until then did they and their servants rush down to fight the fire beside the natives.

While Governor van Mook was too tactful to say so, he knew that we were still on our mountain top watching the natives fight the fire. We could not see that it threatened our own compound. Van Mook went back for the battle of Java. He went all through that ordeal in which superior air power and superior sea power dealt one devastating blow after another. The timetable of disaster was far exceeded in those days of punishing losses and phenomenal heroism. On order of the governor, van Mook finally left on the last available plane for Australia to represent the Netherlands East Indies in London. But he left his family behind. Not all the soldiers in this war fight with guns. Lieutenant Governor van Mook is one of the heroes.

Men from other fronts were in Washington on the same urgent mission that had at first brought van Mook to the capital. One was Maxim Litvinov, the ambassador of the Soviet Union. Here indeed was a veteran of the wars, both civil and external. About his very presence in Washington was something miraculous. When Stalin finally concluded that the Litvinov policy of collective security had hopelessly failed, he turned on his foreign minister the full force of his wrath. Few men have survived that blast. Madame Litvinov went to Siberia for a cooling-off period and her husband was allowed to fall into obscurity. Even in the midst of his explosion Stalin must have perceived the way in which his servant would be able to serve him at a later time.

Leaving Kuibyshev in November, the Litvinovs came by way of the Middle East. They flew across the Pacific just in advance of the Japanese attack. Of official greeters at stops along the way the blunt Max asked embarrassing questions. At Nichols Field, near Manila, where he saw ranks of shining planes, he asked about dispersal fields. The reply was vague and noncommittal, but the canny Litvinov understood perfectly what it meant. In Hawaii he asked similar questions and got similar replies. Arriving in San Francisco on Saturday, December 6, it is possible that the Litvinovs were not as stunned by Pearl Harbor as were most Americans.

Inevitably Washington was a shock for the Soviet ambassador and his wife who had been born Ivy Low, daughter of a British philologist of note. They had come from Moscow, a besieged city stripped down to the bare essentials of living. One thing Moscow had in abundance and that was defensive protection; the anti-aircraft batteries could send into the air a curtain of steel that almost defied attack. Washington was still a capital torn between war and peace, rocked by the blow at Pearl Harbor.

What the Litvinovs found difficult to understand was the way in which life went on as usual. The parties, the sleek, shiny cars jammed in traffic, the hotels crowded with people drinking and dancing. Particularly Madame Litvinov, who has almost as much disregard for the pleasant minutiae of living as though she had been born a Russian Communist, found Washington hard to accept. Reporters asked her about her clothes and whether women in Soviet Russia had permanent waves and the ambassador's wife had trouble remembering that her opinions would after all have a semiofficial sound. What does it matter anyway, she was in the habit of saying, whether I come to a party in this old dress or another dress? America was very strange.

They lived in indifferent simplicity in three or four rooms of the huge Embassy that had been the pretentious, show-window house of the Pullman family. It still has an early Pullman, gilt and red-plush look that makes a curious background for the portraits of Lenin and Stalin and the big pictures of the revolution that the new tenants have hung up. Litvinov's predecessor, Constantine Oumansky, had given huge parties that spared no expense. The new ambassador reduced the scale of entertainment, curtailing the guest list and curbing the caviar and champagne.

In other ways, too, he differed from his predecessor. Oumansky had been a constant visitor at the State Department, depositing on Sumner Welles's doorstep one complaint after another. The urbane Welles almost lost his urbanity under Oumansky's incessant prodding. Litvinov spent little time at the Department. This did not mean, however, that the Soviets failed to register their dissatisfaction with the degree of collaboration between the U.S.A. and the U.S.S.R. in prosecuting the war. It was hardly necessary to register formal complaints when news stories out of Washington

and from neutral European sources made the cause for complaint
so obvious.

America was not living up to the terms of the formal protocol
that had been signed in Moscow by the Harriman mission in the
late summer of 1941. In early 1942 the lag had been a scandal.
Our aid to Russia was on a token basis, in striking contrast to the
generous pledge we had formally signed. The fact was that officers,
both on the military and civilian side, were reluctant to give priorities for the shipment of materiel to the Soviets. Prejudice went
deep, directly affecting official decisions.

What complicated the situation was that the army experts had
been so wrong on Russia. And what is more, they had not concealed their wrongness. A tempest-in-a-teapot controversy grew up
over whether Colonel X had been removed from the general staff
and relegated to a minor post for remarks he had made about
Russian strength at an off-the-record press conference, or whether
the change had been, as announced, a routine one. Of course, experts everywhere, with a very few exceptions, had been wrong
about Soviet resistance and that includes a self-advertised prophet
who goes under the name of Adolf Hitler. Nevertheless within
the War Department there was a defensive psychology.

The President on March 17 made public a letter he had sent to
all officials connected with the program of aid to Russia, ordering
primary priorities for all shipments to the Soviet Union. The letter
was signed Franklin D. Roosevelt, Commander in Chief, and the
significance of that "Commander in Chief" was not lost on those
who had followed the struggle over aid to the U.S.S.R. The President's order marked the beginning of a tremendous drive to bring
the shipments up to schedule.

While he had said, with emphasis, that within a month the
flow of supplies would be on schedule, two months later they were
still not on the mark. But that may have been because Harriman
and his aides were too optimistic when they signed the Moscow
protocol. As with so many other phases of the war program, the
vital factor of shipping was overlooked. The British, more cautious
in what they agreed to do, have kept their shipments up to the

promised level. One of the keenest of the younger correspondents, James B. Reston, has ridden this story hard in the New York *Times*, thereby doing the cause of the United Nations yeoman service. Commenting on the increase that followed the President's order, Reston summed up succinctly as follows:

"Nobody here with any knowledge of the number of submarines operating off the East Coast and the supply and demand situation in merchant and naval shipping can, however, hope for any sudden or decisive improvements in our saltwater problems for some time. The tanks, planes and ammunition we are sending to the Russians, together with the other special equipment they have requested, will certainly bolster their defense but it would be a mistake to expect that what we and the British are doing will determine the outcome of the battles that are to be fought on the Russian front in the next six months. These battles may very well settle the fate of the world for generations to come. That solemn fact is understood both here and in London and, being understood, all the supplies and action that the two great democracies can muster will be sent. But in the last analysis the Russians themselves will decide the issue."

Of the failure to live up to the protocol, Litvinov would say little either on or off the record; merely, in his thick accent and curious idiom, stating the fact that the expected number of planes and tanks were not arriving at Russian ports. Crotchety is the word for the ambassador. He sits in his study wearing one of those uniforms of blue serge with turn-down collar, pleats, and belt, which important Russians in Moscow are always wearing in news photographs. I have rarely met any public figure who was so difficult to talk to. Replying with monosyllables or a shake of his head, he comes to a full stop and waits for another prod. Nothing is volunteered. Although he is not a large man, there is about him something massive and imperturbable. His health is not good and he seems, shut away in his paneled study, curiously isolated from the hurly-burly of Washington, which may be a status he has worked to achieve.

If the cry came from Russia for more and more and more, it

also came from the Middle East, from Libya. News dispatches and broadcasts from Cairo did not conceal the urgent need for far more materiel than was coming from the United States by the long way round the Cape of Good Hope. Libya had been robbed after Pearl Harbor of troops and supplies to buttress Singapore and other points in the Far East. The intimation from Cairo was that if more help did not come, not only Libya but Egypt and Suez might go.

On length of hauls there was almost no choice. All the hauls were long; vistas of water that from Washington looked endless; only three round trips a year to Archangel, the Antipodes, India.

From Alaska came the same call—more ships, more men, more planes, more guns. The construction and supply of bases in that distant territory had been greatly handicapped for lack of cargo space. The haul from Seattle to Juneau is 1,033 miles and everything must be hauled—concrete, steel beams, machines—with which to build modern air and land fortifications against threatened Japanese invasion. Progress was slow and the state of Alaska's defenses hardly one to cheer about. The Japs knew this. The customary laundrymen were arrested on December 8 and 9 and found to have the most elaborate photographic equipment which had been used to record the development of the bases.

In view of the shipping shortage those 1,033 miles were a fearful handicap. Diplomatic bickering between Canada and the United States had delayed selection of a site for the Alaskan Highway. As governor of Alaska and member of the Alaska International Highway Commission, Ernest Gruening came to Washington at infrequent intervals to urge action. When it came, after months of indecision, he was dismayed that the route chosen was the inner, mountainous route which not only Gruening but many others long familiar with the country believe to be all but impossible. The difficulties of terrain, as Gruening had repeatedly pointed out, are such that years of the most difficult and hazardous engineering effort will in all likelihood be required. Old sourdoughs are of the opinion that the muskeg can never be conquered. They say it will absorb anything you try to lay down over it.

I WRITE FROM WASHINGTON

An alternative route was along the coast. Knowledgeable men held that a coastal road could be built within a year or a year and a half. It was apparently the military experts, American and Canadian, who vetoed the coast route. Their argument was that it would be easy for an enemy to land a brigade or two at an isolated spot and pinch off the highway. Another argument for choosing the inner route was that it would link the bases of a military air line between the United States, Canada, and Alaska.

Alaska no longer had a far-off, academic sound. Vice-President Wallace, in one of the most significant speeches of the war, made it plain that an attack might be expected there and on the Pacific Northwest. The winter fogs had lifted. The Japs were enraged by the bold, brilliant blows our Army bombers had dealt to Japanese industrial centers. They could be expected to strike in angry desperation. And it was not long afterward that they occupied Attu, Kiska and Agattu at the end of the Aleutian chain.

Wallace spoke of still another front where danger was imminent. In Latin America the surface was smooth enough, but beneath the surface were rumblings and grumblings that meant no good for the future. And here again shipping was the key.

With the exception of a trickle from the British Isles, South America was cut off from the rest of the world and therefore dependent entirely on the United States for manufactured goods. It was up to us to supply the essentials to sustain modern life in the industrial centers of Latin America. Zinc must come from North America in sufficient quantities to permit the great dailies of Buenos Aires to continue to publish. Coal must go to the railroads of Brazil if we were to continue to get vital manganese ore from Brazilian mines. This was a critical test of our capacity to live up to the splendid promises we had made.

Yet the tonnage available for the South American trade was allowed to fall well below the level that the State Department considered safe. Under the terms of the executive order creating the War Shipping Administration, authority was not too closely defined, so that both the Army and the Navy continued to requisition ships for immediate and urgent use. Often these ships came off South American runs.

At the conference at Rio de Janeiro in January, Sumner Welles had had his back to the wall. Striving for American unity on a declaration calling for severance of relations with the Axis powers, he was confronted over and over with the same question. You are asking us, the Latins would say, to go to war, but can you assure us that we shall not be completely cut off here at the other end of the hemisphere? Have you sufficient shipping and can your Navy convoy on the north-south trade routes? These were difficult questions. What saved the day was the Axis tonnage interned in Latin-American ports. This was enough to make the difference.

It did not, however, solve the problem of convoys. Available merchant vessels lacked guns and deGaussing equipment. Slowly this lack was made up, but it was precarious business sending such unprotected lambs into the jungle of the South Atlantic. After several losses Brazil ordered her ships back to port until more adequate protection could be provided.

Through the spring and summer of 1942 the screw was turned tighter. Narrow squeaks were the rule and not the exception. A cargo would arrive just in time to prevent dire consequences. Vital industries were sustained but the fabric of the Latin-American economy was fraying out under the strain. The time was plainly visible when mounting unemployment would make itself felt in a variety of unpleasant ways. Axis agents were waiting for just such an opportunity. Chile and Argentina had not lived up to the declaration of Rio by breaking off relations with the Axis powers. In Buenos Aires and in Santiago were concentrated the agents who had operated throughout the continent. They were waiting for the signal. When it came, we might expect fifth-column warfare in Latin America. That was the warning in Vice-President Wallace's speech.

There was no dodging the hard fact that shipping was inadequate to the colossal task we had undertaken. It was no secret that the number of finished vessels actually delivered was far less than the number being sunk by Axis submarines. As the submarine warfare was intensified, with subs in the Gulf of Mexico and the St. Lawrence River, a crisis was on our very doorstep. Yet there seemed to be no acute realization of this in Washington.

In the face of this immediate and crying need, shipping officials continued to talk about what they could do in 1943. That had been for too long the emphasis—what next year or the year after that would bring. Twenty million tons of shipping was the amount promised for 1943. On examining this pledge, however, you quickly discovered that there was an "if" in it. Twenty million tons of shipping would come off American ways IF sufficient steel plates were allocated for merchant ship construction. Past failures to live up to the construction rate had been laid to lack of plates.

Here was one of the black spots that seemingly no one had faced up to. If the war was one and indivisible in each and every corner of the globe, then production was one and indivisible too. Not even over our own productive plant had any over-all allocation been enforced. Far too loosely co-ordinated was the division of materials between tanks, munitions, shipping, planes, and civilian essentials. And only the smallest beginning had been made in unifying the production of the United Nations. Canada and the United States had made an effective start, eliminating duplication and waste, tying together the industrial plants of the two countries.

What the crisis demanded was a supreme production council with a total view of the vast productive front and the powers to say when and how commodities and materiel should be allocated. And if this was essential for the battle of production, still another necessity loomed even larger. That was for a supreme war council which from Washington should direct the destinies of this all-encompassing conflict.

The Christmas visit of Winston Churchill had been one of those dramatic episodes that both President and Prime Minister love. Bringing together these two symbols of the democratic faith was heartening for all the world. Out of that meeting went a current of hope that made itself felt around the world. While nothing specific was said by either man, you had the sense of large plans made and strategies discussed.

When he departed Churchill left behind him various military deputies who were presumably empowered to represent the British war cabinet at the council table in Washington. Chief among these was Field Marshal Sir John Dill, a distinguished soldier, who was commander in chief of the British forces during the first part of the war. It was Sir John who flew to France at the time of the collapse and went through the harrowing drama that resulted in the surrender of the French forces. Dill and his aides were installed in the white marble building on Constitution Avenue that had been the headquarters of the Public Health Service. Here too our own chief of staff, General Marshall, established quarters. So did the deputy of the British Admiralty, Admiral Sir Andrew Cunningham. And so did other military and naval men of high rank.

The headquarters of the combined chiefs of staff became one of the hush-hush nerve centers of Washington. If you are important enough to have an appointment with one of the lords of creation who have their being there, you present yourself humbly and wait until the proper verification has been established. Then you are not permitted to go down the corridor alone. A soldier in full war accouterment walks beside you. It is quite possible that the show of authority is greater than the authority itself. The decisions, even the minor decisions, of these British deputies are often reviewed or revised in Whitehall. This makes for harassing delays. It makes for inefficiency and uncertainty. Important visitors are constantly popping over from the other side, some with the unintentional publicity that accompanied Admiral Sir Dudley Pound's visit, others with complete secrecy. And we reciprocate by sending Harry Hopkins and General Marshall to London. Surely much of this coming and going would be unnecessary if real power were concentrated in Washington.

The Pacific War Council was a step forward. Around one table sat representatives of the nations engaged in that far-distant struggle. What these representatives quickly realized was that a decision on the Pacific theater immediately had its repercussions on other theaters of war. To one man in particular was this driven home so forcibly that he spoke out with courage and frankness. This was

Walter Nash, the first minister from New Zealand to Washington, whose mature wisdom gave his words in council a weight far out of proportion to the size and importance of his country.

We have got, said Nash, to stop talking at people and start talking with them. He proposed that on the supreme council, representatives of the British Commonwealth of Nations, the United States, Russia, and China should sit. Representatives should have full power to approve decisions taken by the council. The chairman would be President Roosevelt, and Washington would be in fact as well as in hope and in intention the center of the war.

Talking with people and not at them! If that is important for the war, it is far more important for the peace that must follow the war. Conceivably we might win the war without real collaboration. With one war for Britain and one war for America and one war for Russia and one war for China we might win it, after a fashion. But we could never win the peace in that way. We could never make tomorrow the tomorrow of our hopes and promises if we failed to come together in the course of the struggle.

Chapter XVI

Who Owns the Future?

THE headline in the morning paper said, "200 Congressmen Get X Gas Ration Cards." The dialogue at the breakfast table was as follows:

M. My God, did you see this? Two hundred congressmen got themselves ration cards that say they can have all the gas they want.

B. Yes, I know . . . isn't it maddening?

M. Why the blankety blank . . . ! What right do those blankety so-and-sos think they have to all the gasoline they want?

B. My dear, you don't have to use such violent language . . . especially in front of the children.

M. They're old enough to know the facts of life. Even about congressmen.

That was, I suppose, a fairly typical conversation over millions of breakfast tables as the war began to cut deeply into the well-cushioned surface of American life. We had been told and told again that it was coming. Each day or two there was news of another tanker sunk. But nevertheless we were not prepared when the blow finally fell.

To ration one hundred and thirty million rugged individualists is a formidable undertaking, so a start was made with the Eastern seaboard. Inevitably, perhaps, the beginning was fumbling and uncertain. How could it have been otherwise? Millions of Americans have known the curious independence which ownership of a motor car brings; the untrammeled right to go as far and as fast, or almost as fast, as your money will permit. Now limits were being put on that independence and, despite the grim reality that lay behind the need for those limits, we were filled with resent-

ment toward the civil authorities who went about in such a bum-
bling fashion imposing these curbs.

You could see, and more clearly in Washington than elsewhere,
the beginning of a conflict that might mean much for the future.
Essentially it was between the civilian and the military; between
order imposed from above and order that came from discipline
within. You could sense this warfare within yourself and in the
life around you.

I remembered when I had felt very much a civilian and a champion of civil rights and civil authority. As an air raid warden I
had gone to a series of lectures on incendiary bombs, poison gases,
and the use of gas masks. The lecturer was a naval officer who had
the look of a determined and slightly pugnacious cherub. He did
a good job. He held the attention of four or five hundred men on
a subject that he made not too technical.

Then one night he threw in, gratis, what must have been ideas
of his own. They could scarcely have been a part of the course.
He held up a gas mask and said, "This is a French gas mask. It
contains a union label. That is why France fell." He went on to
say that the union compelled the government to pay exorbitant
prices for everything so that the government of France could not
buy weapons. This seemed to me a slight oversimplification of the
history of the fall of France.

At that point our lecturer launched into a brief discourse on the
art of strike-breaking. It was no good sending in the National
Guard to break the strikes in Maryland's mines. National Guards-
men were sissies. They never shot to kill. And they used tear gas.
You had to use adamsite with those tough miners. He had explained a few minutes before that adamsite was a gas that para-
lyzed the muscles of the stomach and gave the victim for twenty-
four hours a strong impulse toward suicide. Let me say that in this
little discourse our lecturer seemed to bear no animus. There was
on his face the same good-natured, yes, cherubic smile.

A little later he discussed possible targets in Washington. There
was, he explained glibly, only one real target and that was the
Navy Yard where, by crippling a substantial ordnance industry,

the enemy could deliver a real blow. Of course, he added, you had the Capitol, and obviously he thought he'd get a laugh out of his audience on that one. I hope Congress is in session when the bombs fall, he went on, with the same look of genial good nature on his face. And then, he said, there's the White House. After a pause that an actor might have envied, he finished his sentence, casually, ". . . but no one would bother to bomb that target."

It made me angry all the way through to hear that cocky man in uniform say those things. I can criticize Congress if I want to but I do not want any bombs falling on Congress. It is my democratic privilege to say what I think about my congressman. But this man in a uniform had no right to sneer at them as though they were a worthless lot better removed by a few bombs. It was anti-democratic, it was anti-American, and I felt guilty that I hadn't the moral courage to stand up and say so in the face of that arrogant uniform.

Yet here I was at breakfast cursing out those same congressmen. Perhaps it was because I felt they had failed, let me down. I was ashamed that they had not shown more self-discipline. They might have set the example. I knew what that self-satisfied man in a uniform thought about them and I had hoped they would show him he was wrong.

Of course, I knew, too, that our lecturer was not an isolated instance, not a happenstance. Many officers share his attitude. It may be merely the sudden resurgence of the long-neglected military. For so many years they have been tolerated; a necessary evil that with just an ell more of progress we shall finally be rid of once and for all. On ceremonial occasions we have brought them out of oblivion to satisfy our curiosity about this relic of the wicked past. It would be no more than what we call human nature if they should now feel a desire to avenge those years of neglect.

What matters is not so much the attitude of the officers, who are a special caste small in number, but of the millions of men who have been drafted to do the fighting and the dying. That is the real burden that lies on us who are still at home. We have to furnish them with the sinews of war when they need them and where. If we fail, it cannot, it will not, be forgiven. And we have not only to furnish the means of war but also to make sure that they will come home to a future not too unsettled. For when they come home, these millions of young men, they will own the future or know the reason why.

In the mental climate of Washington is an almost unconscious awareness of this fact. There are men who want to make sure that the future will be to their liking. They are ambitious or they are beset by fears and doubts, by a haunting sense of insecurity in a time of overwhelming change. They want to impose order from above. They are impatient with civilians who move cautiously within the existing framework; civilians who are anxious to preserve traditional safeguards.

From the very beginning of the war a dispute has gone on over the Japanese on the West coast and what to do about them. Francis Biddle took the reasonable point of view that most Japanese are loyal and that once those known to be disloyal had been weeded out, there would be no further cause for alarm. Still the pressure persisted and at the end of January the Attorney General specified military zones from which enemy aliens had to be evacuated. This, too, was feasible and reasonable. But it did not satisfy the clamor in California where fear had apparently won out over common sense. All aliens had to go, all Japanese, American-born citizens along with noncitizens.

What happened is not exactly clear. Since his policy had not won acceptance, the Attorney General apparently felt that therefore he must surrender all responsibility. He recognized, perhaps, that as a civil officer of the government he had no arbitrary rights over American citizens. An executive order was prepared giving the military the most sweeping powers. While Biddle brought about some modifications of this order, the President on February 19, less than three months after Pearl Harbor, by his signature opened the way for a kind of martial law to be established in military areas to be designated when the War Department felt that such a step was justified. This was an extraordinary cession of power, with far-

reaching implications of which most Americans were entirely
unaware.

Under the order of February 19 the army proceeded to evacuate
125,000 Japanese. Among them were approximately 75,000 Nisei
whose American citizenship was established by their American
birth. This was a precedent-making action that may well have echoing implications long after the event. Theoretically they went of
their own accord to insure their own safety. But this, of course,
was a convenient fiction. The Nisei knew authority when they saw
it just as their fathers and mothers did.

The mass evacuation was inevitably a drain on men and materials at a time when the need for both was critical. The Army
should not have had the burden of such an assignment at such a
time. Naturally, Lieutenant General John L. DeWitt, in command of the area, was concerned for the security of his command.
It is a tremendous responsibility that weighs on one man in a time
of national danger. He knew, far better than anyone else, the
hazards. And he knew that if the civil authority did not assume
responsibility, then it was up to the military authority. There could
be no easy interregnum at such a moment. So General DeWitt
acted, swiftly, drastically, using civil authority to carry out the
evacuation but making it perfectly clear that control rested with
the military.

His action left a great many questions. What about Italian and
German aliens? Thomas Mann, acting as spokesman for Nazi
refugees in California who were less famous and less fortunate,
told a congressional committee that in many, many instances the
beginning confidence of harried outcasts had been shattered once
again. Letters began to pour into Washington, pitiful letters from
little people who saw a sudden abyss open up. Were they to be
evacuated too? Was this to be France? The longer the uncertainty,
the deeper were the fears that gnawed at "aliens" who had known
so much insecurity.

Then on April 27, Lieutenant General Hugh A. Drum, commanding the Eastern Defense Command and the First Army,
gave out a statement in which he announced plans for establishing

an Eastern military area that would include all the states of the Eastern seaboard. A remarkable document, it made clear that the grant of power from the President gave the military control not only over aliens but over all persons.

"The plan embodied in the administration of the Eastern Military Area contemplates," said General Drum, "the control of conduct within the area on the part of enemy aliens, as well as of all other persons, so as to safeguard the national security, and will be effected by means of general restrictions and orders issued from the headquarters of the Eastern Defense Command.

"The fundamental policy embodied in the plan is not to interfere in any manner whatever with the lives of the great mass of loyal Americans in the states included in the military areas, or with the economic life of the area, but it does express the determination of the military authorities to prevent any enemy sympathizer, whether alien enemy, alien of other nationality, or disloyal American, if any exist, from committing any act detrimental to the national security, and will be effected by means of general restrictions and orders issued from the headquarters of the Eastern Defense Command."

Behind the decision was Secretary Stimson's wrath. On an inspection tour in Florida he had been impressed by the success of the blackout at Miami Beach. Moving up the Florida coast to St. Augustine he found the lights ablaze and heard the story of a ship torpedoed because it was seen in tragic silhouette by a roving U-boat. Stimson swore a mighty oath that if civilians could not learn such an elementary business as dousing their shore lights, then they would have to be taught by the Army.

There is evidence, however, that General Drum's statement caused some consternation among the civilian officers of the War Department. Three days later Stimson issued a vague press release in which he sought to reassure unhappy aliens. He stressed the importance of keeping the coast dark. Altogether the War Department receded a considerable distance from General Drum's forthright words. And when the Eastern military area was proclaimed

it was in terms meek and mild with no intimation of the infinite
extent of military authority.

Within the administration in Washington are many officers of
the civil government who follow these developments with growing apprehension. The nose of the military camel is under the government tent and it seems there is no stopping the bold, forward
rush of the intruders. In almost every department the military is
moving in and with a frank warning that this is only the beginning. Civil action is not swift enough nor drastic enough for military men.

Given Washington, it is probably inevitable that out of this
should come rumors of a "plot." I was taken aside at a party and
told by a high officer of the government that a section of the
military, small but influential, wanted to extend outright martial
law to the entire country. The intention of ambitious military
men, so the story went, was first to establish a military area on
the West coast; next a military area on the East coast; then within
these areas the degree of martial law was to be increased with the
civil authorities superseded by a gradual but nevertheless inevitable
process. From both coasts the zones were to be extended inward.
It was early in 1942 that I was told of this "plot."

One of the first agencies that was to be supplanted was the
Federal Bureau of Investigation. The FBI would be abolished or
made strictly subordinate to military police under the Provost
Marshal General. Even the conversations of ambitious military
men were reported. They were antidemocratic, anti-Semitic, ugly
sounding.

My own conclusion was that the plot story could be put down
to the rumor-befogged air of Washington where, as the President
has often complained, a miasmal swamp seems to engender un-
truths, or, worse, half truths. But at the same time it was true that
many military men wanted to abrogate civil functions and civil
rights under the spur of the emergency and they said so frankly.
In the military area on the West coast the Army was giving its
own orders directly to the FBI rather than routing such orders
through the Department of Justice in Washington as is the nor-

mal requirement. A small point, but it was symptomatic of what might happen in a broader sphere.

There is no reason to look for anything mysterious or sinister in the attitude of the average military man. Total war calls for almost as much discipline within the civilian population as within the army and we are a nation of rugged individualists and proud of it. We are not going to take orders from anybody. But the military has to answer for the security of the country. There is hardly time to wheedle reluctant civilians into changing their lavish and careless habits. Military discipline is clear and unmistakable. It seems to offer a way out of confusion and doubt.

What I had begun to feel was what millions of other Americans must have been feeling. We were beyond the age for active fighting in a war that called for the utmost stamina and resistance. We had families and responsibilities. Yet we felt a deep impatience with the ordinary course of existence; with the limited contribution that the civilian could make. We wanted to do something direct, active and simple, something that required no complicated decision. Escapist, you could call it, but nevertheless there it was.

One day at lunch I was asked if I would go to Sweden. One of the new information agencies wanted to send someone over to try to work out ways through which Sweden could get more news, more books, more magazines, more information in general from the United States. I had been in Sweden several times. I had many friends there. I knew something about the country, its people and its politics. I was told it was my duty to go.

At first I resisted. I had a large order of work ahead of me and it was work that seemed, to me at least, fairly important. I was not at all convinced that I could be useful in Stockholm. There was the suspicion that this might be one of those urgent, quick, hurry, rush missions that came out of someone's febrile mind. And there was the chance that when you got to Sweden, you would find yourself cut off from America, tied up in diplomatic red tape with a vastly more foolish sense of futility than you had nurtured back in Washington.

On my own I made a few inquiries, and I discovered that perhaps there was a job to be done. Sweden was getting from us only a skeletonized news report. The British were doing a better information job. The Germans were flooding the country with expensive propaganda. If I could help to change that balance even slightly then I should have to go. Although my knowledge of the country and the people was very limited, I had a great admiration and respect for their achievement. Many Swedes had said that I had been far too uncritical in the two books I had written out of my visits to Scandinavia. They said that I saw only one side and that a brightly colored side. But I could not help admiring their order, their reason, their calm intelligence. And when they showed me their poverty, I could not recognize it for poverty if only because it was so well ordered and so clearly understood.

Getting to Sweden is not too difficult. You take a clipper or a bomber to England and then from there you take the courier plane that the British operate in the north. If I had to go, I had to go. It began to take on the look of an adventure; a chance to see at first hand just a little of the war that in Washington seemed so remote and theoretical. After two or three days of indecision, I said, Yes, I would go if I could get a leave of absence from my job; and knowing the *Post-Dispatch* I felt that they would be generous in the face of such a request.

I asked about schedules on the clipper and there was a discussion of the inoculations that are a part of wartime travel. It still seemed a little unreal that I should be going on such an errand and abruptly it developed that it was indeed completely unreal. What developed in the course of several conversations, in which on the one side were confusion and apology and on my side irritation and a kind of anger, was that approval of the State Department for such an undertaking had not been obtained. Approval had to be obtained and the State Department was being evasive. At last the State Department made up its mind. The situation, said the State Department, was too delicate; it should not be disturbed by any new factor, any new disrupting force. That had a familiar ring. It was a little funny to think that I should be considered a disrupting force, and I knew that the Swedes would think it was funny too.

I had seen when last I had been there, five years before, how firm was the foundation on which they had built their democracy. There were reports that, under pressure of the Nazis, Sweden had yielded so much as to surrender virtually her independence. I knew those reports were a gross exaggeration, not without malice. And then about this time Alva Myrdal came from Sweden to join her husband who was at the Institute of Advanced Studies at Princeton. Alva Myrdal is one of the most clear seeing people I have ever met. She and her husband, Gunnar, were intellectuals, thinkers, who got into the thick of Swedish politics in order to put their knowledge and their ideas to work. The studies of population trends which they made, showing scientifically the relation of population growth and decline to national well-being, became a great popular political issue, the focus of a political program. Astonished to find such widespread misapprehensions about her country, Mrs. Myrdal in an article in the *American-Swedish Monthly* set down her own findings. She put it this way:

"If I were to venture a personal guess, I should certainly estimate pro-Axis sentiment to be less than 1 per cent. That does not mean, however, that the rest are pro-Ally. I estimate that 10 to 20 per cent of the people would call themselves definitely pro-British, and 60 to 70 per cent just 'pro-democratic.' These latter are the bulk of the people, clear in their own minds as to what ideology they prefer, but unwilling—largely due to the 'psychology of neutrality' with its conditioning to caution—to confess that sympathy as directly related to any foreign power. And there are, finally, some 20 per cent undecided, a factor never to be forgotten in any country. They comprise, first, the ones who prefer to keep themselves ready to profit, whoever is the winner, but also the ones who 'understand' both sides, the ones to be swayed by events, and finally the politically indifferent ones. These groups are the very ones not immunized against propaganda. Yet, even to them the propaganda effects of victory mean much more than any propaganda of arguments."

The propaganda effects of victory had weighed heavily on military minds in Sweden, according to reports that had come to me from time to time. Swedish military men had been greatly impressed by the might of the German war machine. They had close connections with their opposite numbers in Germany. German generals told Swedish generals that it was they who would actually rule after victory; Hitler was an upstart and a bounder and in due time he and his Storm Troopers would be dealt with. This was a persuasive appeal, especially to men who spoke the same language. And military men the world over do speak the same language. They are in a sense a special caste. It seems to be a differentiation that goes very far back, with biological roots; as between the soldier ants and the worker ants, as old as life itself. Even in a country that has had no war for more than 125 years, a country as homogeneous, as peace-loving, and as highly developed as Sweden, you had military men who looked with mistrust if not contempt on the slow processes of civil progress.

"Such an estimate," Mrs. Myrdal went on, "admittedly speculative, since it cannot be submitted to any objective test, is based on a fairly systematic questioning and contact with large groups in many parts of Sweden. One general impression may be quoted in support of the estimate: wherever one goes it is evident that the citizens who are organized are the steadfast ones. And as Sweden is a country so largely stratified by civic organizations of all kinds, it follows that a majority of the Swedes are unshaken in their democratic faith and will so remain even if many years and many hardships still are to tax their endurance. This is only saying in words what the election figures of September, 1940, so drastically said in figures."

Organization, that is the secret of Sweden's democracy. And essentially we in America are so unorganized. Or, rather, we have organizations but they are on the surface, at the top, while in Sweden they strike down to the grass roots. Of course, there is no comparing the two countries. They are so utterly dissimilar.

Yet I could not help but contrast them. In Sweden under the impact of the war crisis the effort has been constant and intensive to keep the inevitable new powers accruing to government distributed throughout local communities. Decentralization has been the unremitting effort of the central government.

Here we have attempted to decentralize but our size and our diversity make it extremely difficult. The curse of bigness was one of old Justice Brandeis's chief convictions. And now Washington is expanding as it has never expanded before. Here is centralization such as not even the wildest critics of federalism ever dreamed of. The statistics make you dizzy.

By the middle of 1942 there were approximately 250,000 civilian employees of the government in Washington alone and by the end of the year the figure would be well above 300,000, more than doubled in less than two years. And this is only civilian personnel. It does not include the thousands of officers in uniform who swarm over the whole town, occupying the numerous buildings that the War and Navy Departments have taken over. Nor does it include the enlisted men who come in and out in a ceaseless current which passes between the capital and the near-by camps, the departments, the great Walter Reed Hospital, and the naval medical center on the edge of the city, to say nothing of the comings and goings of men on furlough.

Nor does it take in the men in uniform who have come from all over the globe. On Connecticut Avenue you can see any and every kind of military rig. Officers of Scottish regiments rarely wear their kilts because of their conspicuousness, but they do wear an exaggerated pantaloon of the proper tartan which causes almost as many stares. There are Canadian soldiers in black berets. Smart British officers in khaki with red facings, carrying bamboo swagger sticks. There are Polish and Yugoslav officers with impressive rows of decorations. Many women are in uniform, American members of the A.W.V.S. in smartly tailored blue, Canadian women in khaki with officers' fatigue caps.

The city is crowded to bursting yet still they come. Newly recruited workers were arriving in 1942 at the rate of about ten thousand a month, according to an estimate of the Civil Service Commission. In every state, in every town the Commission is re-

cruiting more stenographers, more clerks, more statisticians. And
where to put them is the growing problem. Families are warned to
stay home because there are neither houses nor apartments available. Dormitories for girls are being rushed to completion together
with some family units, and although the total is pitifully inadequate, Congress denied the District of Columbia twenty million
dollars that had been requested for wartime housing.

To provide space for these incoming workers, twenty-seven temporary buildings have been constructed in less than a year at an
average cost of $835,000 a building. This is some sort of a world's
construction record. The twenty-seven new Tempos provide a total
net working area of 3,292,156 square feet. Some idea of what this
means may be obtained by a comparison with the RCA building
in Rockefeller Center, the largest office structure in the world.
RCA, 850 feet high, contains 2,924,036 square feet, which provides space for 26,000 persons to work. At the rate of 80 square
feet for each worker the new Tempos will house about 40,000
government employees. Largely prefabricated, the new buildings
have been put together on the site from asbestos wall board cut
to a standard size.

They have gone up as though by a kind of magic. At the start
five hundred men were on the location ready to go to work. As
the building progressed, this number was increased to two thousand. Under this system the Tempos took form like movie sets
in thirty-eight to sixty days for each building. The Tempos are
completely functional, without any ornament whatsoever, and in
Washington's steamy summer they are unbearably hot. With few
partitions in the interior, even relatively important executives per-
force sit in full view surrounded by secretaries and stenographers.
There was a desperate hunt for space on which to grow these
mushrooms. Washington's beautiful Mall, with its sweep from
the steps of the capitol to Arlington across the Potomac, has been
encroached on. Across the river in Virginia the War Department
is completing what may well be the largest office structure in the
world, larger even than the RCA building. Twenty-four hours a

day, under huge searchlights at night, work on this colossus is being pushed.

By comparison the boom of World War I was no more than government as usual. In 1917 and 1918 twelve temporary buildings were put up to take care of wartime workers who at the peak, at the end of 1918, reached a total of 117,000. Of frame and stucco, they took considerably longer to build than the present Tempos. While they also were known, as the present buildings are, as Tempo A, B, C, and so on, they survived for a long time after the war. In fact, when the present crisis broke, two "temporary" buildings from the first World War were still in use. Now they house workers in this new and more terrible conflict.

The figures sound like a boosting brochure issued by a Surrealist Chamber of Commerce. Everything is up in this boom town. The juvenile delinquency rate has jumped 25 per cent. Babies are born of induced labor so that mothers will be able to get into hospitals when there are vacancies. Penal institutions are overcrowded and so are schools, churches, night clubs. In Gallinger Hospital, which could best be described by a Dickens or a Zola, thirty-five nurses and internes contracted tuberculosis from overwork and the fearfully overcrowded condition prevailing constantly.

The per capita consumption of alcohol is considerably higher in the District of Columbia than in any state in the union. The latest figure is 4.26 gallons a year for each individual, comparing with the highest state, Nevada, with a figure of 2.65. The rate for Illinois is 1.64, for New York State 1.35. For several reasons, of course, the Washington figure gives a false impression, one of the chief reasons being that suburbanites in near-by Virginia and Maryland buy their liquor in the District where prices are cheaper than almost anywhere else in the country. But then statistics on arrests for drunkenness—not too reliable since police practices vary from city to city—show Washington far in the lead.

All this adds up to a problem of sizable proportions for after the war. More and more powers are being concentrated in the capital. Correspondingly, states and communities are yielding authority. Centralized power implies rigid controls. And the American people have always resented such controls.

Perhaps it is symptomatic that as the war ground down on the pattern of civilian life, their resentment has been directed not so much at the President or the military, the focus of the new powers, as at Congress; or at something that is lumped vaguely under the term "politics." Perhaps it is merely that Congress is such a convenient target. But in many ways this is disturbing. In this resentment is something essentially undemocratic, away from representative government, the basis of American democracy.

Sharing this concern, and with good reason, is Congress itself. An election in the fall of 1942 threatens to dispossess many a congressman from a job that is, if not secure, at least fairly well paid. There is the strong possibility that the American people may simply vote their resentment and thereby turn the ins out and the outs in. Good precedent for just that exists in the past.

I made a brief excursion to the Middle West in the spring of '42. Some observers predicted a Democratic upset. People would vote their grievances. I disagreed. If you put it solely on that basis, then in all probability the election would go the other way. True, many people had grievances. There were communities that had been injured by the war. On the other hand, millions of Americans were working at high wages for the first time in years. And in the summer of 1942 they could still buy something with their money. The tide of battle in the Far East had been disastrous, but the Southwest Pacific was a long way off and the casualty list of Americans had not yet been sufficiently large to reach into every community.

Then in mid-May the Gallup poll showed that if the congressional election had been held in that week, the Democrats would have gained thirty-eight seats in the House. It was a bombshell to Republicans, many of whom had complacently assumed that disasters and defeats would produce an automatic reaction which would in turn yield the G.O.P. a harvest of votes. That was the illusion they had clung to ever since the Democrats had come into power. While a great deal could happen between May and

November, it was difficult to see how so strong a trend could be reversed with a sufficient force to overthrow the sizable Democratic majority of ninety-five in the House. That would mean that the Republicans would have to capture fifty seats.

Understandably Mr. Gallup's report caused rejoicing among the Democrats and especially among the New Dealers. No one had done very much about the party. The national chairman, Boss Edward J. Flynn of the Bronx, at least three or four cuts below the Farley standard, had involved himself in an odorous scandal and while a jury had duly and officially exonerated him, the smell lingered. Nevertheless the Democrats stood a good chance of winning another election by default.

Looking at it with any detachment, you cannot feel that this is an occasion for dancing in the streets. The end result is desirable because so many individual Republicans—if not the party itself—have demonstrated their complete bankruptcy. But that the Democratic administration should go unchallenged—that is the sad commentary on the state of our politics.

If we are to have a two-party system, then we have to have a second party that stands for something and men who stand with it. One election after another should have taught the Republicans the truth of that ancient axiom—you can't beat something with nothing. Wendell Willkie has labored manfully. At the meeting of the national committee in Chicago he compelled the adoption of his resolution which chucked isolationism out of the window for all time. That at any rate was what it said. But at election time politicians of all colors and complexions have a habit of huddling under the party platform.

It is difficult to see how you can make a party out of men such as Dewey Short, the Ham Fish of the Ozarks, Clare Hoffman, the ranter from Michigan; or even from men such as little Phil Bennett of Springfield, Missouri, who looks out on the world with puckered suspicion, like a frost-bitten apple still hanging on the tree. On the other hand, of course, you have men such as Joseph Clark Baldwin of New York who are courageous and intelligent and self-sacrificing. But the Joseph Clark Baldwins appear to be lonely exceptions.

While this may be venturing into the realm of miracles, it seems to me that an eventuality devoutly to be prayed for is a renascence of the Republican party. That much-heralded, much-talked-of phenomenon—"a new party," "a third party"—seems today farther off than at any time in recent years. Perhaps Willkie can work a miracle. Perhaps he can breathe life into a moribund institution. At any rate he has the courage and the patience to try, and those are qualities that should carry him a long way in his undertaking, if only because they are so rare.

Beyond '42 is '44. Into the November elections of '42 many people are trying to read a cosmic significance. It will be, it is said, the most important election since the Civil War. My own feeling is that, short of an overwhelming disaster, a blow that would put the nation in imminent danger, the American voter will not take the contest too seriously. A change could, of course, come very abruptly following on military reverses that would shatter the penumbra of hope in which most of us lived. But without such a bombshell the voters will tend to return a Congress very much like the one we have had in recent years. They may vote out some of the conspicuous members of the lunatic fringe. The Democratic majority may be reduced or even, by a narrow margin, upset. Otherwise the color of Congress will remain substantially unchanged; that is a neutral gray, shading off into black at one extreme and into a faint blush pink at the other.

I say this knowing how dangerous it is to attempt to prophesy the direction of the political current in a troubled and uncertain time. In Washington any prophecies ventured by the boys in the press gallery are made sufficiently far in advance of the event so that newspaper readers, who have notoriously short memories, will have forgotten if we were wrong. And if we were right, you can be sure that that fact will not go unnoted.

To my way of thinking the tough election will be '44. Then you will want to hang onto your hat for that curve on the roller coaster. Then will come the test, after the corrosive months and years of war have burned deeply into the American consciousness. A great deal of rhetoric has been spilled about America finding her soul in sacrifice and suffering. Perhaps sacrifice and suffering will develop deeper spiritual qualities. It remains to be seen. And the first great test may come in the presidential election, a national test of our political system and of the maturity of the American voter under trial by fire.

Already it is on the Washington horizon. Loyal New Dealers, when they speak of it at all, assume that of course Roosevelt will have to run again if we are still in the war or even if we are moving toward a kind of victory and a difficult peace. That convenient signboard, Joe Guffy of Pennsylvania, has already spelled it out in public. He was one of the first to demand openly a third term and now, as though not to destroy his record for prescience, he has called for a fourth term.

In 1940 many voters with great reluctance accepted the inevitability of a third term. A fourth term will be far more difficult to accept. Millions of voters viewed the results of the 1940 election with a sense of angry frustration. You can't beat Roosevelt, they said bitterly. A fourth term would accentuate that feeling. It might dam up dangerously the frustrated resentment of too large a section of the American public. Any speculation is, of course, idle. Two years, at the pace at which events are moving, could bring anything.

Yet we cannot ignore what must be a momentous decision. We must consider and weigh men and reputations. I remember that almost the last time I talked with Justice Brandeis that was his theme. The choice, he said earnestly, should be between many men who were trained and ready for the highest office of all. We should not merely drift into the convention of a great political party in an atmosphere of uncertainty with a few contenders. The field should be crowded. That should be the end harvest of American public life—leaders with experience, understanding, maturity. The nomination should not be a prize falling to the clever contender, the shrewd manipulator.

The war has tended, of course, to dwarf most reputations. The impact of history in the making is so violent that only a few can stand up to it. Certainly in the politics of '44 a military man may be expected to have a prominent place. And that man, again barring some unforeseen and unexpected disaster, will be General MacArthur. His friends and admirers, fanatically devoted, are determined on the advancement of their hero.

Whether in pushing him for high office they are doing him a service is another question. The course of American history is strewn with distinguished military leaders and conspicuous heroes, from Grant through Dewey to Lindbergh, who have suffered under the political machinations of well-meaning friends. Only that greatest of all Americans, the great Washington, stands out, with his forbearance, his restraint, his profound sense of the national well-being, as a noble and a solitary exception. To challenge that reputation, as unfortunate men have challenged it in the past, would be indeed to dare destiny.

Beyond '44 is the halfway mark of a century already plagued by the four horsemen; by insecurity, fear, terror, and the horrors of mechanized murder and scientific tyranny. And all of this is seen against a background of hope; hope that has come out of the nineteenth century like a glow in the sky. It may be the glow of morning or the last light of an age that is dying in a rain of blood.

One man in the dubious spring of 1942 stood up and talked with courage of the future beyond the next election and the election after that. Shambling, shy Henry Wallace put into words the vague aspirations and desires that are in men's hearts everywhere. It is, he said in a memorable speech to the Free World Association in New York, to be the people's century once the dark forces of evil have been vanquished. His language was simple and direct. It was language that everyone could understand. It came nearer to being a marching rhythm, a rhythm for the future, than anything that had been spoken by any leader. Henry Wallace had come a long way from those patient experiments on seed corn that had won him his first reputation.

In the chaos of the war his words had a lonely, eloquent sound.

So much is still to be formulated. So often the words that are spoken and written seem irrelevant and remote. And, again, words are superfluous.

How can any American, however wretched and impoverished, miss the meaning of the test we are being put to! I have been one of the fortunate ones. Realizing the danger to America, to the free America I have known, I acknowledge that a hundred times over. I owe so much to my country. I can say that, yes, say it with pride. I have known so much of the strength and the breadth and the beauty of it.

I remember riding out of Taos toward the purple mountains, riding down a canyon golden with the late October sun. I remember the hot, sweet breath of the Iowa summer, blown across the long green pasture. I remember the smell of the grapes on the shore of Lake Erie, the heavy tangle of the vineyards and the powdery dust from the roads. I remember the Florida marshes and the narrow, high-crowned highway to the sea, the white birds suddenly flying up, the tall grasses bent against the wind. And I remember the Golden Gate and the long rollers pounding up the shore and the drive up Tamalpais and the incredible world down there below. And New York in the electric air of early spring, and Boston Common, and the dark, uncertain shape of Pittsburgh from a plane.

Yes, and I remember Washington, early December, and the Monument in the beginning dusk, pure and beautiful, the branches of the big elms naked and clear. It is wonderful beyond anything, the people and the country. For all the scandal and the shame that I know, I know this other, too. It is bigger than Washington, bigger than men or parties. The people, it seems to me, want the truth. They can take it. Too often from Washington they get, instead, evasion.

I have not only seen it and been through it but I can write about it. That is being curtailed, that last privilege. Out of the war have come innumerable taboos, not only in the capital but in arms plants, on docks and in shipyards all over the country. It is inevitable and right. It is part of the self-discipline of war to accept the encroachments of censorship. It is part of what we surrender in the ordeal of the present in order to insure such privileges for the future. Knowing America, knowing Washington, I can believe in that future.

INDEX